SAGE was founded in 1965 by Sara Miller McCune to support the dissemination of usable knowledge by publishing innovative and high-quality research and teaching content. Today, we publish over 900 journals, including those of more than 400 learned societies, more than 800 new books per year, and a growing range of library products including archives, data, case studies, reports, and video. SAGE remains majority-owned by our founder, and after Sara's lifetime will become owned by a charitable trust that secures our continued independence.

Los Angeles | London | New Delhi | Singapore | Washington DC | Melbourne

IDEOLOGY, CONFLICT
and STATE CONTROL
in HIGHER EDUCATION

Thank you for choosing a SAGE product!
If you have any comment, observation or feedback,
I would like to personally hear from you.

Please write to me at **contactceo@sagepub.in**

Vivek Mehra, Managing Director and CEO, SAGE India.

Bulk Sales

SAGE India offers special discounts
for purchase of books in bulk.
We also make available special imprints
and excerpts from our books on demand.

For orders and enquiries, write to us at

Marketing Department
SAGE Publications India Pvt Ltd
B1/I-1, Mohan Cooperative Industrial Area
Mathura Road, Post Bag 7
New Delhi 110044, India

E-mail us at **marketing@sagepub.in**

Subscribe to our mailing list
Write to **marketing@sagepub.in**

This book is also available as an e-book.

IDEOLOGY, CONFLICT and STATE CONTROL in HIGHER EDUCATION
A Sociological Analysis

SUSHREE PANIGRAHI

Los Angeles | London | New Delhi
Singapore | Washington DC | Melbourne

Copyright © Sushree Panigrahi, 2022

All rights reserved. No part of this book may be reproduced or utilized in any form or by any means, electronic or mechanical, including photocopying, recording, or by any information storage or retrieval system, without permission in writing from the publisher.

First published in 2022 by

SAGE Publications India Pvt Ltd
B1/I-1 Mohan Cooperative Industrial Area
Mathura Road, New Delhi 110 044, India
www.sagepub.in

SAGE Publications Inc
2455 Teller Road
Thousand Oaks, California 91320, USA

SAGE Publications Ltd
1 Oliver's Yard, 55 City Road
London EC1Y 1SP, United Kingdom

SAGE Publications Asia-Pacific Pte Ltd
18 Cross Street #10-10/11/12
China Square Central
Singapore 048423

Published by Vivek Mehra for SAGE Publications India Pvt Ltd and typeset in 10.5/13 pt Berkeley by AG Infographics, Delhi.

Library of Congress Control Number: 2021944191

ISBN: 978-93-5479-149-9 (HB)

SAGE Team: Aarooshi Garg, Ankit Verma, Shivani Anupkumar, and Dally Verghese

CONTENTS

List of Tables		vii
List of Abbreviations		ix
Acknowledgements		xi
Chapter 1	Introduction	1
Chapter 2	State and Education	42
Chapter 3	Political Activism and Students' Union	100
Chapter 4	Entrenched Hierarchies: Caste and Gender	139
Chapter 5	Issues in Higher Education	185
Chapter 6	The Teacher: Roles, Rules and Challenges	215
Chapter 7	Conclusion	259
Bibliography		292
About the Author		305
Index		306

LIST OF TABLES

1.1	Humanities	34
1.2	Sciences	35
4.1	Literacy Rate for SCs	158
4.2	Literacy Rates for STs	159
4.3	Composition of Students: Periyar University	163
4.4	Composition of Students: Pondicherry University	164
4.5A	Pondicherry University: Students Strength (Admitted) for 2017–2018; Courses: Ph.D./M.Tech./M.A/M.Sc/M.Sc (Int)/M.B.A/M.C.A/Others	164
4.5B	Pondicherry University: Students Strength (on the Rolls) for 2017–2018; Courses: Ph.D./M.Tech./M.A/M.Sc/M.Sc (Int)/M.B.A/M.C.A/Others	164
4.6	Faculty Profile—Pondicherry University	165
4.7	Composition of Students: BHU	166
4.8	Composition of Students: AU	167
4.9	Composition of Students: OU	168
4.10	SC/ST Intake: DU	169
4.11	Composition of Students: JU	170
4.12	Composition of Students: NEHU	171
4.13	Composition of Students: Jamia Millia Islamia	174
5.1	JNU—Original Fee Hike	191
5.2	JNU—Revised Fee Hike	193

LIST OF ABBREVIATIONS

ABVP	Akhil Bharatiya Vidyarthi Parishad
AICMR	Indian Council of Medical Research
AICTE	All India Council for Technical Education
AISA	All India Students' Association
AISHE	All India Survey on Higher Education
AMU	Aligarh Muslim University
API	Academic performance indicator
APSC	Ambedkar Periyar Study Circle
AU	Allahabad University
BHU	Banaras Hindu University
BPL	Below Poverty Line
CAA	Citizenship (Amendment) Act
CCTV	Closed-circuit television
CSS	Central Civil Services
DU	Delhi University
DUSU	Delhi University Students Union
FTII	Film and Television Institute of India
GDP	Gross domestic product
GER	Gross enrolment ratio
HCU	Hyderabad Central University
HECI	Higher Education Commission of India
HEI	Higher education institution
HoD	Head of department
IGNOU	Indira Gandhi National Open University
IIMC	Indian Institute of Mass Communication

IISER	Indian Institute of Science Education and Research
IoE	Institutes of Eminence
ISC	Indian Science Congress
JNU	Jawaharlal Nehru University
JNUTA	Jawaharlal Nehru University Teachers' Association
JU	Jadavpur University
MGAMVV	Mahatma Gandhi Antarrashtriya Hindi Vishwavidyalaya
MHRD	Ministry of Human Resource Development
MP	Madhya Pradesh
NEHU	North-Eastern Hill University
NEP	New Education Policy
NET	National Eligibility Test
NSUI	National Students' Union of India
OBC	Other Backward Class
OU	Osmania University
PG	Postgraduate
PUSU	Punjab University Students' Union
SCs	Scheduled Castes
SFI	Students' Federation of India
SPPU	Savitribai Phule Pune University
STs	Scheduled Tribes
TFRC	Telangana Admission and Fee Regulatory Committee
TISS	Tata Institute of Social Sciences
UG	Undergraduate
UGC	University Grants Commission
UP	Uttar Pradesh
UPA	United Progressive Alliance
VC	Vice chancellor
VRSF	Vidarbha Republican Student Federation

ACKNOWLEDGEMENTS

Writing a book is often perceived as a solitary task. In a sense it is, because the ideas are your own and you want to put them into words in a manner that the reader finds it clear and engaging. However, as you look back, you realize that numerous people have helped shape this book and that you were never really alone.

One of the primary reasons to pen a book was my father, who has always led by example. He inculcated in us, early on, a strong belief in education and reading. My partner, Prakash, patiently helped me through the numerous edits and sorting out ideas. My professors from Jawaharlal Nehru University (JNU), Professor Maitrayee Chaudhuri and Professor T. K. Oommen have always taken out time from their busy schedule for me and continued to guide me long after I left JNU.

I am grateful to the Rajiv Gandhi Institute for Contemporary Studies for giving me complete autonomy to plan and execute the research. The support I received on the administration front was invaluable, considering the nature of the research. Research associates Piyush Kumar and Subhrali Kachari worked very hard, travelling to universities and reaching out to other field researchers. A note of special thanks to Subhrali, who continued to help me even after she left the organization. I would like to thank all the field researchers who painstakingly followed all the guidelines and many completed the fieldwork under very tough circumstances.

Introduction

Democracy needs to be reborn in each generation, and education is its midwife.

—John Dewey

What does education have to do with democracy and democratic ideals? It is not surprising that people often raise the question since there is a visible discomfort with the idea of a democratic educational system. While what we need is an educational system that questions, protests or attempts to change the inherent hierarchical structures present in the society, there are constant efforts to control protest, prevent questions being raised and further institutionalize hierarchy. The education system itself reflects and perpetuates these injustices. In a democratic country, education should provide the means of fighting hierarchies and inequalities that are accepted as part of daily life. Status-quoist education reduces the purpose of education from that of creation of knowledge, ideas, innovation and critical thinking to merely market-driven utilitarianism. Thereby, the role of students and teachers, and that of universities, is relegated to consensus building rather than creating a change. This is of particular consequence at a time when questions on the true nature and functioning of a democracy are being raised, be it in the context of farm laws, Citizenship (Amendment) Act (CAA) protests, arrests for posting a comment on the social media and so on. In such a scenario, ideally, universities should become a part of the larger debate taking place in the society.

Education is not merely confined to books; higher educational institutes (HEIs) provide life experiences that shape and sharpen minds. An oft repeated phrase, 'How could an educated person behave like this?' brings to life the meaning of education. A very basic example would be a person throwing out a bag on the street while driving.

The first reaction is (assuming the person who owns a car must have some degree of education), 'If educated people behave like this, what can be said for the uneducated?' It conveys that education is not merely about obtaining a degree but also acquiring certain traits that justify the purpose of education. Much has been written and said about crisis in education, what a university stands for and the meaning of education itself. This work moves beyond these familiar ideas and presents a larger canvas. The idea of this book germinated in the backdrop of universities across the country reporting conflict within the universities and with the State. However, it is not limited merely to specific instances of conflict or analysis of the same. Educational institutes and the State have been in perpetual conflict; some of the reasons for this conflict are historically similar, for example, recruitment of teachers, infrastructure, lack of funds or student activism.

Of late, HEIs have become ideological battlegrounds like never before. Indeed, a war of opposing world views is on. There have been several instances of conflict in universities in the recent years, due to ideological (political and otherwise) and other reasons. In the light of these events, it is tempting to embark on a study of reasons behind the conflicts, and several eminent academicians did analyse the situation in the perspective of political–ideological conflict. One of the many questions that comes to the mind is whether HEIs provide the grounds and space for conflicting ideologies to emerge and engage; do they shape the ideology (world view, attitudes) of students? The core purpose of this book is to locate the role of ideology in everyday life, especially that of students and teachers. To achieve this, an extensive qualitative research was conducted in universities and technical institutes across the country. It explores how students understand, define and perceive ideology, not in the limited sense of political ideology but rather from a much wider perspective. Do students understand the meaning of ideology? Do they have strong ideological positions, and how do they interpret these ideological positions? This book moves away from a discussion on political ideology. Instead, it seeks to understand the sociological forces that shape ideology, impact of ideology on social and professional lives and impact on teaching and friendships. It explores the social world of ideology.

Students were asked about their opinion on rewriting of history, the merging of science and mythology and the importance of the national anthem to gauge their ability of critical thinking and analysis of contemporary issues. How do students and teachers of science and humanities differ in their views on these issues? Do student activism and students' and teachers' union find support among students and teachers? Do strong ideological beliefs, in turn, translate into political activism or support for politics on campus? This book questions certain myths about linkages between caste and ideological positions; are they valid or are they merely stereotypes? Similarly, women are often portrayed as being apolitical; is this a valid assumption or, again, a stereotype? This is perplexing, considering political participation of women stretches back to the Independence struggle. In the context of gender, the gendered rules and regulations in campuses and the protests cannot be ignored, considering the number of protests that have taken place across the country.

The conversations with the teachers reveal the role ideology plays in not only teaching but also among teachers, the relationship with the administration and its impact on teachers. The teachers spoke candidly on whether they allow their ideological beliefs to influence students and teaching, or their relationships with other teachers in the department. This book also presents their opinion on reservation, the impact of reservation from the teachers' point of view and, consequently, the changing composition of students and teachers in universities and the problem of caste as faced by many teachers in universities. As mentioned earlier, crisis and problems facing education, especially higher education, is much written about. However, no conversation with teachers is complete without it. Among several concerns on this front, fee hike emerged as a major concern by teachers. Through conversations with teachers, this book presents a picture of the freedom and constraints faced by teachers due to rules at the university level and those introduced by the State. The conversations reveal the discomfort with research and attendance rules, lack of recruitment, hierarchy in deciding courses, changing composition of academic councils and how that impacts teachers and their representation and implications of the new reservation policy in universities.

4 Ideology, Conflict and State Control in Higher Education

In the last few years, campuses across the country have been witness to conflict due to several reasons, so much so that even apolitical campuses have become sites of conflict. Many of these conflicts quickly turned into political tussles. A few examples will help illustrate this point. The traditional pattern has been that engineering colleges and institutes report very few conflicts with the State or administration, as they do not have students' unions. However, there has been a deviation from this norm in recent times. Several engineering campuses have reported conflict due to certain measures by the administration aimed at curtailing freedom of speech. Some examples to illustrate the point are briefly mentioned here. IIT Madras (Chennai) courted controversy with a ban on the Ambedkar Periyar Study Circle (APSC) in 2014, following an anonymous complaint to the Ministry of Human Resource and Development, Government of India. The complaint stated that the study circle was holding discussions critical of the policies of the government. This led to protests by students against the ban, and it was reinstated after series of meetings between the students and faculty. The students of the APSC claim that they are being closely monitored and are issued warnings against speaking out against the government. In 2015, IIT Kharagpur issued a notice barring students from holding any gathering apolitical or otherwise, just hours before a scheduled march by the students against violence in Aligarh Muslim University. Students in IIT Madras and IIT Kharagpur protested against the denial of freedom of speech by the State through the administrative machinery of the institute.

Some instances that were reported were based on differing political ideological leanings in the campus. In September 2017, the administration of Jammu University decided to serve only vegetarian food in hostels and also banned students from protesting against the murder of journalist Gauri Lankesh. Students from Kerala, in Jammu University, wrote to the Chief Minister of Kerala, Mr Pinarayi Vijayan, urging his support in their fight against these rules. Earlier that year, pro right-wing students in Jammu University had protested against the disrespect to the national anthem during an event. These are just two instances of conflict driven by political ideology in the same university in the same year. Interestingly, four universities: Central University of

Tamil Nadu, Pondicherry University, Central University of Kerala and Manipur University saw protests by the students against 'saffronization of the campus' (saffronization refers to the right-wing as saffron is a colour associated with Hindutva) in 2018. In Central University of Tamil Nadu and Pondicherry University, students claimed that the right-wing students' union, ABVP (Akhil Bharatiya Vidyarthi Parishad), was being given preferential treatment on issues like permissions to hold meetings or movie screening. The shutting down of Manipur University for four months following protests by students against the vice chancellor (VC) received lot of attention from the press. The protests were about charges of corruption and saffronization against the VC. In the Central University of Tamil Nadu, students claimed that they were warned against holding any meetings or protests against any government policy. The Central University of Kerala received complaints from the Dalit and leftist students and teachers of being unfairly targeted by the administration.

Visva-Bharati University in Shantiniketan, West Bengal, was in news for unrest on campus on two occasions. The first incident took place in January, when a leader of the ruling party at the Centre was heckled during his speech at the university on the controversial CAA. The VC was locked in a room by the students' union for inviting the speaker to speak on CAA. The second incident took place in August 2020, when a boundary wall being built to prevent the university grounds from being used for the 'Poush Mela' (an annual local fair) triggered a protest by both students and the local residents. This was viewed as an assault on a long-honoured tradition. The origin of the fair is traced back to 1843, when Debendranath Tagore initiated a three-day festival in the month of December. In 1951, the Visva Bharati University decided to hold the fair within the campus, inviting participation from artisans and traders. The wall built by the university went against this tradition and, hence, was broken down as a mark of protest by the students and public. The VC complained to the Central and State governments about the violence on the campus. The authorities responded by shutting down the university. The first incident had definite political overtones, but the second incident started off as a combination of factors: problem with the traders and environmental concerns (the National Green Tribunal had pulled up the university authorities for environmental damage in the previous Poush Mela). As the issue escalated, it was depicted as a purely political and ideological issue with both State and Central governments getting involved in the matter.

The above-mentioned examples were a consequence of threats and bans, leading to protests and complaints. However, several other instances of conflict in universities have been violent in nature. In Punjab University, the authorities called in the police to act against students, protesting against a fee hike, while in Banaras Hindu University (BHU), the police attacked students protesting against discriminatory hostel rules. Jawaharlal Nehru University (JNU), India's premier institute, has been at the centre of controversies for a while due to a series of events. It started with a much maligned students' union meeting in 2016, where it was claimed that the students indulged in seditious and anti-national sloganeering. Student leaders were arrested, physically assaulted and charged with sedition. Overnight, the country was divided into pro-JNU and anti-JNU groups with matters reaching a point where people started demanding closure of the university. With one incident, all the achievements and accolades of a premier institute like JNU dissolved into nothing, and the very existence of the university was questioned. In 2020, a masked group of men and women entered JNU and beat up students and teachers assembled to discuss the proposed fee hike and also entered the hostels and assaulted students. It was alleged by students and teachers that administration, police and some of the faculty were complicit in the entire episode. The violence in JNU has been viewed as a clear political ideological battle between the dominant left-wing and the rising right-wing. The popular opinion among teachers and several others is that the rightists want to conquer JNU, the bastion of the left-wing politics. For long, JNU has been seen as dominated by the left-wing both in terms of faculty and students' union and influencing other campuses. The students of Jamia Millia Islamia were targeted in a similar fashion for speaking against CAA and the National Register of Citizens proposed by the government. Students were brutally attacked in libraries and hostels by the police and were in turn accused of having initiated the violence.

The nature of the conflicts highlighted so far have been between students and the university administration (sometimes due to interference from the State). However, there have been reports of violent conflicts not only between students' union groups but also between teachers and students. Take, for example, the threats received by an assistant professor of law in a college in Goa for teaching the class about Ms Gauri Lankesh, Mr Kalburgi and Mr Dabholkar (all three have been assassinated for speaking out against certain religious practices and superstitions) and even the Manusmriti (ancient Hindu code of law) in the class. The right-wing students' union in the college filed a complaint against the teaching of anti-religious subject matter in class. Earlier in 2016, two professors in Maharshi Dayanand University were pulled up by the executive council of the university for planning to stage a play on author Mahasweta Devi's much acclaimed work *Draupadi*. The protest against the play was led by the right-wing political students' group, and as the word spread, the local villages and ex-servicemen joined in. According to the protestors, the play depicts the army men as rapists and this was not acceptable, especially since the Uri attack (surgical strikes carried out by the Indian army across the Line of Control) had just been carried out by the army. There have been constant tussles between opposing political student groups with regard to speakers invited to seminars and conferences. Ramjas College, Delhi University (DU), was at the centre of a controversy due to the outbreak of violence over the choice of speakers at an event, ironically titled 'Culture of Protest'. Students have been embroiled in conflicts over movie screenings. Left-wing students of Jadavpur University, West Bengal, protested against screening of *Buddha in a Traffic Jam*. The film director accused the students of attacking him and damaging his car. In Banaras Hindu University, students protested against the screening of Anand Patwardhan's documentary film *Ram Ke Naam*. A clash between student political groups in Hyderabad University turned into a stand-off with the administration and a caste issue, resulting in the tragic death by suicide of Rohit Vemula, a young PhD scholar.

The State and administration can express authority and control in several ways. A powerful expression of control is the banning of books, and this has seen protests from both teachers and students. A number of books have been banned, meetings interrupted in the past few years, as they represent views that are not in line with the perspective that the government in power, irrespective of political orientation, wants to promote through education. In 2011, A. K. Ramanujan's essay, 'Three Hundred Ramanayas: Five Examples and Three Thoughts on Translation' was removed from the MA history's reading list in DU after Hindutva groups, including teachers and students, objected to it. In 2010, the Shiv Sena in Mumbai, pushed for a ban on Rohinton Mistry's novel, *Such a Long Journey*, for using insulting language against the party and its leader, Bal Thackeray. In 2018, a standing committee on academic affairs of the DU proposed a ban on three books from the MA syllabus of the Department of Political Science authored by Kancha Ilaiah Shepherd—*Why I Am Not a Hindu: A Sudra Critique of Hindutva Philosophy, Cultural and Political Economy; God as Political Philosopher: Buddha's Challenge to Brahmanism*; and *Post Hindu India*. In the same year, the standing committee on academic affairs in DU asked for the removal of Professor Nandini Sundar's *Subalterns and Sovereigns: An Anthropological History of Bastar* and Archana Prasad's *Against Ecological Romanticism: Verrier Elwin and the Making of an Anti-modern Tribal Identity*, from a course offered by the Department of History. Earlier in 2017, the teachers of National Democratic Teachers Front opposed the contents of a book by Professor Nandini Sundar, *Flames in the Forest*, and sought its removal from the MA sociology reading list.

It is evident that conflicts in HEIs occur at different levels of the system and in varying degrees of intensity depending on the underlying causes. It has been observed that new rules, restrictions and policies have acted as triggers in setting off conflict in campuses. Teachers, students and the administration become actors in these conflicts with their own ideological leanings (social, economic and political) colouring these conflicts. Political events at the national or state level or within the campus lead to confrontation between opposing student political groups. The intensity of conflict also varies, with violent conflict most likely between student groups, the administration being subjected to gheraos and lock in and the administration using the powers of the State against students. These conflicts are not new and are part of a historical narrative that tends to repeat itself. What is alarming today is the rapid succession of events that seem to go out of control and their trivial causes, for example, students attending pork or beef festivals or sharing a video. An interconnected world has meant that these conflicts have received attention. Universities within the country and across the world have expressed solidarity and support for students and teachers. Collective and united voices have been raised against attacks on students and universities, through nationwide protest marches, social media support and solidarity sit-ins. The consequences of any action are no longer constrained by isolated geographies, nothing goes unnoticed or unrecorded. The cumulative effect of the events has been a surge in articles, debates and discussions on government funding of education and increasing privatization, the role of conflict and dissent in education, perspectives on student politics, necessity of students' unions and the importance of a liberal education system for a robust democracy. A parallel conversation has been revived on the role of education and students in society and, also, what a university stands for. This is what the next section is about.

Education, as a system and process, has in it some inherent paradoxes. In this book, two paradoxes are discussed—the paradox of student activism and, second, the paradox of homogeneity. Both these concepts need to be seen through the prism of critical thinking. The paradox of student activism is based on the contentious and much-debated topic of student activism. Post Independence, sociologists, in India, engaged in discussions on the role of students in nation-building. Students were to be prepared not only for contributing economically but also socially and politically towards the progress of the nation. Students had already been a part of the national struggle for independence and their role in nation-building was seen as a natural extension. However, due to circumstances and events (refer to Chapter 3), the political role of students beyond that of being an electorate is being questioned. The State, through education, actively inculcates the ideas of nationalism, common identity and the duty of students to work for the welfare of the country. On the other hand, one of the latent functions of education is to develop leadership and other such qualities that would prove to be helpful in their life, professional and otherwise. Here in lies the paradox. Student activism creates a platform for students to develop public speaking and leadership skills and, most importantly, learn critical thinking. Several national political leaders speak of how they began their careers as student leaders. However, despite the fact that many senior leaders today, across party lines, who have stood against the government of the day as student activists, deny the same opportunity to students. Student activism is frowned upon and seen as a waste of time unless they support the dominant social, economic and political positions. Every country wants erudite, seasoned and principled politicians. How can this be achieved if we deny the youth an opportunity to engage in democracy?

Second paradox, which is yet to receive the kind of attention it deserves, is the paradox of homogeneity. The latter is of particular interest and consequence as it has far-reaching consequences for us as citizens of the country and also as global citizens. In the 1990s, globalization had become the buzzword, especially with the opening up of the economy. There were talks, seminars and courses on globalization, numerous thesis and dissertations were written on globalization, opening up new areas of research. Today, we seem to be turning the clock back and are intent on creating a narrow homogenous identity as a nation. This is taking place in several ways and not only in India but in other countries as well. One is through the need to glorify the historical past, increasingly based on false narratives rather than facts. This historical past is based on the achievements of the original inhabitants of the land, which is often based on a religious identity or racial identity or even both. Second is by claiming cultural superiority and one that needs to be recognized by the world. Both these ideas will be discussed in greater detail later in this book.

EDUCATION AND A SPACE CALLED UNIVERSITY

There are two main foundations or pillars of the research presented here and, consequently, in this book. First, this work is structured on the idea and ideal of education. Second is the university which is a space for shaping minds and forming a world view. The framework and analysis are based on the premise of the need for an educational system that encourages students to be aware of the world around them, instil principles and ethics of compassion, humility and honesty and encourage creativity. In HEIs, students are further encouraged to learn to think critically and deal with both conflict and consensus, question the policies of the state and regressive practices and traditions prevalent in the society.

These are not unattainable utopian ideals. We already have examples from history of how students can bring about positive changes in polity and society through concerted activism. In the past few years, European countries like Finland and Denmark have been experimenting with presenting an alternate version of education. They have introduced this new approach right from the primary levels. One such change has been breaking down the barriers of gender identities at a young age. The manner in which a society envisions education is reflected in its schools and universities. The opposing view espouses the linkages between education and employment. With the increasing cost of education, privatization and competitiveness, education is shifting further and further away from its original purpose. It is necessary to revisit some of the approaches to education from across disciplines. Philosophers and sociologists have spoken of education as a lifelong process and one that need not necessarily involve formal instruction through educational institutions. Education, believed to have been derived from the Latin word *educere*, meaning to progress from inside to outside, has been understood by philosophers like Plato as a lifelong learning process. In *Laws*, Plato writes, education 'not only provides knowledge and skills, but also inculcates values, training of instincts, fostering right attitude and habits' (Plato 2018, 644). He expands the idea of education further in *The Republic* and says 'True education whatever that may be, will have the greatest tendency to civilise and humanise them in their relation to one another and to those who are under their protection' (2018, 416).

When Plato speaks of the meaning of education and its impact on society and individual, it could be seen as the beginning of sociology of education. The founding fathers of sociology—Comte, Durkheim and Spencer—were keen on studying education both from the perspective of socialization and seconded the relationship between social development and educational institutions. Later, education was seen as the panacea to all social ills—such as crime, poverty, juvenile delinquency and so on. Sociology 'recognizes education as a social fact, a process and an institution, having a social function and being determined socially. Educational sociology could appear only when it accepted the social nature of education' (Shimbori 1979, 394). Tracing the development of the field, Shimbori writes that the initial view was that the education system, namely schooling, was a representative of the society at large and was, therefore, useful in transmission of culture. A new school of thought emerged, largely led by Herbart, that education needs to be studied from a wider perspective and not only from an individual perspective, receiving a set of formal instructions. But the argument for individual-centred approach to education was,

> The objectives and curricula of education cannot be fully discovered. Since education has a social function, in transmitting a cultural heritage to children and adapting them to the present or future society, education, especially in its aims and contents, should be derived from the needs of society, although education cannot be effective unless it responds to the individuals needs and abilities of children. (Shimbori, 1979, 399)

Over time, the discourse on education has shifted from what it should be to what it is. This is reflected in the sociological theories on education, where the focus of research and academic studies has been largely formal institutionalized education. The essence and role of education as an agency of socialization and that of social control and social change received much attention in the decades of 1950s–1970s, when the world was going through a transition. There was a tussle between the ideas of capitalism and communism, and much of the scholarly work on education was from either of the perspective. Much of this conversation was about access to education in terms of cost and livelihood prospects versus the true meaning of education. For sociologists, education performs many functions; it is an agency of socialization, social control, social mobility and social change. Of all this, the most important role is of the State. Each process is a complicated one and dependent on various other factors at play.

For Berger and Luckmann, education is an agency of socialization reflected through interpersonal relationships between the teacher and the taught, and the impact of course and curriculum, peer and secondary groups and so on (1967). Talcott Parsons focused on social integration and consensus along the lines of the school of functionalism. Education, for some, is a means of developing creative thought (Paterson) and, for others, means of social control (Bordieu) and state propaganda (Gramsci). It may appear conflicting that education is a means of continuity and social change. This is why education as merely an agency of socialization may bring with it the danger of being a conformist, as it prepares an individual for the society by acquainting him/her with only the dominant values, traditions and norms of the society which may or may not be in alignment with the individual's values and norms. Socialization of an individual through education is not a simple process, as it needs to represent the heterogeneity of society which it mostly does not.

As Berger and Luckmann put it, it is through socialization that an adult internalizes the meaning of the world and the social structure. It prepares an individual for what already exists and introduces him/her to the foundation of the society. They refer to it as 'reality maintenance,' whereby, the society must 'ensure that the reality as apprehended in individual consciousness is congruent with what is institutionally defined' (Minnis 1990, 90). A rather frightening aspect of socialization is presented by Berger and Luckmann when they write that whenever a new/alternate idea arises contradicting an existing idea or definition, for example, citizenship, nationalism or religion, there is an attempt to use education to fight it by introducing new courses on politics or religion, as the case may be. This they refer to as crisis maintenance. They write,

> The development of specific mechanisms of social control also becomes necessary with the historicization and objectivation of institutions. The institutions must and do claim authority over the individual, independently of the subjective meanings he may attach to any particular situation. The priority of the institutional definitions must be consistently maintained over individual temptation at redefinition. The children must be 'taught to behave' and once taught must be 'kept in line'. So of course must be the adults. (Berger and Luckmann 1967, 62)

Most of the times, education serves the purpose of what they term as 'reality maintenance'. It can be related to education of adults, whereby several courses in education are based on principles that ensure the 'reality maintenance' against the 'background of a world that is silently taken-for-granted' (Berger and Luckmann, 172). They go on to write that conduct becomes institutionalized and, hence, predictable. What appears to be a spontaneous conduct is actually a controlled behaviour that is a result of effective socialization and taken-for-granted behaviour. The gendered rules and regulations in many universities and other HEIs, especially in hostels, are examples of how behaviour is controlled in the educational system.

Taking forward the idea of both socialization and social control, Lilian McCoy (1998, 111) writes about the labour class and education in Britain:

> Education through schooling was seen by some as a way of exercising control over the working classes and the only way of ensuring continued social stability and industrial prosperity of the nation while others saw such education as a threat to the social order itself. This highlights educations ambiguous relationship with power. Education can control and empower, it can promote continuity or dissent. It can be dangerous if it makes people think.

In our everyday experiences in formal educational institutions, one may recall several instances of how uniformity, continuity and hierarchy are represented and ingrained in the minds of students from a very young age. Take, for example, the idea of school uniforms, punishment by figures of authority, namely the teacher and school administration, in case of any deviance from expected path of behaviour, acknowledging hierarchy and learning the 'right answers'. In all this, education contributes to the idea of social control.

Social mobility through education can, sometimes, become an unintended consequence. Thompson (1950, quoted in Lilian McCoy, 117), too, saw the British education system as merely advancing the interests of the capitalists and the upper class. He writes 'members of every community should be educated for their own sakes, with a view to their own happiness and not be made instrumental to the interests of any class.' This is reminiscent of the views of Bordieu expressed in his idea of 'cultural capital'. He writes in his work, *Reproduction: In Education, Society and Culture*, (1977), 'if proportion of working class students were significantly increased, those students' degree of relative selection would, as it declines, less and less off set the educational handicaps, related to the unequal social class distribution of linguistic and cultural capital' (Bordieu and Passeron 1990, 76). Education not only perpetuates the ideas of the ruling class but also is skewed in the favour of those who have had the privilege to access knowledge and social networks.

Echoing what McCoy writes about how the working class viewed education, in India, the British too wanted to create a steady stream of what were referred to as 'babus' (lower-level administrators), thus saving the cost of having someone come over from England, in today's language, an expat. Indians could be paid less and work without the benefits someone from Britain would expect. In India, social mobility is not confined to just class but also caste. Education was a privilege for not only the rich but also the upper caste. Education was out of bounds for the poor and those belonging to the lower castes, as they were not deemed 'fit' to receive knowledge, and much like how the British wanted to nurture a particular kind of working class, upper caste/class Indians, too, wanted to have steady stream of manual labourers. Education would translate into social mobility, which was not desirable as it would upset the 'natural order' which required that a certain section had to remain poor, submissive and servile. The reservation policy was one such attempt by the State to address this inequality. In most countries, 'Higher education in contemporary context remains as means both for social mobility and for national growth, societal restructuring and national unity' (Lea and Healy 2006, 3, quoted in Weiss and Aspinal 2012, 8). Another unintended consequence of Western education in India was that it opened the doors to the work and ideas of European thinkers and philosophers on liberty and equality. This greatly influenced and shaped the Indian national movement and the making of the Indian Constitution post Independence. Western education has played a significant role in giving direction to the students' movement during Independence and to student union thereafter.

One of the key factors that can lead to social mobility through education is affordability of education. Historically, only the elites (initially defined by caste, later expanded to include class) had access to education across the world. In order to break this cycle, State-led intervention through policies was necessary to ensure that people from all sections of the society have equal opportunity to education. This is one of the markers of a welfare state. However, a shift from a welfare state to a market state decreases the chances of the poor getting an education, as the costs of education goes up. Burd writes about the American experience of how more than 90,000 students from poor families were deprived of education because the Bush administration decided to cut Pell Grants, the nation's largest federal student aid programme (Burd 2005). Universities and institutes in India have seen a steady increase in fees over the past few years. Student protests against fee hikes spurred a debate on utilization of taxpayers' money versus fee hikes. It is rooted in the question of whether the State should continue to subsidize and spend on education. The other question was the extent of State support for education. There was public support for the JNU administration when it hiked the fees due to a popular belief that the existing fees were too low. Several testimonies of students who have studied in JNU said that their dream of an education was fulfilled only because there was a university in the country where world-class education was affordable. This is why fee hikes were met with vociferous protests in a country like India, where a large section of society has been able to access education only because of its affordability. The importance of this comes out in several interviews with teachers. The policy of making education affordable has not been given the attention it deserves. The advantage of social mobility through education may become a thing of the past if this persists.

Functionality and purpose of education get even more defined when one enters the university or a HEI. Societies which have built their education foundations on ideas of freedom and creativity along with learning are more likely to continue to do so in HEIs. But, in a typical set-up, processes of socialization, social control and institutionalization have formed the basis of education, and this is more likely to continue into higher education. This phase of the youth is crucial as ideas can get further entrenched or may be overthrown by newer ones. Peer pressure, influence of teachers and impact of events around them can play a role in shaping young minds. This is reflected in ideological viewpoints, political leanings or even awareness about the life around.

Henry Newman (2016), in his much-acclaimed work called *The Idea of a University*, says:

> If I were asked to describe as briefly and popularly as I could, what a University was, I should draw my answer from its ancient designation of a Studium Generale, or 'School of Universal Learning'. This description implies the assemblage of strangers from all parts in one spot;—from all parts; else, how will you find professors and students for every department of knowledge? and in one spot; else, how can there be any school at all? Accordingly, in its simple and rudimental form, it is a school of knowledge of every kind, consisting of teachers and learners from every quarter. Many things are requisite to complete and satisfy the idea embodied in this description; but such as this a University seems to be in its essence, a place for the communication and circulation of thought, by means of personal intercourse, through a wide extent of country.

Newman's views on education are shaped by a socialization perspective. He sees education not as an individual endeavour but one that is based on interdependency with other members of the society, and it is intergenerational. It is obvious that Newman is not talking only about the formal structures of education but also the informal means of education. Altbach, one of the leading scholars on student activism, writes, 'Without stress on family or caste, the university provided at least a partial model of what a modern society could be like' (1970, 75).

The vision of a university is based on idealism, a mingling of diverse mind, open spaces (physical and cognitive), liberalism, freedom to express one's thoughts and so on. It is a representation of what the society outside the walls of the university should be. It naturally follows that when people with diverse views congregate, there will be disagreements and even conflicting views. This is not to be avoided. Universities should encourage debates and discussions so that an individual can come out of the barriers of one's own thought processes and beliefs that are often result of the socialization in family, school and peers. For a mind to constantly evolve, which is one of the main purposes of education and in that the university, one of the prerequisites is that it should not be bound in walls of its own making. The mind should have the ability to challenge its own positions and arguments and not seek solace in self validation. The university should then encourage conflicting ideas to be expressed rather than giving precedence to consensus as emphasized by functionalists. Immanuel Kant believed that the State should give universities and, in turn, the faculty freedom to teach and also give legitimacy to knowledge produced in universities. According to him, this is beneficial for the State. When Immanuel Kant was charged of misusing philosophy to distort the teaching of holy scriptures, Kant maintained that philosophy is for the benefit of the society and that university knowledge should be given legitimacy and approved by the State. He insisted on freedom of the faculty. This puts faculty on the duty to enquire on behalf of the public. This will include discussion of public issues, directly helping the government in its aim of welfare of all. This will further ask the State to protect the freedom of the faculty. Humboldt, too, sees the State playing a positive role in education and universities. He argues that the State should not interfere in matters of the university and rather encourage teachers and students to research, learn and teach. He believes that universities also prepare students for their life beyond the university. For him, merely teaching is not sufficient, both teaching and research need to go hand in hand. Also, the teachers and students are not silos, rather they have to work in cohesion.

The idea of a university as a democratic space with a broad vision of education is easier said than done. The State withdrawal from public university in terms of funding has opened doors to donors and private players taking away autonomy of university and handing over control to either the State and the private players and donors. As Bhushan writes (2016), 'Modern public university in a democracy is to produce and disseminate knowledge for success of democracy and diversity. Democracy is a pre condition for a university to produce knowledge, which again is very necessary for the success of democracy.' The purpose of education espoused by yesterday philosophers may well seem utopian today. What is being witnessed now is a far cry from the idealistic vision of a university and the knowledge shared through education. Over the years, there has been a shift from knowledge for knowledge's sake to knowledge for commercial and employment purpose. And this is not limited to a particular country; it is a worldwide phenomenon. In such a scenario, several teachers who believe in education, in the original sense of the process, question how ideology, critical thinking and democratic values are to be taught to the students in a constricted education system that is geared to prepare students for employment. One of the reasons for this conflict is rooted in the past. Earlier, the guilds and the family used to perform the task of preparing and training the youth for employment. The clergy would impart religious education, while philosophy and liberal arts were taught by educational institutions. As time progressed and traditional structures broke down, universities were expected to perform all these functions—create employable youth, transmit knowledge about philosophers and thinkers and religion. Thus began a conflict within the system.

Terry Eagleton, in his much acclaimed 'Slow Death of the University', 2015, published in the *Chronicle of Higher Education,* speaks of the push towards the sciences, engineering and medicine in terms of funding and grants in the context of the British education system. He writes in the British context that the teaching process has become so bureaucratic that the teachers have less time for teaching and have to concentrate more on 'produce for production's sake' (Eagleton 2015). The grant/s that a university receives is based on the research output that is shown by each department. As a result, much of the time of teachers is spent in managerial work. Several of these aspects came up in conversations with teachers during the fieldwork. There were both covert and overt ways of controlling faculty. Recruitment, academic councils and research are ways of ensuring that the faculty work within the boundaries set by the State and administration. We will discuss more of this in Chapter 6 of this book.

Eagleton (2015) further writes,

> According to the British State, all publicly funded academic research must now regard itself as part of the so-called knowledge economy, with a measurable impact on society. Such impact is rather easier to gauge for aeronautical engineers than ancient historians. Pharmacists are likely to

do better at this game than phenomenologists. Subjects that do not attract lucrative research grants from private industry, or that are unlikely to pull in large numbers of students, are plunged into a state of chronic crises. Academic merit is equated with how much money you can raise, while an educated student is redefined as an employable one. In general idea is that universities must justify their existence by acting as ancillaries to entrepreneurship. As one government report chillingly put it, they should operate as 'consultancy organizations'. In fact, they themselves have become profitable industries, running hotels, concerts, sporting events, catering facilities, and so on.

Many of the readers may find this relevant in the constant comparisons and questions on relevance of humanities today, especially with the conflict between State and the universities. Why should the State fund students/universities in which humanities are taught, which in no apparent way contribute to economy or economic activities or growth? 'Knowledge is valued for its strict utility rather than as an end in itself or for its emancipatory effects.' Good value for students means taking courses labelled as 'relevant' in market terms, which are often counterposed to courses in the social sciences, humanities and fine arts that are concerned with forms of learning that do not readily translate into either private gain or commercial value. Under the rule of corporate time, 'the classroom is no longer a public space concerned with issues of justice, critical learning, or the knowledge and skills necessary for civic engagement' (Giroux 2009, 118).

As Giroux points out, State funding of education and research diminishes, faculty look for funding outside, namely private donors. This is especially true in relation to research on new products, say in medicine, where the industry is looking out for innovations and new products and ever so ready to back researchers who can deliver on their promise. This further establishes the link between research, outcome and profit. 'Within this symbiotic relationship, knowledge is directly linked to its application in the market, resulting in a collapse of the distinction between knowledge and the commodity' (Giroux 2009, 10). A similar pattern is emerging in India, in the wake of the conflict between universities and the State. The malaise he points out is being witnessed in Indian universities—the rush for publications, paying money for publishing articles and a constant pressure to show the 'outcome'.

The constant point of debate is what is the student studying and how is it beneficial for the State to fund the education of the student. As Udaya Kumar (2016, 29–31) points out,

> The rhetoric around the taxpayer subverts inclusive conceptions of public interest by producing a distinction between 'taxpayers' and 'spongers,' and arrogates a differential right to dictate the terms on which public funds should be spent. Education is seen less as a vital resource valued and maintained in collective interest than as a site of economic investment where he funders, that is, the taxpayers, have a right to set societal agendas and objectives. This differentiation of the public—dividing it on the basis of graded rights in deciding public matters—is interestingly accompanied by a trend in the opposite direction.

While these discussions are of a theoretical and philosophical nature, education has a practical and policy angle to it. Education has been interrogated through the lens of gender, class and, in India, there is an additional angle of caste. There is no dearth of literature on education considering that it has been a challenging task to provide quality education to millions of Indians. This has prompted experts in economics, education and sociology to analyse, comment and suggest on the education policy adopted by successive governments. If one may summarize the challenges before the government and policy planners, they would be: ensuring that more and more people enrol for education at all levels—primary, secondary and higher education, accessibility and affordability of education, quality of education and employability post education. There are, of course, several off shoots which include enrolment of Scheduled Castes (SCs) and Scheduled Tribes (STs) and girls in the formal education system, which had been denied to them for decades. The inclusion of girls, SCs and STs in education has been an indicator of social change and social mobility. From being denied access to education, SCs and STs today have special schemes and reservation. Of course, the impact of reservation and the attitude of teachers and students towards reservation is a separate topic of discussion. Some of the problems plaguing universities, funds, lack of infrastructure, teachers and quality are all linked to the central question of the social role of education.

A question that has been asked often is—Should universities be political or apolitical? One of the apprehensions associated with a political university is the impact it has on its relationship with the State. There have been instances in history, for example, Hitler's regime, when the bureaucracy gained control over all universities, compromising on the type of teachers by interfering in appointments and the moral authority of the teachers thus appointed. Karl Jasper, in 1960, wrote that politics can be introduced in a university but only as a research subject. He did not want politics of the everyday world to enter into campuses. The fear of blind opposition or cooperation have led many thinkers to support the idea of an apolitical university.

Habermas disagrees with Kant, Jasper and Humbolt in a lot of ways. For Habermas, the idea of University meant 'shared self understanding of the university's members—traces of a corporative consciousness' (Habermas and Blazek 1987, 5). He notes that after the Second World War, universities have been moving towards two different directions. One was the emphasis on technology-driven reform, which makes it a system of social labour and cuts it from the public and political domain. For Habermas, one of the primary roles played by the university is to meet the need of an industrial society and provide qualified workforce. Not only should the students acquire knowledge of a subject but also be equipped to deal with the professional word. Here, Habermas is referring to the latent functions performed by education by teaching students how to work in a team, react to authority and so on. But he also speaks of leadership skills, ability to think on one's feet and loyalty towards the organization one is working for, what he calls the unwritten professional standards which may not be necessarily taught but that must be a part of the socialization process. University is a space for reproduction of knowledge and transmission of the cultural traditions of a society, yet another established socialization function of education. For him, 'the influence of interpretation provided by the social sciences and humanities on the self understanding of the general public can be seen easily' (Habermas and Blazek 1987, 'Introduction'). But he cautions that any study of cultural practices must be done in a thoughtful and reflective manner, else it will lead to dogmatism.

The experience of the German universities during and post Second World War shaped Habermas' view on universities. The students were trained 'under the aegis of an apparently apolitical institution and generations of students in the disciplines of knowledge and simultaneously were educated in a politically manner. This process produced the mentality of a university trained professional stratum, it assured homogeneity of university trained elite' (Habermas and Blazek 1987). He says that the apolitical nature of German universities bred a strong sense of loyalty to the State authority, and there were no student political organizations in the university. According to Habermas, universities should build political consciousness in its students. It cannot restrict itself to performing only the 'traditional, socially necessary functions'. Society should not accept depoliticization of the university and should encourage political discussions in the university, and universities should assert themselves in democratic sphere. Not only students but also professors and junior faculty should assert their rights and take part in political discussions, as the university itself is a political issue and this makes it an ideal place for political activity.

Habermas, in his work (translated by Shaprio 1987) on student protest and politics, speaks of the role played by students in the 19th century in China, Russia and Cuba and presents an interesting observation that in countries where army wields control, the students' body exercises the function of putting political pressure on the government. In doing this, the students see themselves as the future elites and also responsible for the modernization process. Like several thinkers before him, Habermas, too, sees the university as an agent of social change and even goes on to say that their mere fact of entering the university system 'promotes an impulse toward entering the struggle against the traditionalism of the inherited social structure .... There is a singular parallel between the socialization process of the individual student and the overall process of social change.' (Habermas and Blazek 1987: Introduction)

As Bhushan (2016) points out, an idealistic view of university is that it is apolitical and the State provides support to the university in its search for knowledge. But if the role of a university is to help in build future citizens, how can it be an apolitical space with apolitical teachers? Udaya Kumar further writes,

> The public university seems placed at the moment at the crossroads of these two forces: the state and a punitive public trying to curtail its autonomy as a space, and the democratization of the student body altering the character, concerns, and relationship of the university to society at large.

> In the new conception being forward by the government, the university is considered as a skill factory which through mass production will address the needs of the country's economy. Critical thought is regarded as an outmoded ambition, an irritant that impedes the smooth accomplishment of this aim. Nationalism is used as a tool to legitimize efforts to determine from outside what the university ought to follow by way of independent thinking. (2016, 31)

Giroux answers this through his idea of public time and says that public time encourages people to question those in power, it encourages critical thinking.

> Public time legitimates those pedagogical practices that provide the basis for a culture of questioning, one that enables the knowledge, skills and social practices necessary for resistance, a space of translation, and a proliferation of discourses. It unsettles common sense and disturbs authority while encouraging critical and responsible leadership and a commitment to linking social responsibility and social transformation.(Giroux 2009, 115)

In contrast to this is the notion of corporate time that is based on the idea of profit and is centred on issues commercial in nature. Corporate time functions on

> The values of hierarchy, materialism, competition, and excessive individualism are enshrined under corporate time and play a defining role in how it allocates space, manages the production of particular forms of knowledge, and regulates pedagogical relations. Divested of any viable democratic notion of the social, corporate time measure relationships, productivity, space, and a knowledge according to the cost-efficiency, profit and a market based rationality.' (Giroux 2009, 116)

Closely associated with the ideas of a university as a political space, two more controversial points emerge. One, ideological positioning of faculty and, in turn, the university and, second, political activism among students and teachers. In expressing either opposition or cooperation with the State, the university may reveal an ideological position. Those who want an apolitical space usually refer to a neutral, non-critical and cooperative relation with the State. A political university may have the same relation when ideologically it is aligned with the State. The problem arises when the university believes in an ideology that is in opposition to that of the government in power.

This inevitably leads to conflict. Ideology finds its way into curricula, textbooks and classrooms.

Giroux (1985) writes,

> Ideology is the production, consumption and representation of ideas and behaviour which can either distort or illuminate the nature of reality can be either coherent or contradictory; can function within the sphere of both consciousness and unconsciousness; they can exist at the level of critical discourse as well as within the sphere of taken for granted lived in experience and practical behaviour.'

He further writes that 'educators working within the critical tradition should support a theory of ideology that is also capable of comprehending the way in which meaning is constructed and materialized within texts or cultural forms such as films, books, curriculum packages, fashion styles etc'.

Higher education, especially social sciences, in India is viewed as being dominated by the left-wing academicians, and the resurgence of the right wing has seen a demand for review of text and academic books and administration of institutes. Education has been used for propagating ideological positions by several regimes. In Nazi Germany, books for children and youth were used for 'identification with Nazi heroes and supporting the support of German youth for the National Socialist cause' (Redmann 1988, 131). The heroes in these books were similar to the Nazi 'heroes' of the Third Reich. Not only that, these books tried to put forth the cultural ideas of a true German family, loyalty to the family and, above all, loyalty to the cause of the nation. Park (1980) speaks of the threat to education due to the 'renewed strength of the political right'. One of the key problems is, according to him, the inevitable religious connect of the far right. In the USA, the far right traces all ills of modern society to progressive, liberal ideas and also lack of belief in God. One far right campaigner says 'We believe we should be in politics as a way of improving the world from a religious concept' (Park 1980, 608). They find the modern theories of evolution and understanding of religion against the Bible. We find echoes of this in the ideological position on education taken by the far right in almost all countries. To this, Park makes an important point when he says that 'We must develop increased sensitivity to the activities and messages of organisations on the political extremes, both right and left.' (1980, 608).

What is essential is the need to be aware of one's own ideological positioning. As Giroux (1983) writes, 'failure to understand classroom pedagogy as a form of ideological production prevents both teachers and students from recognising the centrality of their own epistemological claims for truth.' He makes an interesting point that ideology has a role to play in social transformation. This transformation can take place only through self-reflection and action. Ideology functions through individuals, and while it does conform to the ethos of the dominant group, it also has the potential to bring in social transformation. For this purpose, he sees intersectionality between ideology, culture and schooling.

Giroux's more recent work, provocatively titled *The University in Chains* (2016), delves deep into the problems that assail universities and higher education. He writes that universities are in the grip of chains of 'rigid ideological, economic and religious' ideas that prevent critical thinking. Giroux makes a scathing attack on the American model of higher education, where universities are increasingly getting commodified and losing their touch with social issues and social movements, engagement with democracy and 'non-militarized' forms of knowledge. He alleges that the current form and content of education does not help foster a meaningful dialogue on democracy and dissent or create 'groups of critical citizens'. Universities are being increasingly modelled on the interests of the corporate world. This is influencing the curricula and university policies. He further writes,

> Patriotic correctness, consumerism and militarization have become the most powerful triology of forces now shaping education and redefining the meaning of citizenship and establishing the contour of an authoritarian social order.... Education is now about job training, competitive market advantage, patriotic correctness and a steady supply of labour force for the national security state. (Giroux 2016, Introduction)

For Giroux, democracy cannot function in entirety with an education system such as this. At the heart of democracy are autonomous, self-reflective and independent citizens. To build this citizenship, universities have to equip students to be able to 'make vital judgements and choices about participating in and shaping decisions that affect everyday life, institutional reform and governmental policy' (Giroux 2016). This can happen only when teachers themselves are allowed to function with a sense of freedom and not silenced through university processes of governance.

Writing about totalitarianism, the philosopher Cornelius Castoriadis (1991) insisted that one mark of such a regime is the disappearance of informed citizens who give substantive content to public space, wage ongoing struggles to preserve and expand the public realms capable of educating the totality of citizens to participate in and shape a democratic society and comprehend that civic education is an 'essential dimension of justice' (Castoriadis 1991, 140). What Castoriadis recognized was that matters of agency, critical thought and politics itself were impossible under conditions in which education maintained a passive attitude towards power, democracy and the future. This is especially relevant under the current regime of neoliberalism, when the crucial imperatives of vision and hope have been stripped from any understanding of the future, mortgaged to a demoralized and corrupt 'democracy of money and military power' (Pender 2007, 16). This is also accompanied by campaigns of intimidation and professional and character assassination based on false allegations and fabrications that are employed to question the credibility and reputation of teachers and, in turn, to justify the firing for alleged incompetency or unprofessional conduct.

In India, over the past few years, not only have universities been attacked as anti-national for criticizing the government policies, but the faculty, too, has been constantly attacked for airing views that are critical of the government. As Robert Zemsky (2003) writes, 'When the market increases totally dominate colleges and universities, their role as public agencies significantly diminishes, as does their capacity to provide venues for the testing of new ideas and the agendas for public action.' In the same vein as Giroux, Suman Gupta (2019) points out,

> Though the recent events in the universities are termed on the basis of ideology, it is difficult to term them on those lines, because they are very diverse and variegated. What defines its character is what it is opposing; i.e the government or the idea of exclusionary and authoritarian nationalism.

The academic resistance hence appears to be the opposite of the exclusionary nationalism. The inclusive and rational principles of modern scholarship and pedagogy also make Academia a threat. The government has used neo-liberal tools like metrics, target setting and cost accounting rationales to transform pedagogy to authoritarian nationalism. Most of the protests in the campuses have been about the neo-liberal setting like hike in fees, too much surveillance etc.

The government, according to Gupta, is intent on aligning all universities with a certain ideological framework, and to achieve this end, there is an attempt to control the appointments, especially in the top positions, and there is an increasing dependence on both corporate and bureaucratic governance.

As Louis Wirth said decades ago and resonates with what's happening today around the world,

> The contemporary intellectual world is no longer a cosmos but presents the spectacle of a battlefield of warring parties and conflicting doctrines. Not only does each of the conflicting factions have its own set of interests and purposes, but each has its picture of the world in which the same objects are according different meanings and values. There exists a further obstacle to the achievement of consensus in the downright obstinacy of partisans to refuse and consider or take seriously the theories of their opponents simply because they belong to another intellectual or political camp. (Wirth, XXVI as quoted in Reisch 2019, 198)

ABOUT THE BOOK

After Independence, control of education was a matter of much debate, of whether it was to be included in the Union or the State List. The states were in no mood to concede to the demand of the Centre to make education a Union subject. The result of a series of debates and discussion was that education was placed in the Concurrent List, which would ensure that the states ensure a minimum standard of education, and at the same time, there would be joint collaboration with the Centre with regard to policies and addressing gaps and preventing duplication. Maulana Abul Kalam Azad, Minister for Education, was in favour of education being added to the Union List, as he was of the opinion that there should be uniformity in how the intellectuals think, and this could be achieved only if the Centre was in charge of education.

Conflicts within and with the education system is not something new, and successive governments have either neglected education or tried to control it through various means. It would appear that the past few years have been marked by frequent confrontations between the State and university administration and students. These are the times when society, at large, is getting increasingly fragmented on ideological lines, not merely political but also social and economic. For the purpose of this work, the term ideology is referred to in the larger sense of 'world view, attitude or perspective,' it does not refer to only political beliefs. Hence, the ideological battle of how people view the world and each other is not just the traditional divide between the right wing and left wing, though political usage of ideology is more popular now. Today, the media and especially social media (like popular culture, Facebook, WhatsApp, Twitter, television, newspapers) is said to have deepened political ideological differences and played havoc with friendship and even familial relationships. But the truth is, these divisions have always been there, these platforms have provided the opportunity and, in certain cases, anonymity to present views without consequences. University campuses have never been immune from ideological battles, be it in India or anywhere else in the world. This book is a response to these turbulent times we find ourselves in. It seeks to explore and understand the response of students to the events around them and the role and influence education and the HEIs/universities play and have in shaping and forming their world views. In doing so, it places at the centre the idea of a liberal higher education system in India.

It would appear as if the world today is caught in several ideological battles, be it racism, caste, religion, economic or political affiliations But these definite world views have always existed and found their way into social lives and in education. At the very beginning, it was mentioned that this book takes ideology away from a purely political realm and places it in the social and professional context of a student's life in a HEI. The first question is, therefore, How and where does a student get introduced to 'ideology' as a concept? Do HEIs provide the necessary space for a student to get familiarized with ideology as a concept and function in everyday life? Does it make or break friendships or lead to conflict in the campus? What is the role of a teacher in shaping ideology in a student? At a certain stage in a student's life, teachers play a very important role as imparters and creators of knowledge. The question that arises here is does the ideological leaning of the teacher create a conflict with the student, and does it compromise teaching and the relationship between the teacher and the student. In the education system, in India, the student is in a subordinate position and the teacher, through real and apparent use of authority, can jeopardize or help a student's growth and development. The third aspect in this is political—whether a deep ideological commitment leads to political affiliation and activism. In connection to this, the element that is explored here is the difference between ideological leanings, political affiliation and political participation that emerge during the course of the research.

There is an emerging narrative against students' activism. While the students become a vote bank for politics outside the campus, there is a resistance to students becoming politically active or even to any questioning of state policies that adversely impacts students. With regard to student activism and students' union on campus, the research posed two questions—one, awareness about the events and conflict taking place in other universities and, second, the support from within the student-and-teacher community for students' union and activism. At times, this resistance comes in from students themselves, who lend support to the denial of freedom.

One of the central actors in the higher education system is the State. The State seeks to control education, and this leads to conflicts with students and teachers, examples of a few were discussed earlier in the chapter. The State can create points of conflict by supporting a particular group of academics or even particular universities and institutes, introducing administrative rules, restrictions on teachers and students that go against the principles of liberal education system. This also brings into play the relationship of the students' union with teachers and administration, which is based on control, hierarchy and, at times, political differences. The State also sees itself responsible for inculcating the feeling of patriotism, belonging to a nation and passing on history of the making of the nation to future generations. Education is the perfect tool for this.

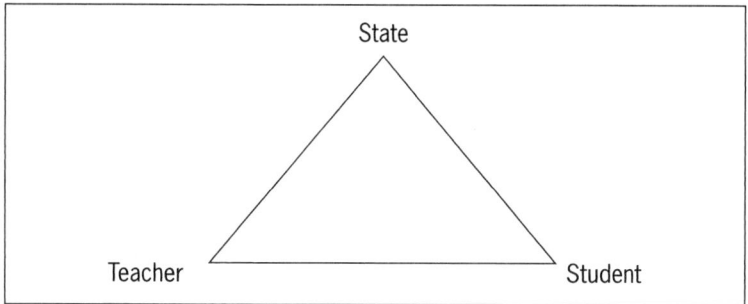

This book explores this in two ways. One is the control that the State exercises over HEIs through policies and administrative structures and processes. This includes infrastructure, funding, reservation policies, recruitment and promotion and research. Second is the use of national symbols like the national anthem, celebration of events of national importance and so on. The State plays an important role in guiding and shaping education. The State may also attempt ideological indoctrination of students in several ways, and one such way is the celebration of certain national symbols: the military, national flag and so on. Enforcing strict rules about celebration on certain days, which have no linkages to HEIs, and penalizing those who don't, can create a backlash and students can emerge as pockets of resistance within the academia, standing up against ethno-nationalism. During the fieldwork, students were asked what the national anthem means to them and, second, their opinion about the current debate on rewriting history and the Indian Science Congress (ISC) promoting certain mythologies as 'scientific achievements' from the past. As a result, today, mythology is being discussed in academic circles as verified facts. How does this impact a young mind? Have young science students abandoned scientific temper? Science students were asked about the blurring lines between science and mythology in recent times. These questions were asked out of the need to examine whether students are capable of examining the events around them in a critical manner, without getting carried away by feelings of nationalism. While some aspects of this were predetermined, many more came up during the course of the interviews with teachers and students.

The scope of the study widened with time, because as the study progressed, it raised several other questions due to the responses received from both teachers and students. For example, the control and idea of research in universities, freedom to speak out against the administration, the concern with fee hikes and lack of representation in the academic council. The interaction between teachers and administration is greater than that between the students and administration or the State. It was not surprising that it occupied a large part of the conversations with the teachers during the field interviews. As a result, issues facing education, which was intended to be a section in a chapter, was converted into a full-fledged chapter, and the problems being faced by teachers has been dealt with in a separate chapter.

Apart from this, this book speaks of institutionalized behaviour and social control as expressed through gendered hostels' regulations. Hierarchy and control in the context of gender and caste in higher education is often expressed through rules of admission, reservation and hostel rules. Rules restricting women from going out, accessing facilities in the campus are a deterrent to their development and also further the gender hierarchies in a formal legalized manner which further indoctrinate expectations and create formal social pressure. The administration can perpetuate entrenched hierarchies of the society. Conservative ideas about gender roles, student as a stakeholder can further restrict the growth and development of the student.

This book also points out achievements of social mobility through both fee structures and reservations. It analyses the implications of fee hikes and the impact of reservation on caste composition of teachers and students in HEIs. Issues like fee hikes and hostel regulations were initially meant to serve as examples of accessibility and exclusion and institutionalized gendered behaviour, respectively. However, as the research progressed, not only had students taken to the streets to protest against fee hikes, but it was also evident that the issue of fee hikes needed greater attention. Students have been protesting against gendered hostel rules all across the country. While the BHU protest and the Pinjra Tod (Break the Cage) movement have received media attention, there have been protests in Rajasthan, Madhya Pradesh and in many more states which have not received the same attention. Therefore, these protests need to be documented and analysed, as many campus hostels tend to perpetuate highly gendered views of how women students should behave and tend to regulate and monitor female students in a bid to exercise societal control over them.

With the scope of book firmly in place, it was evident that a qualitative research is necessary to capture its essence. The research was planned in a manner that the universities/technical institutes would represent the main regions of India—North, South, East, West and Northeast. Since one of the objectives of the research was to analyse whether choice of subjects/discipline of study impacts the understanding of ideology and student activism and so on, it was imperative to include students and teachers of both humanities and science stream. Limited resources, both human and financial, in addition to time constraints, demanded that the total number of universities and science institutions to be included in the study be limited to not more than 30. It helped that some universities had both science and humanities students, and as a result, students from both streams could be interviewed during the same phase. Private universities were not a part of the study.

The initial plan for the fieldwork was to interview at least 20 students and 5 teachers from each university and technical Institute. In universities, where both science and humanities were taught, 20 students and 6 teachers from each stream would be interviewed, taking it to a total of 40 students and 12 teachers. The research also intended to interview professors who had retired, as they would be best suited to give an overall view of the crisis in education and the changing composition of students and teachers. In some universities, the target on minimum interviews were met, while in others, it was difficult to get students and teachers on board due the nature of the topic. A total number of 627 students and 165 teachers were interviewed across the universities listed in Tables 1.1 and 1.2.

An attempt was made for the interviews with students to be distributed carefully across gender, age and courses as far as possible. Similarly, the teachers were interviewed across departments

Table 1.1 *Humanities*

Sl No	University	No. of Students	Teachers
1	JNU	20	6
2	SPPU[a]	19	5
3	Calicut	20	6
4	NEHU[b]	20	6
5	Gauhati	20	6
6	DU	22	6
7	Bangalore	20	6
8	Punjab	20	6
9	OU[c]	19	5
10	BHU	20	6
11	AU[d]	20	6
12	Pondicherry	19	5
13	Gulbarga	20	6
14	Periyar	18	10
15	Jadavpur	20	5
16	Kashmir	19	
	TOTAL	316	90

Source: Author.
Note: [a] Savitribai Phule Pune University; [b] North-Eastern Hill University; [c] Osmania University; [d] Allahabad University.

and positions. An effort was made to ensure there would be two interviews each, from each level—professor, associate professor and assistant professor. Further, it was intended to include at least two teachers belonging to the reserved categories. However, these criteria were not met in every university due to a variety of reasons. In some cases, there were students who refused to mention their caste, and they were not forced to reveal the same; so the numbers here are not absolute but only indicative. Teachers were not asked their caste but several teachers from the SC community mentioned it voluntarily. The word ideology was viewed with suspicion by many, as like most, ideology was understood to be only political ideology. Some refused

Table 1.2 *Sciences*

Sl No	Institute/University	No. of Students	Teachers
1	NIT Warangal	37	5
2	OU technical	23	3
3	IIT Delhi	20	5
4	IIT Madras	20	6
5	NEHU	20	7
6	Punjab	21	6
7	BHU	20	7
8	AU	20	5
9	Pondicherry	19	6
10	FTII[a]	20	–
11	Bangalore	20	6
12	DU	19	6
13	Jamia Millia Islamia	13	3
14	NIT Srinagar	19	6
15	Jadavpur	20	4
	Total	311	75

Source: Author.
Note: [a] Film and Television Institute of India.

to answer what they thought were political questions such as new issues that have emerged in education, the debate of University Grants Commission (UGC) versus Higher Education Commission of India (HECI). Teachers, too, were apprehensive about answering questions regarding autonomy to choose and design course or the problems they faced in the university.

As mentioned earlier, some students refused to mention their caste when asked at the beginning of the interview. Overall, the data indicates that most of the students were from General and Other Backward Class (OBC) groups (106 and 116, respectively) and SC/ST had an equal representation of nearly 13 per cent. It is also to be kept in mind that the number of ST students is among the lowest in all universities. Among the humanities students, 141 female students and 175 male students were interviewed. PhD and MPhil students are very few in number in most universities, but it was important to include them, as being a part of the university for years, they have a more informed opinion. Students pursuing bachelor's and master's degrees form the majority of students in every campus, and a larger number of students were interviewed from these courses. It was not surprising that most of the students were from urban areas, as most of the universities are located in urban or semi-urban areas. The only exceptions were Calicut University, DU, JNU and Periyar University.

Majority of the science and engineering students interviewed were from the General category. But in contrast to the humanities respondents, the number of ST students interviewed was higher than the number of SCs. Although the number of OBC respondents was considerably high at 32 per cent, but the gap between the General category and OBC students was much wider. The number of women in engineering courses and sciences is considerably less in comparison to the men, and this was reflected in the interviews conducted. Unlike the humanities, where there is a gap about 30 students between men and women, in sciences, 205 men and only 105 women were interviewed.

Most of the field research was done by local researchers. This included MPhil/PhD students, alumni of universities, assistant professors and other young researchers. One of the main reasons for the choosing of local researchers was that of language. In several universities, students were comfortable in speaking in the local language, be it Kannada, Tamil or Marathi. The familiarity of existing students or alumni with the campus helped in establishing contact with the students' union groups and teachers. Considering the reluctance to speak on many issues, a familiar face or a known senior from the university, institute added a certain degree of comfort for the interviewee. Three separate sets of interview schedules were administered. One for students of humanities and liberal arts, a second one for students studying engineering or Bachelor of Science, and a third one for teachers. The interview schedules for students were structured, while the one for teachers was semi-structured, leaving it to the teachers to point out more issues and concerns. The interview schedules for the humanities and science students were similar, except for a set of questions on the ISC, importance of scientific temper and relevance of mythology in science. The interview schedules were divided into administrative queries (admission policy, rules in hostels and on campus, new courses introduced, tussle between administration and students), ideology (understanding of ideology, political leanings, support to the idea of students/teachers on campus, whether students are aware of the ideological positions of the teachers, what the national anthem means to students) and the third aspect was to assess the awareness of students regarding the recent trend of rewriting history, merging of mythology with science and history, identifying ideological bias in textbooks and their ability to critically analyse this.

These were in-depth conversations and elicited interesting responses from both students and teachers. The teachers' interview schedules were semi-structured, allowing for new topics of discussion to come up with ease. Broadly, the teachers were asked about the freedom to choose and design their courses, changing caste composition among students and teachers, main issues facing higher education, recurring and recent additions, whether ideology impacts teaching and the interpersonal relationship between teachers and students. They were also asked about their opinion on student activism on campus and the move to replace UGC with HEI.

The combination of fieldwork and secondary research are captured in seven chapters in this book, including the Introduction and Conclusion. The Introduction serves as the first chapter. From the second chapter, fieldwork comes into play and each chapter presents the analysis for a set of interconnected questions that were posed to students and teachers. Further, each chapter is substantiated and strengthened with secondary research.

The second chapter dives into some of the key themes that were explored as part of the field research. It begins with a brief introduction of the theoretical positions of sociologists, political scientists and philosophers with regard to ideology and education. We also took a contemporary look at the crisis in education within Giroux's framework of pedagogy and education. The chapter then moves on to a sociological analysis of ideology, from the socialization perspective of peer group, teachers and the campus political activities using the Berger and Luckmann framework of social reality of everyday life. The second chapter also explores sociopolitical attitudes among students and the role of socialization in shaping sociopolitical attitudes through the agencies of family, teachers or the peer group. Do students really understand what ideology means, and do they let ideology impact their friendship? The interviews provide interesting insights on the students' perceptions of the right- and left-wing ideology. It also discusses whether the student can be truly apolitical. Some of the universities where the research was undertaken have seen conflict outside the campus (conflict areas like the Northeast and Kashmir) and inside (AU, BHU and Jamia Milia). These experiences impact both students and teachers, and in many cases, conflict has made them wary of political activism on campus.

Furthermore, is there a difference between how students of humanities and sciences view ideological positions and their shaping of sociopolitical attitudes? The attitudes of the students towards rewriting of history, mythology and science is analysed from both the prism of political ideology and as an exercise in critical thinking. In this chapter, the conversations with students is analysed at two levels—one, how the State influences feelings of nationalism, nationhood and, also, yields ideological control in several ways through educational institutes and universities, for example, through courses and textbooks. The analysis of the interviews is placed in the theoretical context of Gramscian theories of education as an ideological apparatus in the hands of the state. Primary data in the form of circulars and instructions from the UGC is used to prove this point.

The third chapter begins with a brief overview of the history of students' movements in India and across the world. It traces the role students played in the Independence movement in India and thereafter. It also looks at the changing character and goals of students' movement. Social science students, in nearly all countries, have the most liberal and radical views on social issues (Altbach 1984). Globally, the history of student activism witnesses the struggle of this institution for its existence and autonomy and, simultaneously, challenging the existing forms of knowledge and its production. The much publicized and politicized events at JNU and Jamia Milia raise questions about the student as a 'political' individual. The State ban on student unions is yet another way of controlling the students, especially his/her political views and associations. This chapter looks at the changing nature of student activism and the sociological reasons for it, awareness of students of the conflicts taking place in other universities and institutes, students' opinion about the need for students' and teachers' union. As in the section of ideology, this chapter does not focus on the politics on campus, it does not analyse the actions of the various students' union and so on. Instead, it presents a picture of how students and teachers view the presence of students' and teachers' union and, also, whether students are united as a community and present a voice in unison.

The fourth chapter locates caste and gender in campuses, though not in the traditional manner. There is enough data on caste composition of students in higher education. In this book, the idea was not to just quote data but to have a conversation with teachers of how they think classroom and staffrooms have changed over the years. University records on admission, as available on the website, were scoured to look at the parity between the General, OBC and SC/ST admissions. This chapter examines in great detail the idea of control as expressed in Berger and Luckmann's idea of institutionalization and habitualization through the gender-specific rules and regulations in hostels. There have been several protests across the country regarding discriminatory rules against women in universities. The Pinjra Tod movement in DU received much media coverage, but similar battles have been fought in many campuses. During the field work, students in several universities spoke of discriminatory hostel rules. This is placed in the context of how educational institutes and universities can be arenas of control and perpetuating hierarchy and patriarchal mindsets through habitualization. There have been very many instances of girls speaking out against the patriarchal norms that are perpetuated through something as innocuous as hostel rules.

The fifth chapter focuses on the issues highlighted by teachers and what they perceive are the main problems plaguing higher education. The teachers were asked about recurring and new issues, and one of the issues that stood out was fee hikes. There have been recent protest movements against fee hikes; this chapter gives an overall view of the fee hikes that have taken place over the past few years and their impact on students in particular and universities at large. It also includes the recent debate on HECI versus UGC, about which the teachers were asked their opinion. The New Education Policy (NEP) 2020 mentions the HECI, and against that background, it is interesting to see what the teachers think about the HECI.

The sixth chapter is based on interviews with the teachers on several issues such as recruitment, administrative policies from within the campus and from the government that impact teachers and academic freedom to choose and design their courses. Freire's *Pedagogy of the Oppressed* has influenced the way teaching and education are viewed around the world. Students are seen as passive receivers of knowledge, and this was reflected in the relationship between student and teachers as expressed in the interviews. Henry Giroux's arguments on bureaucratization of teaching and the impact of privatization and private funding on education and pedagogy ring true even more today in the scenario of the rules in universities with regard to teachers, cost of education and the freedom with regard to teaching. The state wields control in several ways—appointments, designing of courses, promotions, etc. The composition of the academic councils of universities and the role of overarching bodies like the UGC exposes the role of the State in trying to control education. This chapter analyses the composition of the academic council of the universities included in the fieldwork. It also explores how teachers view the relationship between ideology and teaching and how it impacts interpersonal and professional relationship among colleagues and with students. The science student and teachers dismissed the notion of ideology influencing sciences, but this position has been refuted through Karl Popper and Thomas Kuhn's idea of falsification and theory of scientific theories and ideology.

The seventh and the concluding chapter ties up all the main arguments in this book and seeks to answer the question as to whether a student can be apolitical and engage in nation-building. It also builds a picture of the student as a citizen of the country and what shapes his/her thinking and world views. It places the current ideological battle taking place inside and outside the campuses and sees its impact on the students and teachers. This book brings to you social narratives from deeply political universities like AU, BHU, Jamia Milia University and also from non-political universities like Bangalore University, Periyar and Pondicherry universities. Kashmir University and NEHU bring to you a totally different perspective.

At a glance, it may seem to be too diverse, but the issues are intertwined in such a way that the work would seem incomplete if not presented in its entirety. This book uncovers several layers of the relationship between the State, teachers and the students and presents it in the framework of a liberal education system in a democracy. Each actor interacts with the other in a specific arena and also have overlapping concerns. The teacher comes into direct contact with the State with matters related to recruitment, promotion, administration, curriculum and with the larger vision of education itself. Students and teachers may express overlapping concerns with regard to textbooks, infrastructure, lack of freedom on campus, caste/class discrimination and so on. The State and student relationship is defined by both covert and overt means. Creating a homogenous body of knowledge with regard to the idea of nation and patriotism, using symbols for the same are some of the examples of covert means, while ban on students' union, changing reservation policies and institutionalizing behaviour are overt ways in which State and students come into direct contact. The following chapters unravel these layers.

State and Education

I am a survivor of a concentration camp. My eyes saw what no man should witness:

Gas chambers built by learned engineers.

Children poisoned by educated physicians.

Infants killed by trained nurses.

Women and babies shot and burned by high school and college graduates.

So, I am suspicious of education. My request is: help your students become human.

Your efforts must never produce learned monsters, skilled psychopaths, educated Eichmanns.

Reading, writing, arithmetic is important only if they serve to make our children more humane.

—Dr Haim Ginott[1]

This is a chilling reminder for all those who have a narrow vision of education as a means to an end. The idealists who had a philosophical vision of education wanted our centres of education to develop students into conscientious human beings who worked for the welfare of the society, whether as active participants in the functioning of the State or by passing on new and old knowledge to each generation which is referred to in theories of socialization discussed in the first chapter. In any democratic society, it is essential that the education system represents diverse ways of looking at the social reality. An education system which represents uniformity and homogeneity of ideas

---

[1] Dr Haim Ginott, a noted educationist and child psychologist, published in his book *Teacher and Child* the letter written by a holocaust survivor.

works against the principles of democracy and in that the true spirit of liberal education.

The chapter is divided into two sections. The first section begins with a brief literature review of existing theories on ideology, and the interconnection between education and ideology. From there, in the next section it answers the questions: How do students form ideological positions? Is it a result of socialization within the university or the family? How do students view teachers, teaching and their experience in the campus? Does the choice of subject of study impact knowledge of ideology, thereby leading to a difference in how science and humanities students define ideology? The most important aspect of all this is the role of the State in education. This is dealt with in the second section with drawing upon circulars from the State to universities on celebration of certain events, icons and the reaction of the students and teachers to the same. The final section uses singing of national anthem, rewriting of history and blurring of lines between science and mythology as examples to understand the ideological moorings of students and the ability of students, from both humanities and sciences, to critically analyse events around them. A combination of interviews with students across disciplines and existing literature has been used to answer some crucial questions.

PART I

THEORETICAL UNDERSTANDING OF IDEOLOGY

Can an individual be devoid of any ideological position or not believe in any particular ideology? The fact that numerous thinkers have written on the theoretical concept of ideology brings home the importance of ideology in not only the political sphere but also societies in general. In this context, students provide an excellent window to the future. This brings us to a larger question: How does one understand and define ideology, and how does it impact our daily life, especially in the context of higher education? Ideology as a concept has been explored by three streams of thinkers: philosophers, sociologists and political scientists. In their own way, they sought to define ideology and its role in society as an abstract and concrete reality. In sociology, ideology found its space in sociology of knowledge (Karl Mannheim immediately comes to mind); however, it did not receive as much attention from political theorists, except from Gramsci, according to Filipini (2017).

To set the record straight, this section is not an exhaustive piece on ideology, as that would be an entire book by itself. It serves to set the context of what is to come next. Several books focused on only theoretical frameworks (some cited here) have analysed ideology from philosophical, political and sociological perspectives. This section first acquaints the reader with the existing theoretical work on ideology and education and ideology in particular. Although this book is not entirely about ideology, it does examine the role of ideology in determining attitude towards various other aspects of a student's and teacher's life in the university.

The initial scholarship on ideology was largely from the Marxist perspective. Marx, in his work *The German Ideology*, connected the concept of ideology to that of domination. According to him, it is a phenomenon of collective thinking, which proceeds according to interests and social and existential situations. It was the ruling class which determined the dominant ideas. Ideology as explained by Marx had its fair share of criticism, and not surprisingly the causal link between class and ideology was one of the main criticisms. As Adams (1989) points out, Marxists tend to classify all non-proletariat ideas as ideological and also false and distorted. The problem being that

> It is only within a rigid framework that allocates world views to specific classes that the history of ideas can be so interpreted that only the proletarian world view is scientific, objective, true and undistorted. Marxism provides no such logical criteria by which we can decide what is ideological what is not and this is true of all sociological theories. (Adams 1989, 10–11).

Here, Adams (1989, 11) makes an important point in relation to ideology in general that 'No sociological theory that defines ideology in terms of social causality or social function can succeed in identifying ideology as a distinctive form of thought.'

Many of the prominent scholars who are viewed as Marxist scholars attempted to address the shortcomings of the pure Marxist way of explaining ideology. Marxist perspective on ideology is viewed by many as abstract, and Althusser and Giddens are credited with 'bringing' ideology to the more practical world. Giddens (1983) defines ideology as 'the mode in which forms of signification are incorporated within systems of domination so as to sanction their continuance'. (In forms of signification, Giddens is referring to the forms of legitimation.) Other prominent Marxist theorists on ideology include Karl Popper, Anthony Giddens and Stuart Hall. Several other theorists who have moved away from the Marxist perspective such as Raymond Williams, Henry Giroux, Philip Wexler and Michel Foucault have worked on defining and understanding ideology from a wider perspective and not just from Marxist view of the superstructure (economic production) determining ideology. For Wexler (1988, 157) ideology: 'Ideology as forms of representation is central to the organization of experiences and subjectivities.' This broader perspective on ideology was espoused by Giroux and Williams.

Any discussion on ideology is incomplete without a mention of Mannheim. 'Ideologies are those complex ideas which direct activity towards maintenance of existing order. Utopia is complex of ideas which tend to generate activities towards change of prevailing order' (Mannheim 1955, XXIII). He goes further back from the times of Marx in situating the history of the term 'ideology'. He also adds that there are several other definitions of ideology that have formed outside the influence of Marxism. In his historical perspective of ideology, Mannheim writes that it is in Bacon's 'idola' that one may find the root of the modern-day concept of ideology. He writes, 'It is extremely probable that everyday experience with political affairs first made man aware of and critical toward the ideological element in his thinking; leading to a methodical search for ideological elements in public utterances' (Mannheim 1955, 55). He also writes of how Napoleon gave a negative connotation to the word ideology. He called all those who opposed him and his ambitions 'ideologists'. This is how the word 'ideology' developed political connotations. It was in the 19th century that ideology from a mode of thought (theory of ideas) became associated with political activity. Mannheim adds that it is this political aspect that is seen even in the Marxist interpretation. However, it is with Marx that ideology is associated with class and class interest, hence the term 'dominant ideology'. Mannheim credits Marx for turning ideology into an economic and political world view. He does not deny class as a causal factor in determining an individual's knowledge and belief but states that it is not the only factor. He sees a gradual progression of the concept of ideology; interestingly, he writes that in the initial stages, ideology was 'devoid of historical and sociological implications' (Mannheim 1955, 59). The second stage he identified with Hegel's view on ideology was a historical perspective: 'The world is a unity and is conceivable only with reference to a knowing subject' (Mannheim 1955, 59). The final stage which shaped ideology as a concept was its positioning in the historical social process. According to Mannheim, it was in the final phase that a connect between social class and the structure of the society was made. This was accompanied by the realization that the society cannot be understood in isolation; it has to be understood in conjunction with the historical past. As Mannheim (1955, 62) puts it, 'Human affairs cannot be understood by an isolation of their elements. Secondly, this interdependent system of meanings varies both in all its parts and in its totality from one historical period to another.'

Further analysing the concept of ideology, Mannheim writes that ideology has two distinct meanings: the particular and the total. Some of us may identify with the distinction offered by Mannheim:

1. *Particular concept of ideology:* This is when one is sceptical of the ideas put forth by one with opposing views. They are seen as disguising or distorting the real issue or situation. This could be done through lies and other ways of deception.
2. *Total concept of ideology:* In this, we are not concerned about an individualistic thought process; rather, we are concerned about a larger picture of 'the characteristics and composition of the total structure of the mind of this epoch or of this group (class, age)'. Most importantly, Mannheim establishes that ideology is not shaped in a vacuum but is influenced by one's life experiences.

> The ideas expressed by the subject are thus regarded as functions of his existence. This means that opinions, statements, propositions and systems of ideas are not taken at their face value but are interpreted

in the life situation of the one who expresses them. It signifies further that the specific character and life situation of the subject influence his opinions perceptions and interpretations.... The particular conception of ideology operates primarily with a psychology of interests, it assumes that this or that interest is the cause of a given life or deception while the total conception uses a more formal functional analysis, without any reference to motivations, confining itself to an objective description of the structural differences in minds operating in different social settings. It assumes that there is correspondence between a given social situation and a given perspective/point of view. Thus interest psychology tends to be displaced by an analysis of the correspondence between the situation to be known and the forms of knowledge. The point of reference in the particular is always the individual (psychological). (Mannheim 1955, 51)

In Gramsci, we find a critique of the limited Marxist understanding of ideology. Also in the historicity of ideology, he differs from Mannheim. Gramsci in *Prison Notebooks* writes on ideology, 'Its original meaning was that of science of ideas', and since analysis was the only method recognized and applied by science and means 'analysis of ideas', that is '*investigation of the origin of ideas*' (1971, 704: author's italics). According to him, 'Ideology' is an aspect of 'sensationalism', that is, of the 18th-century French materialism. It used to mean 'science of ideas', and since analysis was the only method recognized and applied by science, it meant 'analysis of ideas', that is, also 'search for the origin of ideas'. Ideas had to be broken down into their (original) 'elements', which could be nothing other than 'sensations'.

Gramsci traces back his approach to ideology to Destutt de Tracy, a French philosopher, who post the French Revolution saw the study of ideology as a science. For Tracy, it was of utmost importance to study how news ideas are formed when a traditional social order collapses, what impact this new stream of thought has on the society and so on. It was important for Gramsci that any study of ideology be located in its historicity (in this, we find a similarity with Mannheim). As mentioned earlier, Gramsci was keen on marking out the changes that have occurred in the understanding of ideology, from science to ideas to a system of ideas. This is where he connects it to Tracy and the French Revolution. Filipini (2017, 7) points out that in *Prison Notebooks*, Gramsci refers to Tracy's Ideology with a capital 'I', and this refers to the science of ideas based on physiological nature, while for him, ideology with a small 'i' refers to the system of ideas that are historical in context. Gramsci was not in favour of the rigid Marxist approach to ideology as a reflection of the economic structure. Moving away from a simplistic Marxist understanding of ideology, Gramsci writes that people and ideology operate in various ways, as intellectuals, due to one's position in economic production, as a result of 'common sense', as part of the dominant group, and there could be others who do not practise the ideology they believe in and so on. So as a result, there is no one way of 'production' of ideology.

Ideology, Gramsci adds, is necessary as it organizes people and creates consciousness about their position and struggle. For him, ideology is rooted in class, which then determines the productive system and then goes to determine the organization of the society. It shapes organizations, and he gives examples of schools, churches and the media which he views as 'hegemonic apparatuses'. These organizations are run by 'inorganic intellectuals' who are in charge of spreading the ideology and also maintaining class hegemony. For Gramsci, therefore, ideology can be analysed at several levels: religion, philosophy, folklore and even common sense.

Not only Gramsci but several other thinkers and social scientists also sought to move ideology from the grasp of a purely Marxist perspective. Wexler (1982) writes, 'Ideology must be studied not as a collection of entities, ideas, but as itself a production, set of practices, structures or method which make meaning.' McLaren supports this when he says, 'Ideologies are best read as socially constructed relations which constitute the products of numerous histories, institutions, processes of inscription and traditions of mediation' (1988, 157) and in this he critiques the Marxist understanding of ideology and says that it is too orthodox and also 'It ignores understanding ideology as cultural production' (1988, 155). To add to this point, McLaren (1988, 156) writes, 'Ideologies are not symptomatic of some prior cause but constitute both the medium and the outcome of a recursive generation of representation and social practices.'

According to Stuart Hall and James Donald (1986), ideology provides the frameworks of thought which are used in society to explain, figure out, make sense or give meaning to the social and political world. Without these frame works we would not make sense of the world at all. But with them our perceptions are inevitably structured in a particular direction by the very concepts we are using.

Seligar, a political scientist, moved away from the traditional views held by political scientists of ideology representing extremism. According to him, the function of ideology is to 'guide concerted actions of a distinct social group/s'. For him, ideology cannot be non-political—it is a political belief system but all political belief systems are ideologies. He outlines the six elements that are found in all ideological belief systems: 'moral prescription, technical prescription, implements, description, analysis and rejection' (Adam 1989, 13). Others like Corbett and Plamenatz in their philosophical approach to ideology broadly agree on it being 'a set of beliefs and ideas' of a group or community, the way an individual understands the world and society are organized. Only Plamenatz categorically states that science is not ideological. This point is discussed in Chapter 6 of this book in greater detail with references to Karl Popper and Thomas Kuhn.

Ideology shapes the way we think and approach an issue: The opposition to a particular religion, race or group of people, denial of rights and idea of cultural loss become clearer when we look at it from this definitional point of view. The fear of the other can also be explained by what Foucault (1980) writes, 'Ideology does not work to distort or mystify the truth as much as to produce and legitimate a particular regime of truth, a process which in many ways is more dangerous to its victims.' The imagery of an economic and cultural threat, of majoritarianism and of dominant ideas is fed by what is deemed as truth by a group. Foucault (1980, 162) 'wishes to prevent the history of knowledge from being colonised by any epistemological categories. He is more concerned about how truth is produced in discourse and how "regimes of truth" are empowered and deployed in everyday social practices'.

John Thompson (1987) explains that ideology serves both positive and negative functions. Like Hall and Donald, he is also of the opinion that ideology helps understand the political world and also provides concept and categories to understand the political world. The negative function, he says, is that ideology limits our perception. He further adds that the negative functions of ideology are seen in the legitimation of a system of dominance, which is sustained by being represented as legitimate, worthy of respect. This may have other consequences such as dissimulation, whereby relations of dominance are concealed, denied and obscured in various ways, and social processes are described in such a way that they conceal the interests and practices which inform them; it may also lead to fragmentation and relations of dominance that are sustained by the production of meanings in a way which fragments groups and places them in opposition to one another. Finally, he speaks of reification: Transitory historical states of affairs are presented as permanent, natural and commonsensical as if they existed outside of time.

As Ian Adams (1989, 38) writes,

> Ideology is, if anything, a disparate assemblage of all kinds of things; facts and values, explanations and prescriptions, myths, ideal societies and much else besides. To be possessed of a set of political beliefs, an ideology, is to understand the world in a certain way. Whatever other characteristics political beliefs may have they do have moral force: they tell us how we should live and what we should strive for. Insofar as we are Marxists, Nazis or Liberals we are committed to beliefs of how the world ought to be, what relationships should prevail, what is just and what is conducive to human flourishing.'

But as Martin (2015, 10) argues in his article on political ideology, 'When political and social analysts define ideology, they tend to give extremely broad definitions, usually including beliefs, attitudes and values'. As examples, he cites Adorno (1950), Campbell (1964), Jost (2006), Kerlinger (1984) and Tedin (1987). For him, political ideology has a specific meaning in democracies, as it means 'an orientation to political parties, as these are the organizations that have arisen to pursue such a quest' (Martin 2015, 11).

As a result of years of interdisciplinary efforts in theorizing ideology, it has come out of the realm of abstraction to everyday life and subjective experiences. So how does ideology play out in our subjective experiences and what is its significance? Education is one such example which puts forth before us the practical and implementation outcomes of ideology, be it through administrative and governance processes, curricula, textbooks or interpersonal relationships among students and teachers. It was but natural that social scientists and philosophers would look for linkages between ideology and education and by extension the state, education and ideology—the manner in which it impact education and the role of the State.

Ideology, a cultural construct as McLaren, Gramsci and several others also believe, impacts other cultural aspects: like education and mass media. Several researchers have examined how communist ideology shaped education in China, how children's minds were shaped by literature in Nazi Germany and so on. It is essential to Gramsci that his background and struggle shaped his thoughts on education and ideology. His focus was on creating intellectuals from among the working class. Even when he wrote *Prison Notebooks*, he spoke of how education is being viewed from a utilitarian perspective 'in which the pupil's destiny and future activity are determined in advance' (1971, 166). He writes in great detail about his vision of how education should be imparted. He is not in favour of an overly vocational training-based and bureaucratic structure of education; education according to him should be balanced, teaching 'general, humanistic, formative; this would strike the right balance between development of the capacities required for intellectual work' (1971, 166).

Even at the time Gramsci wrote *Prison Notebooks*, he pointed out the issue of teacher–student ratio and also the need for adequate infrastructure in terms of buildings, libraries and so on. One may recall that sociology of education also moved on to focus on the 'implementation' issues being faced after the expansion of education. He makes an important point when he says,

> The traditional school was oligarchic because it was intended for the new generation of the ruling class, destined to rule in its turn: but it was not oligarchic in its mode of teaching.... The social character is determined by the fact that each social group has its own type of school, intended to perpetuate a specific traditional function, ruling or subordinate. (1971, 186)

Gramsci suggests creation of a single type of school which then lets the child decide his/her future profession. This is what we have in a broad sense, of course, with difference in quality of teaching, teachers and infrastructure.

According to Gramsci, one of the most important functions of a State is 'to raise the great mass of the population to a particular cultural and moral level, a level (or type) which corresponds to the needs of the productive forces for development, and hence to the interests of the ruling class' (1971, 258). Gramsci proceeds to claim that the State—which at one point Gramsci asserts is equivalent to the 'fundamental economic group' or ruling class (bourgeoisie) itself (1971, 16)—implements its educative project through a variety of channels, both 'public' and 'private', with the 'school as a positive educative function, and the courts as a repressive and negative educative function' constituting 'the most important State activities in this sense ... [b]ut, in reality,' Gramsci maintains, 'A multitude of other so-called private initiatives and activities tend to the same end—initiatives and activities which form the apparatus of the political and cultural hegemony of the ruling classes' (1971, 258). Hegemony, therefore, is a process by which "Educative pressure [is] applied to single individuals so as to obtain their consent and their collaboration, turning necessity and coercion into 'freedom'. The 'freedom' produced by instruments of the ruling class thus moulds the 'free' subject to the needs of an economic base, 'the continuous development of the economic apparatus of production'" (1971, 242). In a discussion on political parties, Gramsci speaks of the political importance of the educated.

What is essential is the need to be aware of one's own ideological positioning. As Giroux (1983) writes, 'Failure to understand classroom pedagogy as a form of ideological production prevents both teachers and students from recognising the centrality of their own epistemological claims for truth.' He makes an interesting point that ideology has a role to play in social transformation. This transformation can take place only through self-reflection and action. Ideology functions through individuals and while it does conform to the ethos of the dominant group, it also has the potential to bring in social transformation. For this purpose, he sees intersectionality between ideology, culture and schooling.

In Nazi Germany, books for children and youth were used for 'identification with Nazi heroes and supporting the support of German youth for the National Socialist cause' (Redmann 1988, 131). The heroes in these books were similar to the Nazi 'heroes' of the Third Reich. These books also tried to put forth the cultural ideas of a true German family, loyalty to the family and, above all, loyalty to the cause of the nation. Park (1980) speaks of the threat to education due to the 'renewed strength of the political right'. According to him, one of the key problems is the inevitable religious connect of the far right. In the USA, the far right traces all the ills of the modern society to progressive, liberal ideas and also lack of belief in God. One far right campaigner says, 'We believe we should be in politics as a way of improving the world from a religious concept' (Park 1980, 608). They find the modern theories of evolution and understanding of religion against the Bible. We find echoes of this in the ideological position on education taken by the far right in almost all countries. To this, Park (1980, 608) makes an important point when he says, 'We must develop increased sensitivity to the activities and messages of organisations on the political extremes, both right and left.'

Giroux (1985) writes,

> Ideology is the production, consumption and representation of ideas and behaviour which can either distort or illuminate the nature of reality can be either coherent or contradictory; can function within the sphere of both consciousness and unconsciousness; they can exist at the level of critical discourse as well as within the sphere of taken for granted lived in experience and practical behaviour.

He further writes, 'Educators working within the critical tradition should support a theory of ideology that is also capable of comprehending the way in which meaning is constructed and materialised within texts or cultural forms such as films, books, curriculum packages, fashion styles etc.'

Before the next section begins, it is important to establish that ideology is used in its broader meaning and is not restricted to political ideology. The next section examines how students and teachers negotiate ideology in their everyday life in the campus and political affiliation in the campus. There were no questions regarding allegiance to political parties. The only specific political question was with regard to association with the students' union.

Ideology: Students Define and Explain

What do you understand by ideology? Can you discuss about your ideological leanings or position?

This question was posed to students with a specific purpose in mind. This would reveal whether educational institutes encourage and provide the students with alternate world views? Or are differing world views pushed under the carpet in the guise of maintaining the status quo? Do students engage in debates and learn to agree to disagree on ideology? Given the political and other conflicts, has the understanding of ideology been reduced to merely a political one?

It was assumed that the ideological position of students as a world view has been shaped by their own subjective realities. Educational institutes, teachers, peer, family and even political parties influence students in forming their ideological leanings.

In the introductory chapter, it was mentioned that one of the questions which is of extreme relevance is whether the ideological leaning of the teacher can create a conflict with the student and whether it compromises teaching and the relationship between the teacher and the student. In the education system in India and most other countries, the relationship between the student and the teacher is based on hierarchy and real and apparent use of authority. Teachers hold the power to either jeopardize or aid a student's growth and development. Do the teachers play an active role in the exchange of ideas across ideological positions? Another element explored here is the difference between ideological leanings, political affiliation and political participation. A person may have a certain world view but may not want to actively participate in a direct political activity or even associate with a particular political party.

Can all the students who took a firm stand on patriotism during the course of the interview be branded as 'political'? Did they have a clear ideological positioning? Do students want politics on campus? What are the problems identified with student activism on campus, both historically and contemporarily, which have influenced the perception about student and teacher activism? The students (both humanities and sciences) were asked open-ended questions on what according to them ideology is, what shaped their political affiliation and how their current political positions were influenced by their understanding of ideology? Did it push students towards any political activity?

When asked what they understood by ideology, some said that they did not know what ideology meant. Students were not required to mention thinkers or particular definitions, just what their understanding of ideology was. While majority of students in both sciences and humanities had some sort of understanding of what ideology was, and that ideology does not merely refer to political beliefs, there were many who instantly took out their cell phones to look up the meaning and definition of ideology. This was because, the students explained, they did not have any courses which taught ideology nor did they use it that frequently.

One may recall that in the previous section it was pointed out that Mannheim in his theory of ideology presented two aspects of it: as a result of an individual's social position or the attribute of an entire social group to which s/he belongs. For most of the students, ideology was a 'set of beliefs, values'; they often attributed these beliefs and values to a single person. It was encouraging to note that very few mentioned that it was a purely political concept or in relation to political parties. Several mentioned that ideology was a world view and that it impacted the social and economic structure of the society. In this section, some of the answers given by students will be quoted, and their caste, gender and education details will be shared to the extent possible. Answers have been quoted verbatim with no attempt to change the grammar or sentence construction. This preserves the accuracy and meaning of what the respondents want to convey. Another reason was doing so is that the language and vocabulary give an insight into the quality of education imparted in universities and institutes.

Even those from science background who had not been taught about ideology formally had some sort of understanding of ideology. However, there were some views from the science students of AU who saw ideology as only opposing world views. Out of two students who identified with the right-wing ideology, one said, 'From ideology I think that following and supporting some specific emotions, rules, thoughts etc. Ideology is community specific' (rightist, male, AU, DPhil, ST); the other respondent said, 'Ideology is the group of thought on the basis of which, we support or oppose the activity of any political, social, or religious organization' (male, AU, DPhil, General). Most of the science students in AU identified ideology with a person or a group, though they did not identify these groups. According to them, ideology represents the ideas of an individual or a group about life and social realities. The humanities students in AU did not so much attribute ideology to a particular group or individual; they rather saw it from a societal point of view, meaning guiding principles which shape the society. 'Ideology is rules, regulations, and laws, created with consensus of a group, and every group has different ideology' (centrist, female, AU, MPhil [Humanities], OBC).

BHU was surprising in many ways. Science students were more aware of ideology than humanities students. In contrast to the aforementioned responses, science students of BHU spoke of ideology from political and individual points of views, though a handful of students were honest enough to admit that they did not know anything about ideology. A few students said that ideology meant expressing one's opinion. Among the humanities students, while many did not explicitly say that they did not know the meaning of ideology, it was evident from their responses that they were not very clear about it. The following response is a typical example, 'Ideology is for anyone from common to special human, that by going in any specific direction, if they need to change themselves in social structure, they could be humanistic.' Or this, 'Whatever I have written till now and will be writing is my own ideology. Which no one can change except me.' But the other responses centred on that the way a society functions and is structured politically and culturally are driven by its ideology.

Surprisingly, in Pondicherry University (Humanities), several students said that they did not know what ideology meant. One student said that he had heard of ideology only after he came to the campus. Few others said that they were not clear about what it meant. The students of Gulbarga University gave political and issue-based reasons for their political ideological leanings but were not clear about the meaning of ideology itself. Although for them ideology was not merely political beliefs, it had social and religious dimensions; hence, for some religion was an ideology and for some caste. When asked specifically to explain what they understood by the term 'ideology', even though most of the students of Gulbarga University said that they were taught ideology in their course, they were not really articulate about it and spoke of issues of reservation and equality. For example, 'Follow the Ambedkar ideology, but we will accommodate with Hindu also. My ideology is to uplift in education. Practice Hindu ideology also' (apolitical, male, SC). Interestingly, many of the students mentioned equality, that it is very important and also that no one should force his or her ideological beliefs on others. It was during the conversation with teachers that it became clearer why certain students spoke of caste as a world view. Teachers in Gulbarga University said that caste had been the biggest divisive factor in the university. Hence, the students also must have experienced caste in their daily life, which is why they perceived it as their world view. Periyar University also had students saying that ideology was politics and most of them could not say what exactly ideology was. About 2 or 3 students out of 20 responded that ideology was about democracy and human rights. Not surprisingly, barring two, all the students said that they were apolitical. The lack of understanding about ideology was attributed to the policies of the university. One of the students said that the university did not provide a conducive environment for discussion on ideology or politics, and the students mostly talked about their respective subjects. The teachers in Periyar University mentioned this, and it is discussed in detail in Chapter 4.

In NIT Warangal, most of the students said that they were apolitical and many refused to answer to the question on ideology and said that they did not know what it meant. One respondent said that ideology was about ideas promoted by certain individuals or political organizations. OU (Science) responded in a similar fashion; many said that they did not know the meaning of ideology, while some said that they did not want to discuss it. Even those studying humanities in OU (humanities) said that they did not know much about the word 'ideology', and a handful, not more than three, attempted to give a definition of sorts. A respondent pursing his postgraduation said, 'It is a system of ideas and ideas that may be political or economical.' One said, 'It is a democratic way of thinking while for another it means living in harmony together.' But unlike the science students, the humanities students in Osmania University were more politically inclined, and apart from Gulbarga University, OU (humanities) reported the largest number of rightists (including right of centre). NIT Srinagar students, on the other hand, had a clear perspective about ideology, and none of them said that they had not heard of the term or that they did not know about it. Almost all the students of NIT Srinagar spoke of ideology as a set of ideas and principles on which a society is organized. A few attributed ideology to the ideas of certain people, which then create followers. But for the majority, it was opinion/views of individual or people about issues. 'Set of opinion or ideas especially one which from the basis of economic or political theory and policy' (male, MTech). Yet again, ideology was seen in its wider meaning.

Contrast this with what a student in Calicut University said about the meaning of ideology, 'I understood Ideology as a belief or a value that an individual holds, theme may be economical, political or epistemological ideologies. The main purpose of ideology to offer change in society.' (apolitical, female, Calicut University, General). In DU too, students gave definite answers when asked about ideology, for example, 'Ideology generally refers to a system of values and principles that encourage a particular worldview.'

If we had to categorize the definitions of ideology given by students, the main themes were: ideology is a world view, way to understand the world: economic, social and cultural, opinion and an individual view which has now been accepted by many. 'Every individual has a set of beliefs and principles in life. These beliefs and principles concern one's opinions regarding the political/social/economic system prevailing in the society. These set of beliefs exhibit the value this individual gives and follows.' (apolitical, male, Gauhati University, PhD, ST).

As a student at Gauhati University (Humanities) put it, 'Ideology begins with being moral or ethical. But the perspective of morality or ethics changes with every single individual. Family plays a greater role in building the sense of ideology. In case of Politics, Nepotism, as well as Institution both play an important role.' This is a good example of both how an individual recognizes the role of the family in shaping ideological positions and the influences outside the family play a crucial role in shaping perspectives. The responses to the questions on ideology illustrate that students were well aware of the core meaning of ideology without an immediate reference to political parties or specific political individuals, barring a few who mentioned Marx. On the other hand, to have students who say that they did not know the meaning of ideology or never heard of it is worrying. This is a clear indication that most of the higher educational institutes, be it humanities or sciences, do not care to make students aware of ideology. But the life experiences of students, on caste or religious lines, create a particular world view or attitude towards social reality.

Life on Campus: Political Affiliations and Political Activity

During the course of research, some students mentioned that they were not aware of ideology or had a position or view on politics till they came to the campus. The campus introduced the students to the idea of ideology (social, economic and political) in an academic manner. Even though families had given them a lens to view the world, they did not know it as ideology. It is in the educational institutes that they understood it in definitive terms. Mere awareness of politics on campus or the ideological divisions does not translate into activism. This is a misconception that is harboured by many that a campus where students discuss politics or are aware of politics pushes everyone into active politics. It is not so. While many may profess to be inclined to one political group or another, it does not translate into students becoming active political members of campus-based parties. This was reflected in the interviews, as not many students among those interviewed were members of any political group on campus. They were clear about their political affiliations and were aware of the reasons why they chose a certain path, but this did not necessarily translate into concrete political activity through political unions on campus. For engineering students (the Indian Institutes of Technology [IITs]), there was not much of an option, as political unions were not allowed on campus. The only exceptions were the science/engineering students in universities where political unions were allowed.

Like Mannheim predicted, there was an element of distrust towards ideologies and in the people believing in them. This was more so among those who said that they were apolitical and centrists. What were the influencing factors which helped shape the world view of the students with regard to ideological political positions? What made them choose left or right or specifically left of centre or right of centre? In the formation of personal political positions, peer pressure and family associations played an important role. Along with it, the political activity on campus also influenced the students. From the conversations, it was apparent that the key factors were (a) the politics being played out in the country, (b) family and (c) peer influence.

Peer influence worked in a slightly different way in this context. Several of those who said that they were apolitical said that they were so because they wanted to maintain good relationships with others and often strong political positions created a rift. One must understand that this is the age when new relationships and friendships are established and popularity is much coveted. Taking extreme positions may prove to be detrimental to this, and hence the response of many respondents was that they needed to get along with everybody. Those who claimed to be centrists said that they believed that this gave them the flexibility to examine a political issue from an unbiased perspective; a similar argument was given by those who were apolitical but with a difference. Those who professed to be apolitical said that they were not interested in politics; they were disillusioned with politics and politicians and preferred to stay away from even political discussions with friends. The following conversations from JNU help illustrate the point.

For example, a respondent from JNU said, 'I don't like to associate myself with that ideology which emphasizes extreme viewpoint and thus ignores the possibility to have meaningful dialogue with other ideological parties. Centrist ideology allows for constructive criticism and meaningful discussion' (centrist, male, MPhil, OBC), while another respondent from JNU said, 'Being attached to a certain ideology restricts our vision and the ability to personal things from various perspectives' (apolitical, male, MPhil, OBC). On being asked why she was apolitical, a student of Calicut University replied that she was apolitical because 'Being apolitical mean I am not ready to support any political party because each of them have own menu and demands, we should be more humanistic than political.' The positions taken by some of the students bring to mind Mannheim when he says, 'The significant element in the conception of ideology in our opinion is the discovery that political thought is integrally bound up with social life.'

Some students did not hesitate to mention the political leanings of their parents and how it had influenced them. But the family did not always influence the choice of the students. For example, a student of DU, who was a native of Kerala, said, 'Leftist ideology makes sense to me. I have been exposed to rightist ideologies (family) and centrist also. From whatever I have read listened and watched so far, leftist ideology is leftist ideology is the one that stand for power less/voice less. It exposes exploitation. The fight of leftist ideology is what I fight against too' (leftist, female, DU, MA). Since the respondent had very definite and strong views, when asked whether she joined any political group on campus, she added, 'I support SFI, but I haven't joined SFI. I believe that when you become part of a close knit group or when you want to be included, you all have to compromise on many things.' Interestingly, several students in other universities mentioned that they did not join any political group on campus as it would restrict their world view and prevent them from taking an objective position on events and issues. Some of the other respondents also said that their families voted for particular national parties, but they chose to be leftist/centrist/rightist as the case may be; in some instances, the students followed in footsteps of the family. The students were aware of the political leanings of the members of the family, and while this may influence them in the initial years, some mentioned that they were exploring and learning about other political ideological positions on campus. In a twist to the socialization theory, the students' opinions were shaped not in the manner that the ideas were passed down to generations or peer pressure forcing them to join groups. Rather, the students were seen questioning or going against (not necessarily expressed through political activism) what the family believed in, or seeing the friends getting into political tiffs pushed them to being apolitical or centrist.

Only a handful of students mentioned that they were politically active on campus. For example, in AU, three students said that they were part of All India Students' Association (AISA) and one said ABVP. One student, who was a member of AISA, said, 'I don't believe in any supreme entity and religious customs. I choose communism because of rationality. AISA is the most rational one among left-wing groups. I choose it because of its role in the interest of students' (male, MA, OBC). Another said, 'Yes. AISA. The ideology and struggle of the organization is loud and clear. Workers of this organization are always active and they demand the appropriate work through right ways against the inappropriate work of the university administration' (female, MPhil, General). Those associated with political groups on campus were absolutely clear about their political ideological positions and the reasons for the same. The centrist and even the left of centre/ right of centre did not show any inclination to align with any of the political parties on campus, at least among those interviewed for the purpose of this research.

Those who claimed to be left or right of centre said that the extreme right and left did not accommodate their political positions on social and economic issues. For example, one respondent said, 'On the one hand the centrist ideology helps in filling the gap between rich poor by making it accessible through various socio-economic policies on the other hand the rightist ideology keeps us connected with our cultural roots and capitalistic approach of policies gives way for excellence to success to whatever height one with to achieve' (right of centre, female, DU, OBC). Similarly, a JNU PhD student on being asked his political position said, 'In such diverse country like ours, we cannot afford to operate in extremes. We have a traditional society, so we have to adopt an ideology that could have both features and also make reforms for less fortune communities.'

One of the preconceived notions that the research started with was that the students in universities may have been persuaded by the current right-wing wave in the country. Surprisingly, among the 600 students interviewed, the number of rightists and right of centre was very less. Among the technical students, a larger number said that they were apolitical, and among the humanities, centrists were in a considerable number. Gulbarga University was the first and only university where a large number of (nearly 50%) the respondents said that they were rightists. Only two said that they were leftists/left of centre. It is interesting to note that it was in Gulbarga University that of the eight OBC students interviewed, barring one, all the other (across gender) said that they were rightists, and this was because of the influence of the current prime minister. Those who said that they were centrists said that they were so because of the support given to SC/ST, reservation and that they were heard. Recall the conversation on caste in Gulbarga University mentioned in the previous section.

Pondicherry University (Humanities) had the largest number of apolitical and centrist students. Those who claimed to be apolitical said, 'I want to work and connect with everyone in my campus, so I decided to be apolitical' and 'I want to live in peace, so I want to be apolitical. Politics divides people.' Interestingly, it appeared during the course of conversation with students that while many said that they were not interested in politics in campus or otherwise, some showed a leaning towards the right-wing ideology. In BHU, a humanities student said (PhD, OBC) that he was apolitical because 'From all above ideologies only positive influence is contained, but they are somehow influenced by politics only. Because of which they make settlement with their core objective. And that puts me in position to doubt about believing in them. That's why any apolitical thought is close to my heart.' Another respondent said, 'Ideological clashes mostly creates disillusionment about ideology.'

The responses to the question why students chose to be apolitical and even centrist point towards a certain mistrust towards either right or left political ideology, which is explained by Mannheim when he writes,

> Ideologies are situationally transcendent ideas which never succeed de facto in the realisation of their projected contents. Though they often become the good intentioned motives for the subjective conduct of the individual, when they are actually embodied in practice and their meanings are most

frequently distorted. The fact that this ideologically conduct always falls short of its intended meaning may present itself in several forms and corresponding to these forms there is a whole series of possible types of ideological mentality. (Mannheim 1955, 175)

Although not in these words, several students when they mentioned why they do not discuss politics or ideology said that no one could be trusted in that matter and people did not act on the true meaning of the original essence of what an ideology stands for. They were referring to the practice of political ideology in actual politics. As a student in NIT Srinagar said, 'Due to politics, some person hate with each other. Every wants the chair. By remaining liberal. We can do anything.' It was echoed by another student in OU (humanities), 'There is no perfect ideology leftist rightist are not good in their ideology, so my thinking is different from them.'

Students who said that they were left of centre or leftists said that they wanted a more equal society, one where the poor and marginalized sections of the society were taken care of and there was no discrimination. Those in support of the right were not very articulate about the reasons, but some said that it was the need of the hour; the right could protect the culture and tradition of the nation, but it was evident that those supporting the leftist ideology were influenced by factors within the campus, mainly an active left political union or the vision of Marxism. This approach was seen across both science and humanities students. In BHU, some of the science students said that they identified with the left, as they needed to raise their voice for the poor and that they wanted a society based on equality. According to a JNU student, 'Ideology wise it is better them others has equality and resource distribution at its core' (male, PhD, OBC). Another student from Gauhati University said, 'I am completely against the concept of richer getting more rich. The subalterns, proletariats and specially the peasants in India needs to come in equal to others. Though it's accepted by me that Marxist ideology cannot sustain in the world full of capitalism' (leftist, female, PhD, General).

The right-wing supporters, on the other hand, were solely influenced by the narrative of the right-wing political parties at the national level. A student in NEHU said that he supported the right wing, as they were strong and fulfilled their promises. There did not seem to be much of an influence of the right within the campus in most of the cases, and this could be attributed to the dominance of the leftists in campus politics. The students mentioned that they were influenced by the policies of the government at the Centre and the need to protect the tradition and culture of the nation. In Savitribai Phule Pune University (SPPU), only two students said that they were right leaning, while one said that she had not thought why the other respondent (male, PhD, OBC) said that it was better to be a rightist, as 'Atleast they are patriotic and harmless to the nation, unlike the leftists who are Naxalites.'

Similar examples came up from a science student in AU, 'The main objective of this ideology is to respect the revolutionaries who were dedicated towards our culture and national traditions, and to develop the national consciousness, which I like.' Meanwhile in OU (science) where most students said that they were apolitical, the ones who said that they were right-wing supporters said that they were rightists 'To encourage and follow our past traditional and cultural aspect in the nation'. Two other students who said that they were right of centre 'Because it introduces many reforms and changes public policy for the welfare of public' and 'Because Rightist are equal justice and category people.' Meanwhile in OU (humanities), a PhD student defended his support for the right by saying, 'Rightists are smooth and friendly and that is why work and progress is also smooth.' Yet another PhD student supporting the right said that he only 'follows the rightist ideology as it supports and talks about the protection of nationalism and unity'.

As students spoke of their political ideological bend of mind, some explained it by pointing out the inherent flaws in the other ideologies which pushed towards them to the choice they had made. Very few saw the 'narrowness of each individual point of view' as Mannheim put it. The centrists were critical of both the right and left ideologies and saw a problem in adopting what they saw as two extreme viewpoints. This can be explained by the role of social experience in the context of ideology. These extremes which were mentioned by the centrists and also the rejection of any political position were shaped by the events which were taking place in the country. The right wing brought with it an extreme stand on nationalism or patriotism which students rejected when they spoke against the compulsory playing of the national anthem in the theatres or said that the right was creating fissures in the society; similarly, many saw the left as not being patriotic enough or being destructive. It was evident that most of the opinions about the left were influenced by the incidents which had taken place in universities with left-leaning student unions.

According to Altbach, the student community due to the Western legacy of education in India is introduced to new ideas of nationalism, radicalism and ideology. He wrote that because of their 'educational background and socio-economic status, students are politically aware—a crucial factor in societies' (Altbach 1970, 74). But he wrote that in a different time. In the current context, do students discuss politics or ideology with their friends? What do students discuss about politics or even ideology? One of the factors influencing ideological positions was peer pressure or peer factor. The word 'pressure' would imply that there is an element of force, which is not always the case. Surprisingly, teachers were not seen as key forces in determining ideological positions. This was evident from the fact that most of the students—barring in campuses which had a dominant political culture—said that they were not aware of the ideological nor the political positions of their teachers and nor were they interested in knowing. Some said that they guessed from the books suggested or when the teachers openly supported some political figure. The earlier understanding of educational institutes acting as agencies of socialization where both teachers and peer played an equal role seems to be changing at least in this context.

Politics as a Point of Discussion in Campus

A visit to a university or any higher educational institute is marked by the presence of students in groups talking to each other, hanging out in groups in canteens and so on. These moments are what memories on campus are made up of. It was but natural to ask the students whether politics forms a part of these discussions, considering that many of them were vocal and clear about their political affiliations. One of the questions asked in this context of political affiliation and activity was: Do you discuss politics with your friends? If yes, what do you usually discuss? In response to these questions, even 'apolitical' students said that they discussed politics and these discussions centred on party ideology before casting their vote; others said that they discussed how to bring in change in the way rural areas think, while an SC female respondent said that they discussed women's issues. Rest said that they discussed government policies and schemes, reservation and leaders of political parties, who to vote for and so on. The students interviewed seemed to be politically aware and in spite of their assertions, many were not really apolitical; what they probably meant was that they were not politically affiliated to any party. It came as a pleasant surprise that policies of the state and Central government, not necessarily related to students or universities, were frequently discussed.

A politically active Jadavpur University (JU) student said that discussions with friends and peers ranged from films to gossips to economics and songs. In comparison to other universities, economic growth was discussed more often among the students of JU. This was in connection with employment opportunities and education, employment and economic growth. The students were honest enough to mention that more often than not, they spoke about personal matters. In a few universities, students were hesitant in mentioning the content of their political discussions. In Calicut University, an example of yet another politically active left bastion, a PhD leftist student said, 'Ideology and politics are things which we can't keep out of our lines and so we do discuss about these things. Whenever there are issues of importance it comes into our discussions.' Another leftist MA student said, 'Each one has their own ideologies. For my friends each hold different Ideologies which they like. In my view, it is essential to understand all ideologies whether it is left or right to centrist.' An MA student even expressed his dissatisfaction with the discussions, 'I have a very small circle in my campus to discuss. This circle consist different people who adopted different ideology. In it there is political scientist strong left. Liberal left persons. I am not satisfied about the all over intellectual discussion taking place in this campus.' In FTII, students mentioned that they discussed censorship, films and funds, among other things.

The humanities students of Bangalore University seemed to engage in political discussions more than the technical students of the same university. From the conversations, it appeared that the students, even those who said that they were apolitical, discussed government policies, actions of the government and, of course, corruption. Majority of the students had said that they were centrists in their political affiliations; very few said that they were political. In the interviews with technical students in Bangalore University, most students had said that they were apolitical. A PhD student from the SC community said, 'As first voters, political awareness is a necessity. The discussion mainly deals with the recent political activities and trends' (apolitical, male, SC). Many of those who said that they were apolitical said that they did not discuss politics with their friends. But no definitive pattern emerged, as many respondents who otherwise stated their political ideological position clearly said that they did not discuss politics with friends, as it leads to conflicts and many of those who said that they were apolitical discussed politics with friends. But apart from Gulbarga University, where about eight students mentioned that there had been instances of conflict, students from other universities reported very few of instances of physical conflict from everyday discussions among students.

If we take examples of some of the discussions which take place across ideological leanings, we see that often the position taken during the discussion is removed from ideological leanings. For example, a student pursuing a master's course in Bangalore University who had mentioned that he was a rightist said that he discussed with his friends religion and politics. 'Discussion about inter relation between politics and Religion. Religion as a hindrance of growth required changes in administration.' It was surprising to note that his opinion on religion was in direct opposition to the politics of the right wing.

Those who said that they were right of centre in their leanings said 'There is a wide array of opinions between my friends and me with respect to Ideology. Some are communists and some are leftist-liberals

(Indian version) most of the discussion are regarding how politics is portrayed by the media and actual incidents that take place' (male, General). There were few others who also said that they discussed the social media and the news as projected by the social media. None of the other university students so far had mentioned the social media as a point of discussion. The students who said that they were leftists said that they discussed the issues facing the country at large. A leftist pursuing her MA from Bangalore University said, 'Usually we discuss our country growth can be done by a proper political party or the work of politicians in our city state.' Another student said that he discussed a wide range of issues, 'The discussion ranges from current events, current policy, economics, laws and government policies' (left of centre, male, MA). Not many students said that they analysed economic issues. It came as no surprise that in Kashmir University, at the forefront of all discussions was the Kashmir conflict and Central and state governments—their policies, conflict in Kashmir and so on.

As mentioned earlier, none of the students mentioned the teachers influencing them regarding ideology or even their political affiliation. If one looks at it from the socialization perspective, the campus does play a crucial role in shaping ideological positions but what role do the teachers play in this process? When asked whether the teachers are open about their ideological positions or if the students came to know about it through other means, most of the students seemed unaware of the ideological and political affiliations of the teachers. In sciences more so than humanities, students said that their teachers did not discuss with them anything regarding this. Among the humanities students, only Calicut University, JNU, JU and DU said that yes, some teachers were open about their ideological positions, political and non-political.

For those who argue for an apolitical campus, the several examples cited here prove that even if a campus does not permit political activity, it cannot prevent the students from becoming politically active or aware. The idea that politics should not enter campus is based on a very narrow understanding of politics on campus. The number of examples cited here on the discussions among students—about policies and unemployment—show that even campuses which do not have political groups are political and that even several students professing to be apolitical are political. Would we like to build generations which remain blissfully unaware of state policies and actions, what ideology is or what taking a political position means? To argue that one can learn this outside the campus after completion of studies is foolish. Caste, religion as ideology and world views need to be discussed in a manner that students recognize their impact on their lives and the way they view others. A student should learn to accept and accommodate varied viewpoints, argue one's positions and flesh out one's thoughts on several social and political aspects of life. To deprive a student of this and expect him/her to quickly adapt to the 'real' world lacks insight about how minds develop. Also, this is the time when not only education involves what is prescribed in course books and syllabus, but a student also picks up skills and knowledge through interaction with peers and teachers outside the classroom, participating in seminars and workshops which present diverse opinions and perspectives and sometimes by attending political events organized by students. Banning books and speakers and preventing universities from organizing seminars are merely going to create a group of intolerant, conservative, close-minded citizens, who would find no place in a global word.

Merely questioning students about their ideological leanings leaves the conversation incomplete. It is important that one is aware of the various ways in which ideological beliefs come into play outside of political activism. The next section explores this by asking students what the national anthem means to them and their views on the rewriting of history.

PART II

STATE, NATIONALISM AND IDEOLOGY

This section explores the idea of nationhood through symbolism and history seen through the eyes of students. Students get acquainted with the nation through the education system, as they sing the national anthem before school events or celebrate Republic Day and Independence Day. This is common to almost all countries. The

Gramscian idea of education as an ideological apparatus in the hands of the state is well established. There is no denying that the State plays an important role in guiding and shaping education through policies, providing infrastructure and finances and also through curricula, books and so on. Apart from this, the State may also attempt ideological indoctrination of students in several ways, and one such way is the celebration of certain national symbols, the military, national flag and so on. In a subtle way, the State also creates a narrative about citizenship, conformity and nation building.

Giroux (2007), in his work *The University in Chains*, points out that the triangle of militarization, corporatization and ideology can pose a deep threat to education as seen post the 9/11 attack in the USA. National security and increasing importance of the military found its way into the American campus. This resonates with what is happening in India today. Each government, irrespective of their ideological leanings, tries to control education and especially higher education. But whether this can go the other way and instead students emerge as pockets of resistance within the academia standing up against ethno-nationalism remain to be seen. This was evident when the Government of India declared Emergency in India and students were actively involved in anti-Emergency protests. That would be the real test of education. Are we producing a herd of sheep or citizens who know how to break away from the herd? In this context, it is important to find out what the national anthem means to students. What do the nation and patriotism mean to students? In the following pages, we explore this and more.

A discussion on nationalism would be incomplete without a reference to George Orwell and his distinction between patriotism and nationalism. George Orwell, in his *Notes on Nationalism*, distinguishes between nationalism and patriotism. According to him, nationalism categorizes people into good and bad, and by extension these groups of people identify themselves with a single nation/unit and their sole duty is to work in the interests of the nation at any cost. Orwell goes on to say that nationalism and patriotism are two different concepts, though they are used interchangeably. Nationalism according to Orwell is linked to the desire for power and prestige for the nation, while patriotism is a devotion to a particular place which one believes to be the best but does not expect others to follow the same belief.

Now comes in a point which sounds familiar in the times that we live today; he writes that a nationalist in the name of being true to the nation can be dishonest. S/he does not see it as being dishonest, as it is for a larger cause. This involves a certain self-deception too. A nationalist takes offence easily if s/he perceives that someone is speaking against the 'power unit'. If the power unit in question is a country, then the nationalist will 'generally claim superiority for it not only in military power and political virtue, but in art, literature, sport, structure of the language, the physical beauty of the inhabitants, and perhaps even in climate, scenery and cooking' (Orwell 1984 [1945], 4). Even the current spree of name changing of cities and towns which is happening in India can be linked to the idea of nationalism as espoused by Orwell. According to him, nations which have been through a fight for independence tend to change name/s and the emphasis is on the usage of local/national language. Over the past few years, we have seen several changes in the names of places—Allahabad has become Prayagraj and the Mughalsarai Junction is now Pt Deen Dayal Upadhyaya Junction. Added to this, there have been comments by many political figures that English should not be given primacy; rather, Hindi or other regional languages should be the medium of instruction in schools.

Orwell points out that nationalists would overlook any action which is morally wrong by one of their own; this would include genocide, torture, wrongful imprisonment, etc. Not only do they justify the violence and injustice by the State through its machinery like the police and the State, they also try to incite people by spreading fake news and information, thereby further vitiating the atmosphere. Just put this in the context of the recent CAA or even the urban Naxal slogan by the 'nationalists' in the Indian context. They see no wrong in the imprisonment of people on the pretext of mere suspicion, citizens being detained in detention centres in their own country and attacks on students in universities by the state police. Disha Ravi, a young climate change activist, was arrested by the Delhi police (February 2021) for sharing a 'tool kit' for organizing protests in relation to the ongoing farm law protests on Twitter. On the other hand, politicians who have openly supported riots and violence which took place in the capital city of Delhi in 2019 have been left scot-free. As Orwell says, 'The nationalist not only does not disapprove of atrocities committed by his own side, but he has a remarkable capacity for not even hearing about them' (Orwell 1984 [1945], 5).

India's freedom struggle against the British further complicates any discussion on nationalism. Tagore, Nehru and Gandhi recognized the dangers of extreme nationalism even while the freedom struggle was at its peak. Gandhi spoke against the parochialism and hatred which very often follow nationalism. He said, 'My love, therefore, of nationalism, or my idea of nationalism is that my country may become free—free that if need be the whole of the country may die—so that the human race may live. There is no room here for race hatred. Let that be our nationalism' (Habib 2017, 163–164). Nehru constantly questioned the idea of worshipping a nation, Bharat Mata (seeing the country as a mother figure), the symbolism which had become popular during the freedom struggle. For him, Bharat (India) consisted of the people and was not merely defined by territorial boundaries. He focused on economic nationalism post Independence. This was reflected in the institution building he initiated as the first prime minister, the benefits of which we continue to reap today. In the introduction to his book *Indian Nationalism*, Habib (2017) comments,

> Nehru repeatedly said that nationalism as articulated in cultural or religious terms is too narrow and parochial to solve the big problems that the country was facing. For Nehru, an economic programme based on economic nationalism was crucial during colonial times to raise the standard of living and incomes of the people.

As Habib rightly points out that nationalism has potential to divide or unite people, it can unleash intellectual and creative activities or destroy the peace of a nation. Tagore also recognized the danger of falling for the Western ideals of nationalism. He wrote that Europe is racially united but has a history of aggression due to conflict over resources and land. For him, the problem in India is not so much political as social and hence we do not need to ape the Western ideals of nationalism.

CELEBRATING THE NATION, ICONS AND EVENTS

Giroux, Gramsci and several others have spoken of how schools can become grounds for indoctrination by the State. How does this happen? Through the textbooks, the course, syllabus, pedagogy and so on. One of the ways the idea of a nation and a common citizenship can be passed on to future generations is through celebration of certain days: Independence Day, Republic Day and so on. Celebrations such as these reinforce the idea of nation, unity and struggle for freedom. The students in all the universities where fieldwork was conducted mentioned that singing of the national anthem and celebration of Independence Day and Republic Day (apart from festivals) are constant and integral features of university campuses. Some mentioned that these were celebrated with great fanfare and sometimes even at the cost of fund allocation for projects as pointed out by FTII students.

On being asked whether there had been any recent additions to celebrations with regard to the State, the students of SPPU, mentioned that Swami Vivekananda's birthday is now celebrated. Vivekananda, among several other icons, has been appropriated by the right wing over the last few years. JNU, DU, Pondicherry University, SPPU and Punjab University mentioned occasions which are now being celebrated on campuses which were not celebrated earlier. In SPPU, students mentioned Shahid Divas (Martyrs' Day) and Savarkar Jayanti as recent additions. This is significant in the light of the rise of the right wing. Savarkar has emerged as a controversial figure; the right wing has been trying to showcase him as a freedom fighter, while historical records show otherwise. Academic and political articles have been written both for and against Savarkar.

Similarly, the Army has also put in the centre of the debate nationalism by the State. It has become commonplace to cite the sacrifices of the Army personnel and the comfort and safety of the citizens which are ensured by the Army. The State is making a definite push towards placing the Army in the discourse of education. In JNU, students spoke of the plans to install an Army tank in the campus as a reminder of the 'true patriots' in a reaction to the alleged slogans raised by students against India. Among teacher respondents, only one teacher in NEHU mentioned a circular to celebrate Army Day. None of the teachers mentioned any special notification by the government. However, a closer scrutiny of the circulars by the UGC in the past few years revealed that the government sent out explicit instructions on celebration of several of the events mentioned by the students. On 20 November 2017, the UGC sent out a letter asking that universities celebrate 7 December as Armed Forces Flag Day. VCs were asked to organize events/talks to create awareness regarding the sacrifices made by the Armed Forces. The Armed Forces Flag Day is usually celebrated by raising funds for war widows and ex-service men (including disabled soldiers). It has now found its way into the campus in a different avatar. Giroux points out that the perceived threat to national security and subsequent attempt at militarization of campus are typical features of a right-wing government.

The State also directs educational institutions to celebrate symbols of the nation. This serves to socialize the young generation into the idea of belonging to a nation. In a diverse nation such as India, where region/state feelings are rather strong, an endeavour is made that students are taught about belonging to a nation rather than just a region. The UGC sent instructions to the VCs of universities on 27 January 2016 regarding observing 30 January as a day of remembrance for all those who sacrificed their lives for their country during the freedom struggle—Martyrs' Day. Detailed instructions of a two-minute silence to be observed after indicating the commencement of the two-minute silence with the sound of sirens or Army guns from 10:59 AM to 11:00 AM were shared. Efforts were to be made to congregate staff and students unless it hampered work. Another circular directed universities to observe Swachhata Hi Seva (Cleanliness Is Service) campaign. It was suggested that the universities upload pictures of the activities along with details of the number of students, teachers and other staff members who participated in the event. Not related to this event, but a few teachers expressed unhappiness over this kind of attendance marking during an event. They said that it put pressure on them to attend an event even if they did not have time or interest.

26 November has long been celebrated as Constitution Day or Samvidhan Divas (Hindi). In a circular by UGC, universities were

urged to celebrate Constitution Day by reading out the Preamble and Fundamental Duties during the morning assembly. The universities were urged to arrange for one lecture on Fundamental Duties and post the Fundamental Duties[2] on notice boards. Another circular asked universities to visit other states as part of understanding India. This was under the Ek Bharat Shreshtha Bharat programme. Universities were urged to organize tours, dramas, elocutions, songs, etc., in other states as an effort towards cultural exchange. From the Gramscian perspective, this would be an example of what Gramsci meant when he saw the state using education as a tool for indoctrination; the functionalists would view this as a means of building future citizens and also inculcating ideas of unity and duties of a citizen and so on. But students need to be conversant with the Constitution, as every citizen should be aware of not only his or her rights but also those of minorities, SCs and STs. Students need to discuss, understand and debate the

---

[2] The Fundamental Duties in the Constitution read as follows:

PART IVA FUNDAMENTAL DUTIES

51A. Fundamental duties—It shall be the duty of every citizen of India—

(a) to abide by the Constitution and respect its ideals and institutions, the National Flag and the National Anthem;

(b) to cherish and follow the noble ideals which inspired our national struggle for freedom;

(c) to uphold and protect the sovereignty, unity and integrity of India;

(d) to defend the country and render national service when called upon to do so;

(e) to promote harmony and the spirit of common brotherhood amongst all the people of India transcending religious, linguistic and regional or sectional diversities; to renounce practices derogatory to the dignity of women;

(f) to value and preserve the rich heritage of our composite culture;

(g) to protect and improve the natural environment including forests, lakes, rivers and wild life, and to have compassion for living creatures;

(h) to develop the scientific temper, humanism and the spirit of inquiry and reform;

(i) to safeguard public property and to abjure violence;

(j) to strive towards excellence in all spheres of individual and collective activity so that the nation constantly rises to higher levels of endeavour and achievement;

(k) who is a parent or guardian to provide opportunities for education to his child or, as the case may be, ward between the age of six and fourteen years.

Constitution, which is left mostly to law and political science students. The Samvidhan Divas should be used to this end.

On the other hand, sometimes a notice such as this can be controversial. In June 2019, a reminder was sent out to universities to take action on a previous letter circulated by the UGC in July 2015 in which it urged universities to adopt handloom fabric for their convocation ceremonies and take pride in being Indian. The argument was that universities should abandon the British-inspired gown and opt for traditional clothing during convocation and other such ceremonies. It was suggested that students could send across their designs based on traditional Indian clothing and fabric like khadi and post it on the Ministry of Human Resource Development website. IIT (BHU) had already adopted this in 2013 prior to the circular. The reaction to this was mixed. Ritul Madhukar (2019) writes that some teachers and students said that it was a welcome change, while others questioned the idea of forcing a dress code. Interestingly, in the article, most of those who agreed that traditional clothes should be worn were from the IITs and other professional courses. According to them, there was no need to hang on to colonial ideas and embrace our Indian identity. But teachers and students in DU were critical of this approach. A teacher said, 'I have a problem with this "sense of pride". Everything we do is being disciplined and conditioned towards "nationalistic pride" and "being Indian". I have an issue with this forced nationalism, now do we need to see it in clothes also? India is not a homogenous country. There are many traditions and creating a single narrative for everything is not a positive approach.' Some of the students saw it as an attempt to saffronize education. Students of sociology and political science pointed out that this directive subverted the idea of free will. A question was raised as to whether there is a common traditional attire in India and why should universities or the State dictate what students should wear.

In October 2018, the UGC sent a letter to the VCs of all the universities across India that they needed to celebrate the birth anniversary of Sardar Vallabhbhai Patel on 31 October. As per the directives, students and teachers were asked to participate in a 'run for unity', organize competitions, essays, quizzes, debates, etc. Most importantly, universities were directed to invite Army officers to give a talk on unity and integrity, and also a pledge to be taken by students and staff was circulated. The pledge read thus,

> I solemnly pledge that I dedicate myself to preserve the unity, integrity and security of the nation and also strive hard to spread this message among my countrymen. I take this pledge in the spirit of unification of my country which was made possible by the vision and actions of Sardar VallabhBhai Patel. I also solemnly resolve to make my own contribution to ensure internal security of my country. (UGC circular dated October 2018)

Earlier in May 2018, a circular was sent to all universities to celebrate Anti-Terrorism Day. Administration was asked to organize debates and quizzes.

> We the people of India having abiding faith in our country's tradition of non-violence and tolerance, hereby solemnly affirm to oppose with all our strength, all forms of terrorism and violence. We pledge to uphold and promote peace, social harmony and understanding among all fellow human beings and fight the forces of disruption threatening human lives and values. (UGC circular dated 18 May 2018)

This circular, originally from the Ministry of Home affairs (8 May 2018) was sent to all government offices, public sector undertakings and other public institutions by the UGC on 18 May 2018. The letter specified that the state governments had to ensure that schools, colleges and universities organize debates, lectures, symposiums and the above-mentioned pledge. The circular also mentioned that the media—newspapers, journals, magazines, the All India Radio and Doordarshan (State-owned television channel)—should be roped in to create and disseminate messages on the 'ill effects of violence and terrorism'. A mention was also made that merchandise such as T-shirts are made with 'attractive anti terrorism/violence slogans'. In a separate letter, dated 8 July 2015, the departments of mass communication and journalism education across universities were urged to 'avoid such elements which may advance the agenda of terrorism' and that 'media policy should include principles of self restraint'. This was based on the recommendations of the Eight Report of the Second Administrative Reforms Commission—*Combating Terrorism: Protecting by Righteousness.*

The various examples from the UGC circulars make it apparent that universities are not isolated campuses where the State intervenes only to provide infrastructure or the curricula. It also involves the active engagement of other agencies like State-owned media and military to slowly prepare the students for their role as citizens—respecting the Armed Forces and fighting terrorism are examples of such instances. It is apparent that State and education are not two separate binaries; rather, the state constantly uses the education system to reach out to students and propagate a certain imagery of the country. One may argue that there is no harm in students going in for exchange programmes or learning about unity and integrity of the country, but when the universities become a breeding ground for the kind of nationalism Orwell warns us about that we need to critically examine the role of the State.

In recent times, the emphasis on a certain kind of nationalism that is built on external symbols such as singing the national anthem or the national song, the emphasis on the valour and sacrifices of the Armed Forces, celebrating 'surgical strike' day and proposal to place Army tanks in universities points to the growth of a dangerous jingoistic nationalism. The reader may well be aware of the numerous debates that have taken place on television channels on 'Vande Mataram'. The controversy on Vande Mataram is a one that dates way before India gained independence. Bankim Chandra's evocative poetry invited controversy on religious interpretation of the idea of India. Television channels were rife with debates on how communities that refuse to sing the national song or national anthem are less patriotic than those who do. Similarly, the introduction of compulsory singing of the national anthem in cinema halls/theatres gives many an excuse to take recourse to violence in order to literally and figuratively beat people into accepting what they believe to be a sign of nationalism. There have been incidents where physically challenged people have been beaten for not standing when national anthem was played in cinema halls. Quick to judge and react, people have resorted to violence without even cross-checking facts/reasons and second forgetting that no citizen can 'punish' another citizen for not standing up for the national anthem. The terms 'nationalism' and 'patriotism' have distinct meanings as explained by Orwell but for most, these are interchangeable.

The debate on nationalism also includes in it the subtext of patriotism. For all those who argue that students should steer clear of politics, can students remain untouched by these events and should they be?

CONTEMPORARY NATIONALISM

What does singing the national anthem mean to students? This was a great way to grasp the critical understanding of issues by students. Can students see beyond what is narrated to them and analyse an issue objectively? It also provides a window to the way students are thinking regarding the increasing association of national symbols and nationalism. Also, at no point were students asked about the compulsory singing of national anthem in theatres. (Please note that the conversations have been presented verbatim without any attempt to change or correct grammar.)

HUMANITIES STUDENTS ON NATIONAL ANTHEM AND PATRIOTISM

The two extreme opinions came from Gulbarga University and Calicut University. The former was the only one with an overwhelmingly large number of right-leaning students and, of course, Calicut University had students who were largely left-leaning and a few apolitical. The following conversations bring to you a comparison of the views expressed by students on national anthem and patriotism from opposing political world views.

A female student in Gulbarga University belonging to the SC community said about singing the national anthem, 'Feel happy, increase the feeling and desh bhakti (literally meaning worshipping the state), felt that people should be in Military. Even I want to join Military to serve country.' Pride and unity were a recurring theme when asked about singing the national anthem in most universities. However, in several universities like DU, Calicut University, JU and BHU, most of students, about 16 or 17 out of 20 students, said that singing the national anthem does not instil patriotism. BHU was a close second with only about three students saying that singing of national anthem leads to a feeling of patriotism. Rather, some students had strong opinion against it.

A Calicut University student said, 'In my opinion, as centres of higher education excellence, universities should try to inculcate the values of humanism, internationalism and secularism over patriotism which is restrictive and rudimentary. Reciting National Anthem must not be forcefully enforced on any citizen of India. Finding solace in Nationalistic symbols can be dangerous sometimes, as they show one's vision to the geographical territories. Moreover, forceful imposition of such symbols remind me of the arrival of fascism in my country' (leftist, male, OBC). Similar views were expressed by another student in Calicut University, who said, 'But I believe that I have some commitments and responsibility to society. I believe in love, compassion universalism' (left of centre, male, MA). One student went on to say that the singing of the national anthem only promotes pseudo nationalism. In DU, a student remarked that rather than forcing people to sing the national anthem to show their patriotism, 'National anthem/ song is way of building and fostering respect and brotherhood for the nation. However there are other means as well for achieving this end, like social work, aiding the needy, value based life etc. Hence a blanket imposition of national anthem to build up patriotism is not sustainable in nature.'

In BHU, while students did not speak of universalism or compassion, they saw a political motive behind the obsession with nationalism and forcing people to sing the national anthem, 'Patriotism stimulates only by singing National song? I don't think so. Personally I think that in making nationalist/anti-national hierarchy, dominance of radical mindset is a big cause. What is there to ask for proof of patriotism? Because of this people gets divided, groups get formed and violence happen. This ideology does not establish peace, but only changes the narrative Diversion gets created from issues. These oppressive/repressive norms seems like escape route' (General, female, MA). Yet another student took it a step further, 'The feeling of patriotism develops on unity. This unity depends on equality, equal distribution of resources, and social welfare policies of a liberal government. Only singing National anthem and song, is not going to develop patriotism. This is also true that those who cannot pronounce National anthem and song properly are calling themselves nationalist.' (male, MA, SC). Similarly, in JU, a student pursuing her MA said, 'You can't inculcate any extra respect or love for the national anthem by forcing it upon people. It only leads to a perverted form of nationalism which is harmful for the national integrity and culture of democracy' (leftist, General).

Several students across universities said that while they did get a sense of pride while singing the national anthem, they did not want it to be under duress. So comments like 'Patriotism cannot be build under pressure' and 'It cannot be forced' were mentioned at several instances. As one student from BHU said, 'Patriotism gets build by National Anthem but some people especially nationalists started treating it as certificate for nationalism.' As mentioned earlier, the response of students in Calicut University to patriotism and national anthem were very different. In other universities, several leftists also supported the idea of national anthem instilling a feeling of patriotism, but here only the apolitical students spoke in favour of it contrary to the popular perception that the leftists were against the ideas of patriotism and were devoted only to the idea of class.

Interestingly, in Bangalore University, while the responses were largely in favour of singing the national anthem, out of two students who said that they were ideologically inclined towards the right of centre, one pursuing LLB said, 'I don't generally believe that a sense of patriotism has to come about with only the singing of either the National Anthem song but should instead be a concept and principal that already exists in a person' (male, General). The second respondent said, 'I believe that singing of national anthem should not be made compulsory at university level. It can be done only at elementary upto class 10. Patriotism is feeling within a person not to be created by singing national anthem song (female, OBC). Although the respondents' ideological leanings were more towards the right, their sentiments towards the national anthem were not.

What about in Kashmir? The fieldwork in Kashmir was conducted post the abrogation of Article 370 in Kashmir. While speaking to the students of the University of Kashmir, one of them remarked, 'I don't believe singing a song that is not written in native language can bring emotions unless it touches one on religious front.' Interestingly, this respondent identified himself as a leftist, but religious feelings were central to him. Of course, one can cite many examples of leftists, especially in West Bengal, with strong religious feelings, contrary to the idea of 'religion of opium of masses' espoused by Marx. Another male respondent in the University of Kashmir said that the feeling of patriotism for him was not directed to a nation but to a region. 'Kashmir being conflict ridden impacts the way we think about patriotism. Having your own identity to imbibe nationalism can be there. So yes it does inculcate patriotism but should be regional in nature.' This point was mentioned by a few in Osmania University, where they said that they wanted to celebrate their state rather than the nation. At a time when borders are shrinking, some students are still embedded in parochial identities which Gandhi spoke against. Kashmiri students have a reason to be region-centric due to political factors and therefore the push towards region- and religion-specific nationalism and patriotism.

While most students saw in the national anthem an opportunity to celebrate diversity and unity, they were not in favour of the recent move by the government to play the national anthem in movie theatres. A student from Gulbarga University who professed to be apolitical had an interesting perspective: 'Feel proud, happy because it includes all the states, unity. But avoid singing National Anthem in Theatre; there it is not respect but disrespect to the National anthem. There we do not give respect, instead disrespect the National Anthem.' In an indirect reference to the same, a student pursuing MPhil from Calicut University said, 'Singing national anthem is good and respectful. But the problem is where is singing it personally. I do not believe that the singing of anthem everywhere is not help to build up patriotism' (left of centre, male). A young female student had a different take on the practice of singing the national anthem in theatres/cinema halls, 'Patriotism is an inner feeling, it cannot be felt under any pressure, but yes I do not have any problem singing it in cinema theatre unlike others. After all there is nothing, I could contribute to our freedom struggle, the least I can do is sing and pay respect' (leftist, MA, General). In JNU, several students mentioned the mandatory singing of the national anthem in movie halls/cinema theatres as follows: 'My opinion is one cannot be and should not be forced to love our country in very specific defined ways which is decided by someone else. We are a plural society and we should be allowed to love and demonstrate our love for country in plural ways. The choice should be ours. Singing national anthem/song on certain occasions in time (like Republic day or Independence day) but it's not okay to make it mandatory in other context. Forcing one to sing doesn't do anything (in my opinion) in building patriotism.'

Similarly, in Gauhati University, students expressed that the main problem was that people were being attacked and shamed in theatres for not standing up or singing the national anthem. Students in Pondicherry University and SPPU had majority of students saying that singing the national anthem helps build up feeling of patriotism, but several also mentioned that they were not in favour of it being forced in cinema halls or even otherwise.

Contrary to the current narrative in the country about the ideological positions on patriotism and nationalism, it was seen that students, irrespective of political ideological leanings, said that singing the national anthem is a matter of pride, binds people together irrespective of caste and community and creates patriotism. They said that it reminds citizens of the sacrifices made by the freedom fighters and also that the campus consists of students from across the country and when the national anthem is sung together, it reinforces the idea that India is not defined by a specific region.

'It is the proudest feeling ever. I believe it's a mixture of pride, submission, dedication and melancholy. In the same spirit, if one takes action and participants in nation building which would complete the idea of patriotism' (centrist, male, BA LLB, Bangalore University, OBC).

SCIENCE STUDENTS ON NATIONAL ANTHEM AND PATRIOTISM

Students from both science and humanities were interviewed in BHU, AU, NEHU, Pondicherry University and Punjab University. This provided an opportunity for a comparative analysis on whether the subject influenced one's world view? In this, BHU stood out, where majority of the humanities students said that merely singing the national anthem does not make one patriotic and science students said the exact opposite. The students also mentioned that the national anthem is a sign of unity; it shows how in spite of regional differences we are united. On the other hand, in AU, both humanities and science students had similar responses on singing of the national anthem. Majority said yes, singing the national anthem is a matter of pride and arouses feeling of patriotism. Similarly, in Osmania University, barring a few who were in favour of cultivating a more regional feeling than a national one, most said that singing the national anthem is a matter of pride and brings people together. 'Yes. National Anthem is constitutionally mandatory for everyone and this is constitutionally directed democracy. Although Vande Matram is not mandatory but personally I think that it is important for building feeling of patriotism' (rightist, male, MA, AU, General). In Bangalore University too, most of the respondents said that the national anthem does promote feelings of patriotism. Some of the sentiments expressed were on the lines that it is essential to create awareness about the country and especially among students, while another remarked that the national anthem helps students in understanding the country and will make them great citizens. It will help build patriotism and express it in public. Another (leftist, female, SC) said that it may not make people patriotic but it will make people think about Indian history. It brings people together and creates a feeling of unity. 'There should be awareness of the importance of patriotism and creates a sense of oneness among people.' Among the few who had contrary views, one said that instead of the national anthem, the Karnataka song must be promoted.

In contrast, at FTII, some students were upset that money from their workshop funds was being used on Republic Day/Independence Day celebrations. They also mentioned that in the past few years, Savarkar Jayanti, Kargil Diwas and Vivekananda Jayanti have been added to the list of celebrations apart from other national holidays. It is worth noting that SPPU also based in Pune mentioned that Savarkar Jayanti and Vivekananda Jayanti were being celebrated in their campus. Some students also mentioned that Hindu festivals were celebrated with fervour in their campus and also Sadhguru (well known for his Isha Foundation) had been invited for a talk but the programme was later cancelled. In Punjab University, students said that there had been an increase in cultural activities promoting certain leaders. On being asked whether singing the national anthem instils a sense of patriotism, it was interesting to note that in contrast to the responses of the students in Bangalore University, most of the students in Punjab University did not support any compulsory singing of the national anthem. One respondent replied, 'No it does not. Instead it promotes Jingoism. This patriotism lacks the will to serve people of the nation. It only respects the symbolism. So I completely reject' (left of centre, male, PhD scholar, Punjab University, General). Another PhD scholar, a female respondent, also echoed the same thought that singing of the national anthem does not lead to patriotism. There was no particular pattern of political leaning that emerged in terms of caste and gender, as in several universities students spoke against it being imposed.

Meanwhile in NEHU, two students spoke of Martyrs' Day and Anti-Terrorism Day that was now being celebrated on campus. Some students said that these programmes have always been there, but majority said that these were recent developments. When asked whether the singing of the national anthem instils a sense of patriotism, barring two respondents, everyone else said yes. Following are some examples: 'Yes, I think it helps us realizing that we belong to the same country. It shows unity when we all stand together and participate in signing the National Anthem' (female, PhD, NEHU, ST). Echoing similar beliefs, another female respondent (postgraduate, General) said, 'Yes, it does help. It is the common and only means for showing patriotism at a given point when residents of the country are multi-linguistic. There is nothing wrong in standing up for 53 seconds of nation's glory.' For most of the students, the national anthem was a reminder of the diversity of the country in terms of geographical territory and also religion and culture and that in spite of these differences, we all belong to one country. A male BTech student pointed out that it was essential for students as it teaches them to respect their country and how valuable it is. 'By singing National Anthem if produced a sense of oneness, brother hood and strengthening our love and bond with other people living in the campus even though we come from different state with different culture of the country' (male, BTech, NEHU, ST).

Like many in the humanities stream, students in NEHU were uncomfortable with the rule regarding playing of the national anthem in cinema halls. For example, a female PhD student said, 'Yes, to a certain extent, but not in places such as theatre where people come to enjoy. It certainly helps the younger generation to feel proud of our country.' A similar sentiment was echoed by another female PhD scholar (General), 'In some way it does, but however I felt that patriotism need not be become by just singing patriotic song. Patriotism comes from within and it reflects in our actions. It cannot be forcefully done.' The only respondent to state his political preference as left of centre said, 'In my opinion singing National anthem/song is a pride to every citizen of India. I don't think it helps in building up patriotism for country because it has been in our blood since the day we were born in this country.' An MSc student remarked, 'For those who love their own country then yes it helps in building up patriotism otherwise no use for those who don't love their own country.'

In NIT Srinagar, a few students said that yes the national anthem does build up a feeling of patriotism, but majority of the students disagreed with this idea. The focus on Northeast and Kashmir is deliberate because of the geographical and political disconnect which is often pointed out by those residing in these areas. We are well aware of the politics of alienation in Northeast and Kashmir, which has resulted in conflict of the states and the Centre. Keeping that in mind, it was surprising that in NEHU there were several students who spoke in favour of the national anthem. On the other hand, in Kashmir, most of the students mentioned the freedom of choice. Of course, there were at least four students who said that yes, indeed the national anthem reminds one of the sacrifices made for the freedom of the country, but majority said that it should not be forced or made mandatory: 'Forcing someone to something can never build patriotism. Everyone should her/his own choice.' There were several who echoed this, indicating towards the politics that takes place, especially during Independence Day in Kashmir with regard to unfurling the flag and singing the national anthem. As another student from NIT Srinagar put it, 'Singing of national anthem can never build patriotism forcing someone for singing national anthem can in turn spread hostility, disturb peace there should be liberty to everyone.' Interestingly, a student from NIT Srinagar, who was not a Kashmiri, said that he does not understand all this debate on nationalism and patriotism and does not think that national anthem and patriotism are linked. In contrast, in JU, a few students said that it should be made mandatory in schools. A larger number of students studying sciences thought that singing the national anthem was important, that it was a beautiful song but that patriotism is something which comes from within and is not merely linked to a song. The connect with the national anthem could be stronger in Bengal because it was written by Rabindranath Tagore, a much revered figure.

For the students across universities, the national anthem was a symbol of unity in diversity. There were a few who felt that it should be made compulsory and said that they got emotional when they heard it or got goosebumps when they sang the national anthem. In Pondicherry University, almost all the students felt that singing the national anthem was a matter of pride and should be sung. In other universities, even those who agreed spoke of unity and diversity, but in Pondicherry University, students largely spoke of a sense of pride, duty and making it compulsory. The students in almost universities repeatedly mentioned that singing the national anthem is a matter of choice and there are more ways of expressing your love for your country and doing something concrete.

There were definitely more instances of critical approach among those studying humanities, but across both streams, there was discontent on the national anthem being made mandatory in public spaces. Rather than a forced nationalism, the students overall viewed the national anthem as a symbol of unity; it reminded them that the students in the campus had come from different parts of the country and with it they brought regional and cultural differences and that they needed to understand this diversity. Appreciating differences is crucial in a democracy, rather than forcing a homogenous identity. The other important aspect that came through is that contrary to popular linkages between ideological positions and nationalism, there were leftists among students who remarked that the national anthem should be sung and promoted patriotism, and there were right-leaning students who spoke of the right to freedom to sing or not sing the national anthem. This is important as it questions the way we slot people ideologically; it is a positive sign that students who lean towards the traditionally orthodox right do not support the notion of thrusting down ideas of nationalism.

The final section, here, covers the second example of how students apply critical thinking to an issue which may affect them in ways they may not comprehend today.

REWRITING HISTORY AND SCIENTIFIC TEMPER: APPROACHES TO KNOWLEDGE

One of the key concerns in social sciences has been that of subjectivity and conversely objectivity. History and historical studies have found themselves in the mid of controversy in the past few years with allegations of Indian historians having neglected the cultural heritage of India and pandering to the Western perspective. The ideological divide in history is not new, but it has found its way into popular cinema. It is alleged that left-leaning and leftist academicians dominated social sciences, especially history; as a result, most history books and departments in universities were helmed by left-oriented historians. Of late, this debate has been revived, and there is an attempt to build a popular opinion against the existing textbooks of history which glorify 'invaders' and not the 'original inhabitants'. In the guise of building national pride, there is a concerted effort to discredit the existing books, textbooks and otherwise, and the legacy of work by labelling it as anti-majority. The accusation against current history books, interestingly largely targeting the school textbooks, is that the glorious past of India and its achievements have not been given their due place and instead the Mughals and other invaders have been given the centre stage. Not only books, but cinema is also being used to propagate the new history which needs to be told. It is absolutely crucial for a student to understand the importance of history and the consequences of its being rewritten, not in the light of new facts or findings or analysis but merely on grounds of nationalism.

History is written by conquerors. Orwell (6) writes,

> Every nationalist is haunted by the belief that the past can be altered. He spends part of his time in a fantasy world in which things happen as they should in which, for example, the Spanish Armada was a success or the Russian Revolution was crushed in 1918—and he will transfer fragments of this world to the history books whenever possible. Much of the propagandist writing of our time amounts to plain forgery. Material facts are suppressed, dates altered, quotations removed from their context and doctored so as to change their meaning. Events which, it is felt, ought not to have happened are left unmentioned and ultimately denied.

In 2014, a committee of 14 historians headed by K. N. Dikshit was constituted for a 'holistic study of origin and evolution of Indian culture since 12,000 years before present and its interface with other cultures of the world'. The committee was instructed to organize and present archaeological data to suggest that Hindus are the original descendants of India, and that the ancient Hindu scriptures are not a myth. These 'facts' would then find their way into school textbooks and academic research so that the earlier theories of invasion and migration are replaced by a linear theory of natural descendants. One of the first steps in this direction is to negate the historical fact of migration of people from Central Asia, Africa and other parts of South East Asia into India thousands of years ago. According to the historian Romila Thapar, the question of who first stood on the soil was important to nationalists because 'if the Hindus are to have primacy as citizens in a Hindu Rashtra (kingdom), their foundational religion cannot be an imported one.' To assert that primacy, nationalists need to claim descent from ancestors and a religion which were indigenous (Reuters 2018).

There have been continuous attempts by the government to use various fora, like the Indian Science Congress (ISC) or the Indian History Congress, to establish the glorious past of India and through it the achievement of the Hindus. The elephant head of the Indian god Ganesha is seen as a proof that plastic surgery existed in the ancient past. Similarly, the battle of Mahabharata is seen as a nuclear war (with reference to the dangerous *Brahmastra*, which could be used only once in case of extreme emergency as it brought with it dire consequences) or the technology of aeroplanes in the Ramayana, the *Pushpak Viman* (flower-shaped vehicle) and so on. There is deliberate effort both by the State and individuals to establish the cultural superiority of Indians in every field and to prove that every possible discovery was made in India and by Indians. There are several memes in the social media speaking of how Indians have not been given credit for several discoveries due to racism. The problem with the approach is that this process of history rewriting is not backed by scientific knowledge, rather a blind sense of pride. Even history in this context has to be approached not with an emotional, nationalistic perspective but from a dispassionate and scientific viewpoint. Of course, it also means not distorting scientific facts like DNA and archaeological finds to suit one's purpose. The nationalist approach to history is common to most countries, irrespective of political leanings. The Chinese government has asked for history to be rewritten from the Chinese perspective for the students in Hong Kong, as they are not aware of the great heritage of China. Similarly, in France and Britain, there is an attempt to downplay racism and colonialism. In Britain, colonialism as a subject is not taught; rather, it is presented as historical victories and control. The State plays a crucial role in building a narrative about the country in a way that it instils pride among citizens.

During the course of the research, both science and humanities/social science students were asked if they were aware of the debates regarding rewriting history, and the science students were asked whether they had heard of the mythology versus science debate in the ISC. It was surprising that in all the universities, both humanities and technical institutes, students were largely unaware of the attempts of the State to rewrite history textbooks. DU and JNU were among the few where students had heard about it. Science students were equally clueless about the ISC and did not seem very conversant about the mythology versus science debate either. Closely associated with the idea of the mythology debate is that of scientific temper and objectivity. During the conversations on whether ideology can influence subjects or teaching, majority of the students mentioned that this was only possible in humanities and not in the sciences. The subjective nature of humanities made it susceptible to ideological influences. Yet in certain universities, some of the responses came as a surprise. For example, in NIT Warangal, when asked if objectivity and scientific temper were important, nearly half of the respondents said these were only slightly important. Majority of them had heard of the mythology and science debate, not of the ISC. Only about two said that they had 'heard something' about history books being rewritten but had no definite opinion other than that the 'books should include contemporary issues'. In NIT Srinagar, more than 50 per cent of the students said that scientific temper and objectivity were very important, but none was aware of the mythology and science debate. Among the respondents from the University of Kashmir (Humanities), only about two commented on rewriting of history books. One said that the history and political science books should include dissent; this is not surprising coming from Kashmir. Another student said that this is the worst time for books to be rewritten.

IIT Delhi students had heard of the ISC, and all of them said that scientific temper and objectivity were crucial. When asked about rewriting of history and other social science books, some students said that the history books were biased and it was important that non-Congress leaders be given their due importance. All of them said that the books should be written in a neutral fashion. In Pondicherry University too, a few of the science students said that the freedom movement and Mughal rule need to be rewritten. This indicates that some biased information on history had reached the students. Fewer number of students said that scientific temper is important (only about 9 out of 20) and about 4 said that in the 'name of objectivity we cannot ignore our historical past'. In BHU (Science), barring a couple of students, most had not heard of rewriting of history. Only one said that history should be rewritten, as it should be representative of people across religion, caste and community. Interestingly, most of the science students had no opinion regarding the current blurring of lines between mythology and science; they had not heard of the ISC, barring a few.

In IIT Madras, a student said that he found the events at the ISC shameful in context of the mythology and science. Many of the students had heard of ISC but were not aware of the events that had taken place. Only one said that she had heard 'something' about history books being rewritten but was not sure about it. It was the same in Osmania University. In FTII, one or two students remarked on the proceedings at the ISC and one student said that it was like spreading fake news. Quite a few students (seven) said that yes history should be rewritten. The reason given for suggesting rewriting was that most history books are from the rulers' perspective and should be rewritten from the common man's perspective. Another felt that whatever has been written is fabricated, hence needs to be rewritten. In Bangalore University (Science), interestingly most of the students had no opinion about the relevance of mythology in science. Only one said that she thought it was a waste of time. In Punjab University (Sciences), the respondents who were vocal so far on ideology and students' unions did not have much to say about the current trend of classifying mythological events as scientific facts; though most of them had not heard of the ISC, they agreed that scientific temper and objectivity were important. Only one female respondent, a PhD scholar, said, 'I think it is overrated. Science is developing the country though limited of funding remains. The groups emphasising on mythology have not studied science and are not known in the science community of India. So I once again say that this all stuff is overrated so don't bother about them.' The Punjab University (Humanities) students showed a decided left leaning in their responses. With regard to rewriting, while many did not know about it, two students said, 'Actually, we have been constantly taught manipulated and taught class biased history of ruling classes. Real history of toiling masses rarely gets space in front, NCERT has deleting chapters on caste struggle colonialism and democracy etc. Peoples history can be written and taught only with revolutionary struggle advances' (male, PhD, OBC). Another added, 'Look at the recent events. The BJP has removed class struggle and Dalit movements and other chapters, so they are trying to show that no such things happen in the history. They are just putting nationalism and bullshit cartoons' (male, MA, OBC). Unknown to the students, quite a few reiterated Mannheim, 'How one looks at history and how one construes a total situation from given facts, depends on the position one occupies within society.'

In NEHU (Science), other than two students, most others declined to comment saying that either they did not know about it or they did not have any views on it; only two gave their opinion about it. A female PhD student said, 'I do not have much idea about the emphasis it is putting on mythologies historical part but as a student in school, I had once participated in it and I can safely say that I had learned a lot from it mainly because of exposure.' A zoology student said something similar, 'Along with scientific ideologies, keeping up with our history and past is also important. Because knowing our roots and from where we come from strengthens our principles.' Most of them replied that objectivity and scientific temper are very important.

AU (Science) students were surprisingly aware of the history book debates. Several of them said that yes, history books needed to be rewritten. It must be mentioned here that in universities where students did speak about rewriting history books, the number did not exceed 5 (out of 20) in most cases, baring DU where nearly 8 students wanted history books to be rewritten. In AU, those who wanted history to be rewritten were a mix of apolitical and rightists. Two apolitical respondents in AU said that the legacy and role of Hindu rulers needed to be emphasized. One said, 'History of Jammu and Kashmir, terror of Firoz Shah, cruelty of Aurangzeb, Destruction of Indian Culture, these things should be included (in history and social sciences). Also Rani Laxmi Bai, Mangal Pandey, Kunwar Singh, Maharana Pratap, Shivaji Maharaj, Bose, Azad, Bhagat Singh' (right of centre, male, General). In the context of myth and science, the same respondent said, 'Myth and history have different meaning (are different). "Ramsetu" had been considered a myth until NASA proved it. (Discovery communications, The Gita of J. Robert Oppenheimer). A proud history helps in building a greater future.' The respondents who did agree that myth had a role to play in science were of the view that the scientific achievements of the past have to be connected with the present. Among the AU (Humanities) respondents too, a similar number of students said that history should be rewritten, but the reasons were different. The respondents felt that the history books needed to rewritten (meant translated) in Hindi; another said that it should be made neutral.

Only one student among all those interviewed in total was aware of the committee set up to rewrite history.

In Gulbarga University, on the other hand, several students who had said that they are rightists surprisingly said that there was no need to rewrite the textbooks. As one female student said, 'We can't modify history, We can write about present but not history' (rightist, OBC); similarly, another student said, 'They were based on experience. Now the written work will be based on assumptions so no rewrite' (rightist, male, SC). Very few believed that the leftist academicians had received support or that there had been bias against rightist scholars.

In Calicut University, surprisingly, when the rewriting of textbooks was discussed, there was not much of an opinion or awareness among the students who so far had given very detailed replies on ideology and politics. The few who wanted history books to be rewritten had reasons diverse from what the government was proposing to do. A PhD student said, 'Books must be unbiased. They should not glorify a single person or group.' An MA (Sociology) student said that books must be rewritten to include some groups which have been excluded from the historical narrative. Majority had no opinion about it. Even PhD students had no opinion about it, considering their greater involvement in academics. Majority of the students did not see any ideological leanings in the social science textbooks. JU (Humanities) showed similar trends where most of the students had no opinion on rewriting history. There were few who said that it needs to be neutral and one said that history should glorify foreigners. Among the JU (Science) students, one said, 'The truth of our Indian history needs to be told. Manipulating the history according the ideology of the ruling party in the government should be stopped.' With reference to mythology and science, a number of students spoke up. A few said that it should be ignored and that it was a result of the current ruling party. Only one said that we need to be aware of the achievements of our historical past.

In Bangalore University (Humanities), where most of the respondents said that they were not interested in politics, quite a few students said that history books need to be rewritten. This group of students was most vocal on this issue in comparison to other universities. An apolitical student (male, General) said, 'Some history books and political science books. They talk highly about few freedom fighters. Kings and dynasties that ruled Indian while they speak loudly about few. There is no balanced approach towards the chapters and some books project the author's ideology more than the content.' Another apolitical female student said, 'Most of the CBSE social science books need an overhaul and need to provide a filler and detailed picture of the past without hiding an important facts and instances.' A PhD student (SC) made an important point, 'Many history text books have failed to include the history of southern India.' This point of exclusion of certain regions was raised even in NEHU. Students said that Northeast history needs to be written about more extensively.

In DU, a student made a pertinent point about writing history, 'One doesn't need to obliterate existing work. One can always write new books. If I don't agree with the centrality accorded to the Mughal state by the Aligarh historians. I can read Sanjay Subramanyam, Muzaffar Alam, Farhat Hasan and Chris Bailey. I don't need to stop publishing Irfan Habib.' It was in DU that a large number of students (when compared to other universities) said that there is a need to rewrite books on social sciences. One said that social science books are written from the left-wing ideological perspective and hence should be rewritten; another student felt that some debates need to be revisited.

As Orwell (7) points out,

> The primary aim of propaganda is, of course, to influence contemporary opinion, but those who rewrite history do probably believe with part of their minds that they are actually thrusting facts into the past. Indifference to objective truth is encouraged by the sealing-off of one part of the world from another, which makes it harder and harder to discover what is actually happening. There can often be a genuine doubt about the most enormous events.

It is disheartening to note the lack of information and interest among students on the very vital issue of history being rewritten. The history books written by the (in)famous Dr Batra for school children are full of historical inaccuracies and serve no purpose but to manipulate young minds. Now there is a shift towards slowly sifting out books which speak of different interpretations of say the original inhabitants of India, the role of migration or even the defeat of Hindu kings. Removing A. K. Ramanujan's 'Three Hundred Ramayanas' from the reading list in DU is an example of introducing a linear history. One cannot stress how crucial it is for young students to be aware of such moves by the State. This is where critical thinking encouraged by universities comes into play. A mind which is not trained to think beyond curricula cannot envisage how false histories can destroy a nation. A vibrant thinking campus should consist of students who are aware of the nuances of such attempts by the State and fight for their right to knowledge which is not tempered by political motives to present a distorted history against a particular community or religion.

Any move to dismiss scientific temper and study, in any field, is in complete opposition to the very notion of science. The IITs were set up in the 1950s, AIIMS in 1956 and ISRO in 1962, as the vision of Pandit Nehru was to inculcate ideas of scientific thinking and innovation among the young generation. He wanted the scientists of India to be an essential part of nation building and spearhead innovations and also help in building dams, industries and power plants. In *The Discovery of India*, Nehru writes that science and technology are not merely about application, but they also need to be guided by

> The scientific approach, the adventurous and yet critical temper of science, the search for truth and new knowledge, the refusal to accept anything without testing and trial, the capacity to change previous conclusions in the face of new evidence, the reliance on observed fact and not on preconceived theory, the hard discipline of the mind. (Nehru)

He expressed his concern that the India of those times did not reflect scientific temper, and thar was including among the scientists. He believed that scientific approach was to be a way of life and every aspect of life: thinking, acting and interacting with others.

For Nehru, knowledge was not merely the possession of facts but also the advancement of individuals towards becoming better men and women. He believed that even in institutes such as IITs, humanities and social sciences should be integral parts of the curriculum, but this was not to be so and today the social sciences are totally sidelined in the technical institutes and considered a waste of time by many students. IITs have also been heavily criticized for not developing scientific temper or bring in any change in the structure of the society. Professor Rukmini Bhaya Nair (IIT Delhi) points out, 'A university is meant to be inclusive and universal, whereas an institute stands for specialisation and technical knowledge' (The Wire 2018).

In the introductory chapter, the paradox of homogeneity was mentioned. No country in the world can claim absolute ancestry to a single race or religion. However, today we are moving towards a world where boundaries are closing in, rather than opening up. The USA saw the emergence of the trend of true 'Americans', making America great again and so on. In India, the rewriting of history is an example of one such attempt to create a narrative of a homogenous past which needs to be recreated. We want the world to recognize the great achievements of India, applaud India-born citizens who became leaders in other countries and Indians who run successful businesses in foreign land. We want Indians in Australia, America and Europe to remain loyal to India, but ironically, we do not want the reverse in our own country. Laws are being made to enable foreign universities to set up campuses in India, but our own syllabus and content have become parochial. This is a dangerous trend and will harm the future of the youth as students and as aspiring professionals. One of the chief requirements of the workspaces today is the ability to work with a diverse team of people. An education system which promotes a narrow and false sense of understanding of cultural and historical superiority brings with it the danger of closed minds and opportunities.

Education is not restricted to the classroom. It is not necessary that the students' expectations will be met on campus—maybe the infrastructure will not be good enough or the number of teachers will be inadequate or administration will be too bureaucratic. Similarly, a teacher who opts for the profession may find herself/himself caught in department politics, teaching indifferent students, excessive paperwork and so on. In that sense, education and universities are far away from the ideal that some philosophers envisioned. In campuses, students may encounter gender bias, caste and class discrimination, and all the barriers they face in society outside the walls of the campus. Far from being places where the ideal society is recreated, universities represent all that ails our societies. As a result, a student leaves with a reinforcement of the status-quoist ideas of society, rather than that of change. This is unfortunate.

Political Activism and Students' Union

Historically, the relationship between students and the State has been an uncertain one. It may also seem to be an instrumental relationship, where the students are roped in by the State when mass movement and mobilization is required. There are several events in the past which bear testimony to this fact. Post Independence, students were seen as a key force in nation-building, but over the years, the relationship between State and students has become an uneasy one. There is a discomfort when students take to the streets to protest and speak against the government. The narrative from nation-building has now moved to, as Giroux points out, students as consumers and the future labour force. To this end, control over students is exercised through administrative processes within the campus and, also, by laws that ban student unions on campuses. 'Students political potency is in part a function of self identification and mobilisation, but these dimensions are tied intrinsically to the shape of higher education, regime dynamics, the scope and nature of the rest of the civil society and socioeconomic development' (Weiss and Aspinall 2012, 7). In the light of the larger framework of this book, higher education in a democracy, the role of students' union needs to be discussed not politically but in the social context.

This chapter deals with a topic on which most people have very definite opinions. In light of the several instances of conflict between universities, State, teachers and students, mentioned through the chapters, a strong sentiment against student activism is evident. Unfortunately, there have been other instances, historically, which further give credence to the belief that student activism can only harm the education process. This chapter presents the story from both the teachers' and students' perspective. It seeks to answer crucial questions on how student activism impacts the campus, the relationship with teachers and administration/State. It also puts forth the answer to another question or probably misconception of the student community as a united whole. Are students across the country aware of the universities turning into sites of conflict or lending each other support in political crusades? It has been established that for all their clarity on ideology and leanings, very few students actually take part in political activism. Most remain passive bystanders and only take a stand on issues that affect them directly. Some may briefly help in campaigning to help a friend or join a protest march out of enthusiasm; full-time dedication to campus politics is pursued by very few. It is here that the paradox of student activism will be discussed in the context of the narratives from the field. First, a brief historical overview of students' union and activism and its impact with examples from world over.

The resurgence of student activism in India in 2019 is reminiscent of the decades of 1980s and 1990s, when Asia saw powerful governments bite the dust in face of student-led protests. China, Taiwan, Hongkong, Indonesia, Thailand, Malaysia, Burma and Philippines have been the site of student resistance movement against the State. The protest at Tiananmen Square by students against an oppressive Chinese government in 1998, Reformasi Movement of 1998 in Indonesia, against dictatorship in South Korea in 1980s, and the ouster of President Joseph Estrada in 2001 are examples of how students have led a strong opposition against a dictatorial and repressive regime. Weiss and Aspinall locate the above-mentioned instances of student-led protest movements in '*developmentalism*', which they define as a 'state ideology that entails cooperation between civil and military power holders and technocrats to implement an export driven growth strategy to win popular support for non democratic rule' (Weiss, Aspinall, and Thompson 2012, 2). They further add that in order to understand and study student activism, we need to locate it in the 'higher education policies, structure of civil society and political regimes and transnational connections' (Weiss et al. 2012, 4). Scholars of students' movements and activism, like Altbach, argue that students bring with them idealism and often fill a political vacuum in society.

The current wave of dissent in India against the CAA and National Register of Citizens, which is being led by students to a large extent, is being attributed to a political vacuum created by lack of cohesive opposition. It is important to note a point that Altbach makes when he says that:

> It does seem clear that students have served as the vanguard of political dissent and activism in many countries, and often reflect the unarticulated concerns of larger groups in the population. Thus, when student movements are stimulated by a major societal issue, the potential for major activism which has the support of at least a segment of the non-university population is considerable.

However, current research indicates that there has been a decline in the involvement of the youth/young people in politics, 'this is reflected in voting patterns, other forms of institutional politics (trade union, political party), disengagement from formal politics (ignored by politicians) and have low levels of political trust' (Brooks 2017, 2). She refers to a study carried out by Pilkington and Pollock (2015) in 14 countries in which they point out that 'the paradox to be understood, it would appear is that these young people are not so much anti-politics but profoundly disillusioned with the current democratic system, while continuing in principle, supportive of democratic forms of government and seeking to be heard through it' (Pilkington and Pollock 2015, 88 quoted in Rachael Brooks). Kimberlee (2002, 92) speaks of four perspectives that can be used to interpret the changes in political behaviour among young people. One perspective is that of individual trait and behaviour, like apathy or social background. Second, young people are put off by current politics and the political system (as pointed out by Pilkington and Pollock). Third, the alternative provided by new social movements that are oriented towards culture rather than power tend to attract more young people. Fourth perspective is that of generational change; young people do not participate in formal politics due to certain developments that have taken place.

Most of the research on student activism is focused on student movements or even short-term protests rather than the students' union, and this is in spite of students' union having played an important role in campuses and influenced student lives. Brooks (2017, 8) uses the work done by Crossley and Ibrahim (2016) and Hensby (2014) on students' union to illustrate the importance of the students' union. For Crossley and Ibrahim, the students' union helps in network formation in the campus and also links the students with political parties and resource mobilization. It also gives the students the space and resource to support their campaigning activities. For Hensby, one of the several roles played by the students' union is to socialize students into political activity and help them get engaged in politics. Leadership provided and created by unions has been much discussed, and in this, it has been pointed out that certain social networks attract new leadership, while in some cases, it may act as a deterrent (Brooks et al. 2015).

Linkages have also been drawn between the influence of students' union and the political climate, demonstrated by the impact that students' union have had in different countries. Klemencic (2014) gives the example of students' union protests against fee hike in countries like Chile, the UK and Canada. The union was successful in preventing a hike in tuition fees through its protests in Chile and Canada, where it had support of the general public. In contrast, in the UK that was inclined towards neoliberal economic policies, the government was assured that the public was more in favour of students sharing the cost of education and, hence, could disregard the protest by the students' union. Education reforms in both the UK and the USA based on neoliberal principles resulted in the higher education student being treated more as a consumer and have also impacted the role of the students' union which is now more of a representative body rather than a politically active body and also has promoted individualism in the student community. In contrast, Africa has seen an increase in student representation, and student leaders have established linkages with national political parties. Students are part of decision-making bodies both at institutional and national level (Brooks 2017, 8). In Russia, the students' union has traditionally been successors of labour unions, and because of this, they tend to fight for causes like financial aid and other social benefits for students.

Williams (2013, 106) writes, 'What it means to be a student at any given point of time, is a social construction, it alters with the prevailing social and political condition with society at that time' (quoted by Brooks 2017, 5). Political behaviour and attitudes among students and the role of students' union are determined by the fact that, 'the wider context influences both the opportunities that are available to students to contribute politically and the substantive political attitudes they take up' (Brooks 2017, 9). But as Weiss and Aspinall (2012) have pointed out, student mobilization is not 'automatic'. Students have to first come together and form a collective identity that is beyond the classroom. Second, students should be deeply connected with the issue in a way that it prompts them to take action (Snow 2001; Mansbridge and Morris 2001). It is well known that majority of students are not involved in protests on campus. Students' unions do not have a set pattern of functioning—while in some countries/regions, they have valued autonomy, in others, they have joined hands with other social movements and political parties.

'Students represent a form of strategic group a loosely structured category formed around shared material or ideal interests' (Weiss and Aspinall 2012, 10). Pinnar (1972) clubs the students in the elite category like military leaders and the clergy. He calls them the marginal elite as they are supported by the larger community but yet are not part of it, as are the clergy and military. In countries that that are pro-development, students are a part of nation-building and economic growth. For Altbach (1979), who focused on student politics in Asia, the geographical location of universities played an important role in determining politics on campus. He writes that in developing countries, most of the universities are located in major cities dominated by politics, which then seeps into politics on campus. Student leaders see a role beyond the campus for themselves and speak up for the population outside the narrow confines of the campus and also far removed from cities.

Weiss and Aspinall (2012, 13–15) point out that the expansion of higher education in South East and Northeast Asian countries has had a tremendous impact on student politics and composition of students' union. By the 21st century, education widened its reach in most Asian countries. Higher education was both a cause and consequence of development; education was seen as necessary for a developing nation for nation-building and, at the same time, economic changes led to expansion of higher education. The middle class, too, were now economically well off, and their children were part of the university system. This also meant the mushrooming of private universities in 1990s amidst demand from the lower middle-class families, who wanted to educate their children so that the next generation could move up the social ladder.

Many of the students who joined universities were first-generation learners from rural and poor backgrounds. They moved into unfamiliar surroundings and, as students, developed awareness about the larger social and economic problems. Immediately after the Cold War, most of the students were part of the elite, and hence, they were not attacked if they participated in protests. Once the composition of students changed in university to include those from the middle- and lower-middle class, it impacted the nature of student activism and, also, the reaction of regimes to student protests. Meanwhile, another change that had crept in was the setting up of universities in smaller towns, which further broadened the socio-economic strata of the students in the education system. Contrary to expectations of more students now participating in activism, the larger number of students meant 'status and potential of students as a strategic political group often declines as their numbers increase with higher education seen as more and more routine and expected stage in an ordinary member of society's life' (Weiss and Aspinall 2012, 17). Higher education was no longer the privilege of a few, and students did not think beyond their limited role. Students were further divided in their political attitude depending on whether they were enrolled in private or public universities. Private universities are expensive, forcing many students to take loans. Once students take loans, they are wary of participating in politics—especially in protests against the government, as it may jeopardize their future. At the most, they may fight for campus-related facilities.

According to Lipset (1967), students tend to be more active politically in poorer countries and in the absence of strong political institutions. Other scholars have also pointed out that students' movements and protests often move in to fill the vacuum created due to lack of a credible opposition, collaboration of the industry, religious elites with the ruling dispensation and repression of the labour class. In kind, political regime also plays an important role in determining increase or decrease in student activism. Democratic societies with multiple political parties are less likely to have student protests than in an authoritarian regime. According to Habermas (translated by Shapiro 1987), students played revolutionary roles in Russia, China, Cuba, Africa, Latin America and South East Asia. Similar to the idea of repressive regimes, he writes that societies where the army was in a strong political position, students were a constant political presence. Habermas further elucidates that the three conditions have to be met for politicization of student consciousness. One, students see for themselves a role in national building and as the future citizens. Second, the university itself is an arena of social change (discussed in greater detail in Introduction), and it provides a platform to the students to fight against traditional social structures. Third, the process of socialization of a student's personal life—family and kinship based on traditional structures and in contrast socialization in university—revolved around social change. Taking a strong position on politics in campus, Habermas said,

> We must not be satisfied with depoliticisation of the university. Current politics must be able to become part of the internal university community. It is an ideally suited place for the discussion of political issues, if and to the extent that his discussion is fundamentally governed by the same rules and rationality within which scientific reflection takes place. (Habermas 1987)

He adds, students should be active and fight for their rights within and outside the campus and, also, be a part of discussion on policies regarding education and the university, as it directly concerns them. Not only students but the faculty too should assert themselves.

India has seen student mobilization since the freedom struggle and later during the Emergency, which was a national issue, and later on the issue of caste in higher education (Mandal Commission). Today, we are witnessing probably one of the largest organized protests which has now spread across the globe. Students (along with members of the civil society) have taken the government head on, and the police atrocities at a university (Jamia Milia Islamia, JNU) triggered off a chain of reactions across the globe. Teachers and students from Oxford, Yale, MIT, Harvard, Heidelberg, Columbia, Stanford and many more have written open letters, organized meetings and marches against State atrocities on students. For the first time in many years, students from even non-political campuses like IIT have joined in the protest.

BRIEF OVERVIEW OF HISTORY OF STUDENTS' MOVEMENTS IN ASIA

Students have played an important role in both supporting and opposing governments across the world. The students' movement in India can be traced back to an initiative by Dadabhai Naoroji in 1848, 'The Student's Scientific and Historic Society', as a forum for discussion. In the initial years, the student movement that emerged in India consisted of a variety of political discussion groups in the colleges, and thus, students were not really an integral part of the national movement.

> The political ideology of the early discussion circles such as the Bombay Students' Brotherhood and similar groups, and later the All-India Students' Federation was well articulated and coherent. It certainly influenced many key intellectuals. But whether it significantly changed the nationalist movement is still open to speculation. The links between political and cultural movements in the developing countries were often close, and the impact of Western intellectual influences, primarily through the universities, was important in the cultural spheres too. In India, for example, early attempts to combine aspects of traditional Indian culture with the values of the West spurred nationalist thinking. The Brahmo Samaj in Calcutta, for example, was an intellectual base for many individuals who later played active roles in political movements, and included many students among its rank. (Altbach 1970, 75–76)

As a part of these discussions, students questioned the education system set up by the British. Ironically, the ideas of nationalism, liberty and equality were brought in by the Western system of education and taught by European teachers. It was at King Edward Medical College, Lahore, the first student strike took place at, regarding academic discrimination between the English people and Indians. The strike was successful, and soon more and more students got involved in the freedom struggle, and at the second all India College students Conference held at Ahmadabad in 1912, the students declared 'Charka Swaraj first, and education after'. Students boycott colleges and actively involved themselves in the freedom struggle.

> The emergence of the Congress as a mass movement under Gandhi's leadership in 1920 coincided with the growth of a major student movement which provided significant assistance to the adult nationalist movement. Students were key elements in the terrorist campaigns in Bengal and Maharashtra as early as 1905. After 1920, leftist Congress leaders, men such as Nehru and Subhas Chandra Bose, counted on student support in their efforts to push the Congress toward a more radical political and tactical viewpoint. Radical nationalists emerged from the student movement to become important in the Congress. (Altbach 1970, 76–77)

According the Altbach, while the students may have played an important role during the national movement, it would have still succeeded even without them.

At the 'All India College Students Conference' held at Nagpur in 1920, during the Non-Cooperation Movement, a resolution was passed that students would boycott schools and colleges, and this became an integral part of the non-cooperation movement. This was the beginning of students organizing and leading processions, strikes and even courted arrest. The students became an important link between the underground leaders and the movement. 'The student movement also provided a training ground for various leftist groups. The emergent Indian Communist Party, for example, placed great stress in the 1920s and 30s on education and recruitment among students, and many Communist leaders emerged from the movement' (Altbach 1970, 76). In India, students were part of the national movement; by 1930s, a parallel movement emerged for an independent Muslim-based state that was supported by Muslim student groups. The person leading this movement was Muhammad Ali Jinnah, and it was under his aegis that the All India Muslim Students Federation was formed as an opposition to the Congress-oriented student organizations. As with other movements in Asia, this too consisted of Western-educated Muslims and gradually built up a sentiment for a separate state for Muslims, eventually leading to the creation of a separate State of Pakistan in 1947.

Post Independence saw the emergence of several student led political organizations. Many of these were off shoots of main stream and regional political parties. The National Students' Union of India (NSUI) is the student wing of the Congress party. Several left-leaning student organizations came into existence, among other such student political organizations like Young Socialist League in 1948, formed as a result of the socialist group breaking away from the Congress. The All India Youth Federation and the youth wing of the Communist Party of India was founded in 1959 and consisted of progressive and democratic young students. One of the most prominent students' union of today's times is the Students' Federation of India (SFI), which was founded as the student wing of the CPI (M) in 1970 'to organize the students to fight a democratic and progressive education system and for the uplift and betterment of the lot of the student community.'

Over the years, as student activism was seen as vitiating the atmosphere on the campuses, especially at the regional level, the declining quality of education and students was blamed on university politics. Amid all this, the Progressive Student Organization was born in 1983, and it concentrated solely on campus-related issues. Much later in 1990, the AISA was formed as a student wing of the CPI (M–L). Both AISA and SFI represent the left-wing ideology and are popular among students, though AISA is seen as more radical than SFI. Last but not least, the ABVP student wing of Rashtriya Swayamsevak Sangh (now known as the student wing of the Bharatiya Janata Party) was formed in 1949 by leading educationists, students and teachers in Delhi. The major aim of this movement is to mobilize student power towards the task of national reconstruction.

There was a change in attitude of the State towards student movements post Independence. It was no longer keen on students being politically active. As a result, student movements became splintered and concentrated on university issues and, sometimes, local-area issues and moved away from larger national or even international questions. (Incidentally, this is the role of a students' union that many students and teachers, too, envisage, as was evident in the interviews held. They want a students' union that will ensure that the demands of the students for better facility, infrastructure, fees, etc., are met). The students become a source of opposition rather than support, and this was seen not only in India but also in several Asian countries like Japan (Zengakuren) and Indonesia. In Japan, the student-led demonstrations against the US–Japan Security Treaty in 1960 led to a political crisis, and the Kishi government was forced to resign under student pressure. Japanese student groups have also been active in rallying against university policies, and Altbach mentions how militant students occupied Tokyo University, leading to its closure for six months and police entered the Tokyo campus to take charge of the situation.

The Indonesian student movement is probably one of the best examples of how a student movement can change the course of history of a nation. The students of Indonesia gave voice and direction to the protest against the Dutch rule, by aligning with movements outside Indonesia, writing extensively on it and also forming organizations. The students are credited with initiating the move to develop an Indonesian language from Malay student initiative and helped to develop an Indonesian language from Malay. As in other Asian countries, early radical and nationalist movements were heavily influenced by students. China provides one of the early examples of students leading movements against monarchy. In 1880, the Chinese imperial government tried to contain the number of students who were going overseas and also kept an eye on them. But in spite of all their efforts, Chinese students turned out to be formidable and became a militant group by the late-19th century. As in India, exposure to Western values was one of the core reasons for the 'awakening' of the spirit of protest among Chinese students. While in India, it was a result of the education system put in place by the colonial rule, in China, it was because the students moved out of China to study. Whatever may have been the reason, the result was a more politically active and aware student community. Chinese students wanted a shift away from a traditional society, freedom for women. The monarchy did attempt to assuage the feelings of the students by establishing more colleges and funding education of those who wanted to study overseas, but it was not enough. The movement against monarchy intensified from all quarters, and it was soon replaced by a Republican government in 1911. But discontent continued to brew, and by 1919, students had organized themselves against the Republican government. It allied with the communists and helped them establish control in 1946–1947. Students in several Asian countries, who studied abroad, became a part of freedom movements in their respective countries. Singapore, Burma and Vietnam were some of these countries.

Burma and Vietnam provide examples of strong student movements. The elite of Burmese society were part of the student movement—Rangoon University Students' Union—fighting for the freedom of Burma. As seen in the Chinese experience, Burmese students went abroad and brought in with them the understanding of a new ideology which further contributed to the freedom struggle in the 1920s. In Vietnam, the students rallied under the leadership of Ho Chi Minh and built up the nationalist movement which overthrew the French rule successfully. Ho Chi Minh was a student activist himself and was part of student politics in France, China and Vietnam. The Vietnamese freedom movement was based in both the communist ideology and a feeling of nationalism.

In India, the Emergency in 1974 provided a rallying point for students. After Independence, it was probably the first time that students found themselves organized for a national cause. In fact, several news reports and articles from the Emergency era have resurfaced in the light of the recent violence by the state in JNU and Jamia Milia Islamia. In West Bengal, the Naxalite movement attracted lot of students. In it, they saw a certain idealism fighting against the landlords for the rights of farmers, tribals and labourers. Refer to the conversations with the students in the universities where some of them mentioned that the left stands for equality, for the poor, or that it fights for a better society—it were these sentiments that drew students to the Naxalite movement. The movement then spread to Bihar, Odisha and Andhra Pradesh. Similarly, students found a cause in the Chipko movement in 1973 and protested against the decision to auction trees to a private firm. Students along with activists marched for 44 days and went from village to village talking to people about the movement.

Navnirman Andolan (Reconstruction Movement) of 1974 was led and organized by students in Gujarat against corruption; it consisted of not only students but also the middle class who were tired of corruption and in 1973–1974 saw clashes between the State and students on the issue of 20 per cent fee hike in hostel fees. On the 3 January 1974, another strike by students led to violence between students and police in Gujarat University. The protestors organized another strike on 25 January, demanding the resignation of Chief Minister of Gujarat, Chimanbhai Patel. This strike again led to a fresh round of clashes between the police and protesters. The army was called in and curfew imposed in many cities and towns across Gujarat. Finally, the Central government gave in to the pressure and asked Chimanbhai Patel to resign.

Several other regional and even caste-based student organizations and movements came up to represent the socially and economically backward communities. Ambedkar founded 'All India Scheduled Castes Federation' to fight caste and to provide protection to SCs. Republican Student Federation, later known as Vidarbha Republican Student Federation (VRSF) was formed in 1967 to follow the ideals of Buddha and Ambedkar. VRSF has been actively involved in college and university union elections as well as organizing rallies and dharnas against social discriminations. In later years, the Mandal Commission agitation became a turning point in student politics and activism with regard to caste. Students were divided on the merit versus reservation criteria. One was either for or against, there was no middle ground. Things came to a head with the self-immolation of Rajiv Goswami. Students in Rajasthan, Bihar and Delhi protested against the recommendations of the Mandal Commission and planned agitations and boycotted classes. The debate on economic grounds for reservation and merit became intense and is a point of discussion even today, as was evident in the interviews with the teachers.

The question that comes up next is then what happens to the movements once they achieve their objective—do they continue to keep fighting for their rights or change their objectives? What is the nature of their relationship with the new government, which they have been instrumental in bringing to power in the first place? Altbach explored all these questions and said that the student movements became opposition groups based in universities, much to the discomfort of the leaders.

> Loyal allies in the struggle for independence and radical social change became 'indisciplined' elements or anti-social forces. Student movements also altered their own self-image and orientation. Sectarian politics—the politics of opposition—became a key element in many student movements and criticism began to be voiced against nationalist ruling groups. These shifts have meant that student organizations in almost every Asian country have become opposition groups, both within the universities and in the broader society.' (Altbach 1970, 80).

He further wrote, the main source of dissent was the slow decline of idealism that is perceived by the students in the very leaders they helped in coming to power. The dynamics of fighting a colonial or foreign power is very different from that of opposing one's own; it becomes more of an ideological fight. When leaders are seen making 'pragmatic' choices, students view it as a betrayal to the cause, and the leaders they saw as infallible are now seen as men with feet of clay.

> Seeing injustice remaining in their society, students demand radical social change in addition to national independence, and are impatient at the pace of change instituted by ruling elites. All of this creates political conflicts between the more 'pure' ideological students and pragmatic nationalist adults who have to deal with the day to day problems of government. (Altbach 1970, 80).

This also meant a shift from national issues to the problems in the education system and the campus. As is evident from the interviews with the students, there is a demand and expectation of representation by the students' union to the administration for better facilities like food, library, infrastructure, etc. Among the larger issues facing the education system, the union is also expected to fight for reservation or against fee hike and so on. The students are also faced with other problems which surfaced in higher education: rising cost of education, growth of private institutes and lack of quality in government universities, decline of regional universities, student–teacher ratio was of deep concern to the students and also the teachers. Students wanted that the universities continue to be critical of the government and, also, not be controlled by the government, which naturally led to a conflict between the State and universities. Instances arose of students sometimes taking up larger causes originating outside the campus. The Emergency has already been spoken of. Prior to that, students agitated against the imposition of Hindi in the southern states, leading to the defeat of the Congress in several state elections in the 1967 general elections.

The composition of the student community in India has undergone a change. Post Independence, concerted efforts were made to make education accessible and affordable. This led to more and more students from lower and lower middle-class families and often rural areas to join universities. As mentioned earlier, most of the student leaders belonged to the elite groups as they could afford education—abroad or in the country. Many of these students are the first-generation learners in their family and bring with them their life experiences, which they then weave into their political lives. In the wake of the fee hike protests, several alumni and present students have written articles on the need for affordable education so that the children of a manual scavenger or a vegetable seller are not denied education. For those who feel students should be able to pay ₹500 or say even ₹1,000, they just need to get this. If a family is earning say ₹4,000 a month, can it afford to spend ₹500 or ₹1,000 on one child each month? When students, who have seen a life where their families are struggling for a proper meal, enter into education or politics, they are influenced by their social realities. Their ideology and political vision are shaped by lived-in experiences of poverty and deprivation. This, in turn, may influence the agenda of political activism on campuses.

Several student protests have taken place over both regional- and university-based issues. Some examples of student activism from across the country ensue. In Tamil Nadu, students led by the Students Federation for Freedom of Tamil Eelam, in 2013, demanded that the Government of India vote in support of the UN resolution for an independent international investigation against alleged war crimes in Sri Lanka. The police arrested students of Loyola College in Chennai who were fasting and protesting against the war crimes committed by Sri Lankan army against the Tamils. Jadavpur University in Kolkata (West Bengal) has been at the centre of several student protests. One such protest was in 2015, when the VC of the university refused to take action in a molestation case on campus. The students ensured that he resigned from his post, organizing and getting together a large number of students in protest. So much so that 100 students refused to take their degrees during the convocation in solidarity with the cause. The arrest was followed by large-scale protest at the Raj Bhavan, in which over 500 students were arrested. More recently, Rohit Vemula's suicide, a student at Hyderabad Central University (HCU), sparked outrage in the student community all across the country.

The FTII protest against the appointment of the new Chairman Gajendra Chauhan grabbed headlines in 2015. Traditionally, the post of chairman of FTII is reserved for eminent personalities regarded and respected for both their skill and body of work. However, Chauhan had the dubious reputation of starring in films of extremely poor quality (classified as C-grade films), no great body of work to speak of and, in addition, was seen as a right-wing hardliner. The students refused to accept him as the chairman, and the agitation continued for over 150 days. Several alumni of FTII returned their awards as a mark of protest. But the government refused to budge and did not reverse its decision. Among larger education-related issues taken up by students, sometimes led by students' union, the students of JNU, on Wednesday, staged a protest outside the Union Ministry of Human Resource Development against the seat cuts that have taken place due to UGC's 2016 Gazette Notification.

References have been made to instances of protests that have resulted in the exercise of State authority; here are a few more examples which show the range of issues on which student protests have taken place. In the first instance, UGC found itself at the centre of another controversy on 7 October 2015, on its decision to scrap the non-National Eligibility Test (NET) scholarship, a scholarship given to students who haven't cleared the NET examination. This would impact several students who, otherwise, could not afford to continue their research. This was seen as a larger private versus public university debate, as the students saw in this an attempt to open up the education sector to private investment with the signing of the World Trade Organization's General Agreement on Trade in Services by the Central government in December 2015. The government responded with lathi charge and surprise police raids on the protestors.

The second instance provides a fine example of how students can safeguard not only democratic traditions of freedom of speech but can also critically engage in matters of national interest. Students at the University of Hyderabad (UoH) organized protests and public discussions on the government's move in Kashmir of splitting the state into two Union Territories and also revoking Article 370, which granted special status to Jammu and Kashmir. But the university refused to grant permission to hold any such event on Kashmir and even went a step forward to deploy the police and the Rapid Action Force to prevent protests. The students and teachers saw this as a deliberate attempt to stifle democratic voices. Several student organizations—SFI, Ambedkar Students' Association, Muslim Students' Federation, Dalit Students' Union, AISA, Students Islamic Organisation and the Jammu and Kashmir Students Association—got together and planned to protest against the bifurcation of Jammu and Kashmir and the abrogation of Kashmir's special status under Article 370. But the registrar of the university informed about police presence on campus and also that Section 144 of the Code of Criminal Procedure, which prohibits an assembly of five or more people, has been enforced on campus. Students were prevented from getting together and discussing the Kashmir issue by the police.

Not to be beaten so easily, the Social Science Forum, a student group from the social science department, and Abhiyan, a cultural organization, organized a panel discussion on the abrogation of Article 370 in Kashmir with the support of faculty members. But they were informed that the permission to hold the event had been withdrawn and the police and Rapid Action Force have also stepped in to stop the organizers from holding the event. Defiant staff and students held the discussion in the presence of the police outside the auditorium. The administration, on the other hand, accused the students of misrepresenting the topic while asking for permission. Apparently, the students had sought permission for holding a talk on 'Democracy and Dissent' and not on Kashmir.

Since then, police presence during events has become a permanent fixture. So much so that the university issued a circular in July 2016 banning public talks and protests in common areas. Not only Kashmir but students have also been prevented from holding film screenings—Anand Patwardhan's 1992 award-winning documentary *Ram Ke Naam* or *In the Name of God*. The documentary, which chronicles Vishva Hindu Parishad's role in the demolition of Babri Masjid in Ayodhya and the movement to build a Ram temple in its place, was not allowed to be screened. The students decided to play the movie on their laptops, which were then confiscated by the police. According to the administration, students were denied permission to screen that particular movie, but they insisted on doing so, which resulted in action by the police. But as an associate professor rightly questioned—why is there constant police presence on campus, especially during events? As per the university press statement,

> It is only under extreme provocation and apprehension of disturbance to peace on campus that the administration has had to resort to calling the police. We would like to emphasize that calling the police for resolving issues within the campus is not normal University policy. (The Caravan, 24th August 2019)

According to G. Haragopal, a human rights activist and the former dean of social science at the UoH (as told to The Caravan Magazine, August 2019),

> Campuses in India are becoming increasingly authoritarian, which is a negation of every democratic structure. The authoritarian culture of the university is the result of a deep economic crisis and also a cultural crisis. But it is also a result of the increasing democratic consciousness of the people. The students' community is becoming more conscious of its dignity, its freedom. I think the dismantling of institutions is part of the model of development and also incapability of governance. But students at the same time are increasingly asserting and this assertion will release democratic forces.

This brings one to the larger question of the relationship between State and students' union. Some historical references from various parts of the world—China, Indonesia and Vietnam—have been made at the beginning of the chapter to illustrate how students' movements/students' union and the State may align or oppose each other. In India, students played an important role during the freedom movement, but post Independence, the relationship underwent a change.

RELATIONSHIP BETWEEN STATE AND STUDENTS' UNION IN INDIA

It is evident that students all over the world have expressed interest in political activity and have been involved in protests, sometimes, through the students' union or as a student community. But the tussle for control over education itself is a political fight. This was reflected in the fight between the Centre and State government on the inclusion of education in the Union List. State policies, administrative control and appointments are all politically motivated. The problem is not only keeping student politics out of campus but also ensuring that the policies and appointments are made for the benefit of students and with a larger vision of higher education. But excessive political interference in the campus has proven to be the downfall for many universities in India.

Professor Nayyar, former VC of DU, writes,

> Starting in the late 1960s, state governments began to interfere in universities. For one, it was about dispensing patronage and exercising power in appointments of vice-chancellors (VCs), faculty and non-teaching staff. For another, it was about extending the political influence of ruling parties. Unions of students, teachers and employees became instruments in political battles. Campuses were turned into spheres of influence for political parties. Provincial politics also played a role, with an implicit rejection of national elites and an explicit focus on regional identities. Just as important, political parties and leaders were uncomfortable with, if not insecure about, independent voices and critical evaluation that could come from universities. (Nayyar 2017)

Batabyal (2014), too, echoes similar thoughts speaking of regional universities of Rajasthan, BHU and Lucknow, which saw a rapid downfall once the State and Central governments started interfering in the functioning of the universities.

Violence on campus, usually accompanied and facilitated by the presence of political parties especially during the student elections, often results in the State taking action. The State also tries to control student activities by banning students' union on campus. One such example is that of Karnataka, where students' union have been banned since 1989–1990 based on court order which cited that campus politics was primarily responsible for the caste-based violence seen in the campuses during those years. There were allegations that the student elections were serving as an extension of the electoral politics. From 2001 to 2016, there have been no student representatives in Bangalore University's academic council. Student councils have, time and again, been demanding for elections, and Bangalore University's student council have often shown their interest in student politics going on in different universities in India. A few student councils from different colleges in Bengaluru have held demonstrations outside the city's town hall in support of the march that JNU students took out for the release of Anirban Bhattacharya. In the month of September 2019, there were media reports that said that plans to bring back elections in the campus were being considered. However, no such official note has been out. As pointed out by the head of student council of St. Joseph's College, unlike an elected students' union, students' council cannot take up serious issues, and a union also helps to develop national leaders and take up grassroots issues.

In Haryana too, student elections were banned in 1996. The ban was imposed by the government due to the unruly behaviour of some student political parties. In February 2018, it was announced that student union election will be held in September/October 2018 itself. The decision was taken after an ABVP delegation met the chief minister. In the year 1997, BHU Students' Union too was dissolved after the death of two students. When it was restored in 2007, indirect elections were conducted for student council, but the clash between the students and police prevented the elections from taking place in 2015–2016. The elections in BHU are still indirect.

In 1984, Punjab banned the student's election due to militancy. Indirect election was held in Punjab University in 1993, after a student leader went on a hunger strike, and it was in 1996 that full-fledged election took place. However, campuses still remained the hotbed of militancy. There were demands to lift the ban, but the assassination of Beant Singh made things worse. After 34 years, in 2018, elections were held. In Maharashtra, student elections were banned in 1993, in the light of murder of a student. This was revoked in July 2019. The erstwhile Andhra Pradesh government, in 1988, after violent murders, banned student elections. In Telangana and Andhra Pradesh, the universities do have different student bodies but not one single elected one. An administrative head in OU said that the elected student union will help, as then there will be only one body rather than multiple bodies.

THE LYNGDOH COMMITTEE

Violence was one of the main reasons for the ban on students' union and student elections in the universities. The Lyngdoh Committee was set up to deal with this and draw out a map for holding elections on campus without compromising on the sanctity of the university as a place of learning. The *Lyngdoh Committee Report* (2006) laid down guidelines for the conduct of student elections on campus. The committee was set up following the intervention of the High Court in the matter of student elections in Kerala.[1] Regional meetings were held in Chennai, Kolkata, Lucknow, Mumbai and Delhi, and it threw up the

---

[1] Pursuant to the order of the Honourable Supreme Court, dated 12 December 2005, the Committee was mandated to examine, inter alia, the following broad aspects of students' elections:

(a) Criminalization in student elections; (b) Financial transparency and limits of expenditure in the conduct of such elections (such as ceilings on election-related expenditure, indication of the details and sources of such expenditure, the filing of returns by students' unions in respect of their transactions and the scrutiny of such returns); (c) Eligibility criteria for candidates seeking to contest such elections (such as maximum age limits for candidates and minimum standards of educational performance attained by candidates); and (d) The institution of a forum to address grievances and disputes arising out of students' elections as regards procedural fairness, eligibility of candidates and/or the non-observance of norms during the conduct of student elections.

different challenges being faced by the universities in each state. In the meetings in Chennai, representatives from universities, human rights organizations and engineering institutes came forward to give their feedback to the committee. One of the main concerns was the increasing number of private higher education institutes and the withdrawal of the State from education. Many of the higher education institutes owned by politicians were used to further political agenda and particular ideologies. As a result,

> Involvement of political parties in the students' elections in the universities and colleges, unwanted and illegal practices like criminalization of students' election, unwarranted monetary transactions, sexual harassment/ exploitation, and unfair means of conduct of election, have crept into the election process, as well as into the day-to-day academic atmosphere of the universities and colleges. (Ministry of Human Resource Development [MHRD] 2006, 13)[2]

Regional meetings held across the country revealed the state-wise situation.

During the deliberations of the Lyngdoh Committee meetings, West Bengal put forward a different problem. It was observed that in most of the colleges and universities in this region, the principals of the colleges were the ex-officio presidents of the respective unions, and consequently, it was observed that political parties in power in the State use political affiliation of the college principals to manipulate indirect elections, so as to perpetuate their hold on college unions. 'In some colleges, even outgoing unions, with the collusion of the principals, have nominated their own successors in the students' unions, while formally showing these nominations as indirect elections. It was also

---

In addition, the committee was empowered to examine and consider all aspects relating to the conduct of students' elections, such as aspects affecting the academic atmosphere in educational institutions including, but not limited to, indiscipline and divisions on the basis of political beliefs and such other avoidable considerations. The committee was also empowered to focus on the need to ensure that elements undesirable to the academic atmosphere in universities do not enter students' unions.

[2] *Report of the Committee Constituted by Ministry of Human Resource Development, Government of India, as per the Direction of the Hon'ble Supreme Court of India to Frame Guidelines on Students' Election in Colleges/Universities.*

common for students with affiliation to students' groups, other than the one in power, to be threatened with violence and be coerced into not filing nominations or into withdrawing them.' (MHRD 2006, 14)

In the Delhi meeting of the Lyngdoh committee, not surprisingly, the main cause of concern was the enormous sums of money being spent in student elections and, also, the participation of political parties in campus elections. Some universities such as Indraprastha University did not want to hold student elections, the argument being that universities offering professional courses did not leave students with the time to participate in student elections. The unanimous demands of all the regions were: ceiling on expenditure, prevent political parties from controlling or interfering in campus politics, no attendance and exam arrears, a time limit within which elections are to be held and an age limit of candidates. Maharashtra had problems similar to that of Chennai; politicians owned educational institutions. In fact, student elections were banned in Maharashtra due to the lobbying of these educational institutions 'secured the enactment of the Maharashtra Universities Act 1994 (ostensibly on the murder of a student in 1989 and quoting unspecified violence thereafter), which prohibits students' elections throughout the state and has student representation entirely on merit-based nomination' (MHRD 2006, 17–18).

The worst situation was probably in Uttar Pradesh, as revealed in the Lucknow meeting. The feedback given by representatives revealed the appalling state of affairs. The student leaders owed allegiance to national and regional party leaders and not to the university; extortion of money from businessmen, violence during student elections, brandishing of guns and open display of power were but few of the problems.

> After elections, elected leaders extorted contracts from the university, particularly the works department, forced entry into all important university decisions and exacted protection money from government contractors. They also sported the latest cars, had their own gunmen and strode the university overawing and coercing college principals and university vice-chancellors to do their bidding. They did not stop at university authorities, but extorted money and goods from local merchants, ostensibly to 'fund student activities'. (MHRD 2006, 19)

Not only students and political leaders, even the teachers were complicit in these matters.

Based on these data from universities, the *Lyngdoh Committee Report* sent in elaborate guidelines on each point raised—from expenditure to campaigning modes to age of candidates and so on. However, the recommendations of the Committee invited a lot of controversy. It was felt that the guidelines were not practical and unrealistic. For example, one of the suggestions was that only handmade posters and a limited number would be allowed; no printed posters or pamphlets were allowed. In DU, which consists of around 51 colleges, candidates said that it was impossible to spread their message only through handmade posters. Each candidate was allowed to spend only ₹5,000. One of the most controversial clauses was that there should be no record of disciplinary action against the students. What was meant by disciplinary action was not explained, and this created a lot of problem. For example, in JNU, disciplinary action was taken against a student for taking part in a protest; as a result, she was barred from contesting in elections. A lack of a common definition and criteria of disciplinary action left it open to arbitrary interpretation by each university/college. Added to this was the rigid rule that a person could not contest for the post of an office-bearer more than once. This clause was included to prevent the same candidates from controlling certain posts. But the other side of the coin was that every year new candidates had to be fielded, and as a consequence, there was no accountability of those who won the elections, since they would not contest again. Furthermore, the age limit was set as maximum 22 years for graduation, 25 years for master's and 28 years for MPhil/PhD. This did not take into account those who enter the education system late or after a break or even after working for a few years. In September 2006, the UGC passed an order that all universities have to follow the recommendations of the *Lyngdoh Committee Report*.[3] Elections were not held in JNU between 2008–2012, as the students did not agree with the recommendations. After much negotiation, there was a relaxation of

---

[3] Read the entire notification and details of the Committee report here: https://www.ugc.ac.in/oldpdf/students_pdf/lyngdoh_committeemhrd2712.pdf

some of the suggestions, following which elections were held.[4] But every year, complaints are filed against student unions for not following the rules and regulations set by the committee.

This does project a very pessimistic picture of students' union and activism in India. But there is more it. What do students themselves think of activism on campus, considering that they are the most impacted by it? Second, how do teachers react to politically active students on campus? The following section brings forth the conversations held with both students and teachers from the field.

DO STUDENTS SUPPORT POLITICAL ACTIVISM AND ACTIVITIES ON CAMPUS?

Altbach, one of the leading scholars on student activism, writes, 'Students have been a major force in the national development of many important Asian nations, and are still a source of political power in their societies' (1970, 84). In his analysis of the student movements and protests across the globe, Altbach writes that the 1960s saw the students speaking up against the Vietnam War and the 1970s saw a decline of student activism in the West. Asia, on the other hand, witnessed resurgence of student activism as a response to the dictatorial governments in power in the region. According to him, 'without stress on family or caste, the university provided, at least, a partial model of what a modern society could be like' (Altbach 1970, 75).

According to him,

> Students are also freer of societal constraints than other groups in the population, and are therefore better able to act decisively on political issues. They are usually not working for a living, they have no family responsibilities, and they often live away from home in a peer group subculture. While the concept of 'generational revolt' has been overworked in analyzing modern

---

[4] The JNU letter on students' elections speaks of relaxation of age limit to 30 years of age for research scholars, for JNU, use of hand-made posters and photostat copies not exceeding 5,000 copies, for elections, and since JNU does not follow the attendance system, the 75 per cent attendance rule for candidates does not apply. https://jnu.ac.in/sites/default/files/circular_notices/Guidelines%20for%20JNUSU%20Elections%202019-20.pdf

student unrest, it no doubt plays a role, particularly in societies in which the values of the older and often highly traditional generation may conflict dramatically with newly acquired modern ideas of young people. University students are often easy to mobilize, since they are located on a campus, or are at least easily reached through the press. (Altbach 1970, 74)

While most of what Altbach says is relevant today in terms of students being easier to mobilize and often leading from the front on issues facing not only the campus but also the nation at large, students do not form a homogenous group. They are diverse in terms of caste, class, gender and also in their attitude towards politics, union and about education itself. The students interviewed during the fieldwork were quite clear about their position on politics on campus and students' union. It was not surprising that campuses like BHU and AU, which had been adversely affected by student activism on campus (dealt in greater detail in Chapter 4), saw an aversion to student politics. It was identified with hooliganism and conflict leading to deterioration of the university itself. In AU, strangely, many of the bachelor's degree students in science were not in favour of students' union and politics on campus. This could be because of the reputation that universities such as AU and BHU have regarding student politics and students form an opinion about the role of the students' union based on prior knowledge.

In AU, students across humanities and sciences seemed disillusioned with the political groups on campus. The students felt that there was no difference between the politics on campus and outside. One respondent, pursuing her DPhil and identified herself as a centrist, commented, 'They take approach of party-based politics. After getting posts here, they start working for Parliamentary and Assembly elections and stop paying attention to the basic problems of the campus.' Another female respondent, pursuing her Bachelor of Arts, added that, 'Political groups have both negative and positive role in the campus. On the issues of walk-out, fee increase and to provide justice to the students, they were positive. But, also, they are the one responsible for hindrance in academics (during elections), anarchy and violence (programme of Akhilesh Yadav) because of which students face problems.'

As mentioned earlier, the feedback to the *Lyngdoh Committee Report* was also marked with references to violence and lack of adherence to any rules during elections in most universities in Uttar Pradesh. This is what the science students also mentioned in AU. Some of the students pursuing their Bachelor of Science degrees were disillusioned by student politics and how elections meant disruption of studies. On the other hand, some of the senior research scholars and even those in master's degree programmes spoke of a larger vision for society, which included socialism, liberty and rights for women, and for this, both students and teachers need to come together and take an ideological stand. Some previous studies seem to suggest that longer association with higher education help develop a clearer sociopolitical attitude. While the senior students do seem to have a wider vision for the role of students and teachers in society, the trajectory of the younger students part of this study will confirm whether their opinions change after spending a few more years at the university. Another point of interest was that most of the students who said they were rightists were against the students' union and were happy that it had been disbanded by the university. They saw the students' union speaking up against the current regime, a right-wing government and, therefore, did not support it.

There was a clear difference of opinion between the science and humanities students in BHU. BHU has had a turbulent history with regard to students' union and elections and has been the hub of political activity for decades. Understandably, students were wary regarding student union, considering the past record. As a PhD student (male), belonging to the SC community, put it, 'No, I am not associated with any (political group). I focus on studies. Political ideology sometimes encourages extremism.' Another respondent from BHU said, 'Earlier I was with ABVP, but because of differences in opinion left it.' Apart from two or three students, all the other respondents in BHU (sciences) said they are not interested in politics. The response to the idea of a students' union was not positive; hardly three students spoke up for the need of a students' union! The overall feeling was that politics on campus takes focus away from academics. Also, majority of the students mentioned that students' union just led to violence and said that it is a waste of time and that students should only study. This could be reflective of the role students' union has played in the campus. Only a couple of students mentioned that the students' union represented the needs of the students and actively pursued it with the administration, and organized students to understand government policies. Surprisingly, majority of students were not aware of incidents taking place in other universities, but there was no clear support for the students protesting against the State or administration in other universities. Among those aware of the incidents taking place in other universities were ambivalent and not sure of exactly what happened.

The response among the humanities students in BHU was different with more students not only supporting students' union but one of the few set of students wanted teachers and students to work together. Also, the humanities students were more vocal and aware of the events that had taken place in other universities and mentioned about the fake news and propaganda against JNU and, in particular, Kanhaiya Kumar, the case of the missing student Najeeb (student from JNU reported missing for many years now) and Rohit Vemula's suicide (student from HCU). The students took the names of their own volition and were not prompted by the field researcher. This is an important point as, in most of the other universities, students mentioned the JNU incident and some mentioned Kanhaiya Kumar, but there was little awareness about the Najeeb case or that of Rohit Vemula.

OU provided an interesting case in study, given its deeply political background. OU, which was deeply involved in Telangana movement, both student and teachers, expressed a disinterest in student activism and student union. Students said that the students' union is largely apolitical, and while the students themselves may not be actively involved in student politics, the general consensus was that the students' political groups fight for student's welfare; some mentioned that they pick up issues related to female students. The extreme political role played by the students in OU during the Telangana movement has now been relegated to the past and replaced by a very university-centric vision. The students want the union to fight for the welfare of the students and seek no larger involvement in other issues. This was reflected in their lack of interest in the controversies with regard to other universities, and the few who mentioned it spoke of only Telangana-related incidents. Some even went on to say that students' union should not go against the nation. The Forum for Protection of Universities in OU highlights that political leaders should stay out of campuses across the country.

In Gauhati University, the students' union seemed to be quite active. As one of the students summed it up, 'They organized some talks of their ideologies, tried to raise question to the authorities and tried to popularize their ideology' (male, General, MA). It appeared that the students were satisfied with the role the union was playing on campus, which was mainly that of representing student issues to the authorities and organizing cultural and academic events. The students also saw the union as a means to raise voice against unfair government policies and for protecting the democratic space of the country. Two of the respondents hit the nail on the head when they said, 'If we need educated politicians, they will come from educational institutions only. Students should be encouraged. Universities are centres where everyone should be encouraged to form their opinions.' While another said, 'Yes, the students of JNU and some other universities are doing good work, because if we do not raise our voices in the name of democracy to fight against the evils and atrocities of the authority, then the value of a democratic country will vanish away. If we do not question for our rights, then nobody is going to provide us a welfare society.'

In several of the universities, such as BHU, AU, NEHU and Pondicherry University, not only students but many teachers also were against the idea of students being politically active on campus. However, more teachers were in favour of students' union than there were students in favour of teachers' union. When asked whether students' and teachers' union are required on campus, most of the students spoke in favour of students' union but not a teachers' union. Very few seemed to see teachers and students collaborating together on issues related to the campus or larger ideological matters.

Students clearly did not want their teachers to be 'political'. This is the reason why in response to the question about the ideological position of teachers or if the teachers should be open about it, majority of the students replied in the negative. The students were overwhelmingly against teachers openly stating their political and ideological positions and also a teachers' union in campuses. Not only students but several teachers themselves said that a teacher had to be 'professional' and, therefore, keep subjective opinions on ideology and political affiliations outside the classroom. One of the fears expressed by teachers openly was that of groupism among like-minded faculty members (which is there in every university and cannot be prevented) and that of favouritism towards students who have similar ideological or political leanings. Furthermore, it may push students towards positions whether they truly believe in it or not, in order to ingratiate with the teachers. This is a problem that does exist in many universities and cannot be overlooked.

Both students and teachers had similar apprehensions about politics on campus, that of students being manipulated by political parties. The teachers said that the students would learn the wily ways of the politicians at a young age. There were both moral and disciplinary concerns. It was also noticed that universities which had both students' and teachers' union and that too political ones shared an uneasy relationship often resulting in conflict. This was also mentioned by a DU science professor, who said that very often the students' union is aligned with the government in power and, in that case, does not support any protest against the government policies. This results in the teachers' and students' union moving in opposite directions rather than together. Not only between teachers and union, but the administration also added a third element of conflict. An active students'/teachers' union invariably resulted in some conflict with the administration with regard to rules of admission (for students) and appointments (for teachers), fee hike, hostel/library and other facilities for students, syllabi, teaching method and other regulations with regard to teachers.

In Pondicherry University, a student mentioned that it was the teachers who urged the students to speak up and protest against an event as they felt it promoted a particular religion. This incident was mentioned by one of the students (female, belonging to a minority community) who said that she doesn't have much of an opinion about politics in the campus but recalled an incident where the Ramakrishna

Mission organized a rath yatra (chariot procession) and the teachers encouraged the students to speak up against a religious activity on campus. Most of the students in Pondicherry University were averse to the idea of politics on campus. It came as no surprise that students who mentioned that they are apolitical said that campus politics was a waste of time. Some were centrists but still did not support any political union on campus. So much so that a PhD student, at Pondicherry University, belonging to the SC community, said that he is a centrist and a member of a national political party, but when asked whether he was a member of any political group on campus, he said 'no', and nor should there be any politics on campus. The reason why the students of Pondicherry University appeared to be against a political students' union on campus was due to conflict between groups and also misbehaviour by political leaders/members of the union. Several students mentioned that a student union should only represent concerns of the student instead of becoming political. One student said that the teachers were promoting right-wing groups on campus, but then the rath yatra episode showed that there were teachers who were against the right wing, too.

Contrast this with the Periyar University (humanities) responses. The students said that none of the universities in Tamil Nadu have political students' union, as it has been banned by the government about 10 years ago. But majority of the students said that they are in favour of students' union in universities, as they felt that it helps create future leaders and form informed opinion about the policies of the government. The teachers in Periyar University also expressed unhappiness about the ban on students' union. Some teachers were in favour of students being more informed about ideology and politics as they did not want students to be deprived of the political experience that occurs through union and election and also through discussion in classrooms.

In SPPU and Bangalore University (sciences), majority of students said they did not want student politics on campus. They said that this disrupted studies and, also, some feared that this might result in favouritism among teachers. In both the universities, students said educational institutes should not have students union. On being asked the reason for their answer, they replied that students and politics don't mix and students should only study. Some also said that campus is no place for politics.

In NEHU, most of the humanities students said that they did not want any students' union on campus, as they would disrupt the peace on campus. But, in contrast, the NEHU science students largely spoke in favour of students' union and was also one of the few universities to speak in favour of teachers' union, too. It was equally surprising to note that nearly all the PhD students were against student activism, as they saw it as a waste of time. A couple of students agreed that the government excesses against the students were uncalled for, but they do not endorse the idea of students' union on campus, especially political ones.

The responses in Jadavpur University among science and humanities students differed on this issue as it did in BHU. In Jadavpur University, yet another politically charged university, surprisingly only about four students (humanities) said that they were associated with SFI, rest said that they were not interested in being a part of any such group and some declined to comment. This was against the general perception that a leftist campus implies more activism among students, rather it further lends to the theory that a minority of students are politically active. The politically active students said that they were in agreement with the vision of the students' union with regard to education, class and society, in general. Interestingly, on being asked about the role played by the students' union on campus, many of the respondents refused to comment. The few who did have something positive to say were either SFI members or others, who otherwise were apolitical and said that students' union was necessary to fight for the rights of students. Barring those who refused to comment, the other answers were in support of students' union. The students said that students' union was crucial in representing the voice of the students. They put forward demands before the administration, composition of executive council, admission rules, etc. As a leftist female respondent from Jadavpur University put it, students union is necessary 'for raising political awareness inside and outside the campus, about issues that are not just limited to the campus premises. They maintain the democratic political culture.' The science students were more openly in favour of students' union and spoke about it more openly than humanities students. But none of the science students mentioned SFI, rather Democratic Students' Front (DSF) seemed to be a popular choice, as it has no parent political party and, therefore, seen as more independent. Even though the students said that they were not part of active politics on campus nor do they desire to be part of partisan politics, they acknowledged that the campus helped them get acquainted with ideological positioning and find their own. Not surprisingly, students from both humanities and sciences spoke in favour of JNU and against the actions of the government.

In Punjab University (humanities), a few students were active politically and were clear why they were with that political group. For example, a leftist respondent said that he chose to be a member of Students' For Society (SFS) as they fight feudal and capitalist forces. Another student mentioned that she is apolitical, but she became a member of Punjab University Students' Union (PUSU) as they fight for welfare of students; she added that in the beginning it was not a political party but has become so now. But many others who said they were leftists or right of the centre did not belong to any political group on the campus. Those who were associated with political parties or the students' union were not blind to its faults. For example, in Punjab University, a respondent said that he was not in favour of violence and mentioned an incident in Indian Council of Social Science Research, where student political group broke out into violence; he said that he doesn't support violent student parties. Another respondent, though a member of the PUSU, said that political parties are 'self-centred', but at the same time, they do fight for some student issues like hostel or some issues in the department. Several respondents in various universities said that they wouldn't mind a students' union as long as it fights for only students' rights and does not align with political parties. Several teachers spoke in a similar vein.

A common sentiment in this regard was that politics corrupts. Among the science students in Punjab University, the students expressed disillusionment with politics and the way political parties function, and hence, very few students were politically active on campus. Only three mentioned being part of NSUI, SFI and ABVP, respectively. One respondent, who was pursuing his engineering and belonged to the SC community, mentioned that he was earlier a member but now no longer so. Most of the students had positive things to say about students' union, in general, while some spoke of what they thought the students' union should be doing. The latter felt they should organize for academic events for the students such as science fairs, visits, demand better facilities and infrastructure, prepare budget and present it to the administration. A few PhD scholars spoke of how students' union is crucial in a democracy.

In Calicut University, all the students were aware of the various political parties on campus and they named the SFI, ABVP, Kerala Students' Union (KSU), freethinkers and so on. Majority of the respondents said that they belong to some political group or the other. Those with SFI said that they believed in the leftist ideology. An MA student said she was with SFI because 'student political groups play important role inside the campus in the issues especially related to the academic problems of students. In my campus, SFI took a positive approach towards a student in the problems related to exams, hostel problems, etc.' Similarly, another student said, 'It plays a vital role in safeguarding our culture and values which ensure all rights to student. Such student politics is mandatory' (MA, male, OBC). The only NSUI supporter said he is so because, 'They influence administrative and every matter of university. Also, I believe in the ideals of leaders like Nehru and Gandhi.'

In Calicut University, even those who were not part of any political group on campus had positive things to say about the union. An MPhil student said she has no time for campus politics, but 'they help us to protect student rights, they question the authority in order to get proper facilities or the betterment of students and academic activities.' Another MPhil student echoed similar thought, 'Students' unions are responsible for providing services to students and act as a mediator between the administration and students.' We see that overall students were either active participants in the political life on campus or were at least aware of what the union was doing for them. The students were also aware of the teachers' union—Association of Calicut University Teachers. They even mentioned some of the teachers associated with it and said it was dominated by the left and the Congress. In DU, students did have some complaints against the students' union and the way elections were carried out, but they did not wish the union away. They said with all its ills, the students' union was crucial in putting forward the demands of the students.

University of Kashmir was the only one where the students were aware of the teachers' union but not the students' union. There are no political unions on campus. Most of the students said that freedom of speech and expression is crucial and students should have that democratic space. Students in Kashmir felt that the students' union in JNU is effective in creating political awareness among students. One student, though apolitical, said, 'We wish to have that kind of political space here in Kashmir. Also, the JNU problem was hyped by media. Students being the forerunners in nurturing the nation towards development should have a say and should not be scapegoats of the capitalism/dirty politics.' One of the points made by early researchers on student activism is that the proximity to political centre impacts student political activity on campus. This has proven to be true in several of the examples, be it DU, JNU, BHU, AU, Gauhati University and so on. Kashmir, mired in politics, does not permit political unions on campus, probably due to the fear of deep politicization of the campus. But the students want a union not only for protest but also because they think that it will lead to intellectual growth among students and broaden their vision about society and nation. This brings to mind what Professor Pathak points out,

> If politics as a vocation means an awareness of the structure and practice of power in society, its possession, dissemination and distribution, and simultaneous urge to intervene and move towards a new order with higher principles like equity, justice, peace and plurality, young students ought to be political.' (Pathak 2019)

The conversations with students and teachers make it clear that there is a support for students' union on campus but with majority supporting a non-political students' union that deals with immediate needs of the students. Altbach pointed out way back in 1970 on the changing nature of student activism.

> The current emphasis of student movements in both the advanced and the developing areas with solely campus concerns was also almost completely absent from the militant student organizations of the nationalist period. Student movements were outward looking, using the campus as a base of operations and recruitment and often of discussion, but aiming their agitational campaigns at issues in the broader society. Even the student strikes which took place in Indian universities during the pre-1947 period were largely directed at nationalist goals, and were only incidentally concerned with university issues. (Altbach 1970, 75)

The broader issues of nation-building, democracy and right to dissent were mentioned by very few. But all those who did speak of the need for students' union on campus said that that it is instrumental in developing leadership qualities and leaders and also created awareness about government policies. The idea of a non-political students' union that organized seminars and cultural events is a popular one. The fear of external political influence, the ills of politics of the state entering the campus and violence pushed students towards a non-political students' union. As Pathak rightly points out,

> This apolitical orientation or indifference to larger issues beyond books, exams and jobs is a major hindrance for the creation of a vibrant political culture, or politics as some sort of catharsis. Second, in the absence of higher dreams, even young students allow themselves to be manipulated and used by self-indulgent/corrupt political bosses. As a result, the play of money, the culture of violence, and utter instrumentality begin to pollute the political environment in colleges and universities. (Pathak 2019)

Like Professor Pathak, several other academics, who otherwise are in support of students' union, also warn against the 'misuse' of students' union.

> Associations which once provided ideological spaces for fruitful discussions shrunk to infinitesimally narrow spaces wherein the identity of students gained primacy. Universities have become proxy battlegrounds for caste groups and political parties. Student politics has undergone a change in terms of the issues it addresses. The fundamental purpose of a students'

association or union in a university, was to address basic issues of the students and bring them to the focus of the administration. But such organisations have now become breeding grounds for communalism, casteism, vandalism and regionalism. (Narayan 2016)

But the dichotomy here is that students want the students' union to fight for the right of students, and this could mean conflict. The students may not always have the option of making a safe choice. The students also mentioned in certain cases, as they did in Punjab University, that the main problem was the VC who supported the government and not the teachers and students. In many instances, it was the rigid stand taken by the administration or policies implemented by the Central government and endorsed by VCs that led to a tiff between students' union and the administration, thus making it political.

The political control of the State is not limited to influencing students' union. Politics is played out in various other ways with administration and teachers being the other points of manipulation. Both Batabyal (2014) and Nayyar (2017) have pointed out how national politics played into universities there by ruining several regional universities. Nayyar (2017) writes,

> The turning point, perhaps, was 1977, the end of the era of majority governments and one-party rule. It gathered momentum after 1989. There were short-lived coalition governments. And there were regime changes after almost every general election. The competitive politics unleashed by changes in governments soon spilt over to universities not only as spheres of influence but also as arenas for political contests. The discomfiture with independent or critical voices, even if few, grew rapidly. Central universities were no longer immune.

> The decline of public universities in India has been an inevitable consequence of this process. The first set to bear the brunt were the universities of national standing in states. The obvious examples are Allahabad, Lucknow and Patna among the old, with Baroda and Rajasthan among the new. These are not even pale shadows of what they were until around 1980. The next set to be progressively damaged were the oldest national universities in the states—Bombay, Calcutta and Madras—established more than 150 years ago.

Appointments made on political grounds and affiliations rather than merit and leadership have led to the downfall of many universities.

Political appointments are made in universities to gain control over the system, as those who have been appointed on purely ideological or political grounds rarely stand up against or oppose those in power. This leads to a chain of events where teachers also form camps and groups for gaining favours. Those who speak out are targeted and lose out in terms of promotions. The student union may either become very active or be totally suppressed through the State action—ban on union and protest, violence against students and so on. The events at JNU, Jamia Milia Islamia and HCU are examples of how the State can use its authority to control universities.

> The essential concept of universities, as autonomous spaces, where freedom of expression, exploration of ideas and advancement of knowledge are an integral part of the learning process. There are bound to be differences in views, but these must be addressed through discussion, with open minds, It would seem that the political class and the ruling elite do not have an understanding of the critical role of universities in society and democracy. It is a serious mistake to think of universities as campuses or classrooms that teach young people to pass examinations, obtain degrees, and become employable, where research is subsidiary or does not matter. Universities are about far more. For students, there is so much learning outside the classroom that makes them good citizens of society. For faculty, apart from commitment to their teaching and their research, there is a role in society as intellectuals who can provide an independent, credible, voice in evaluating governments, parliament, legislatures, or the judiciary, as guardians of society. This role is particularly important in a political democracy. (Nayyar 2017)

Professor Pathak, too, points that while students may be politically and ideologically inclined, it would defeat the purpose of a university if students refuse to engage with those with diametrically or merely different ideas.

The disillusionment of the students with politics and politicians influenced their opinion about students' union and activism on campus. When students speak on the lines of caste and community, it goes against the idea of the university. Universities are meant to create the kind of societies we want outside the campus. Unfortunately, students involved in politics often pick up the negative aspects and start imitating the behaviour, mannerisms and strategies of the reality that exists outside the university. In cases where student political unions are linked to a parent national/regional political party, the 'reference group' is the leaders of the political parties. This, in turn, leads to the display of power and money, arrogance and disregard for rules by the student leaders. The students' unions become mirror images of the parent party. If the parent political party is in power, this also implies that the union will not oppose the government or speak against the policies of the government. Hence, instead of charting out their own course, student leaders become mere imitators of their reference group. It has led to students losing faith and moving away from political activism. Of course, the number of students actually keen on being part of political unions on campus is very low.

This study revealed the following interesting points. One, a very small percentage of students actually translate their ideological leanings to political activism. Second, some students may be clear about their ideological stand and have strong reasons for it, but this may not translate into actual politics on campus or even support for the students' union. There were several respondents who were ideologically leftists, left of centre, rightists but did not want students' union on campus. Third, it was observed that students may categorize themselves as apolitical, but they have strong political views and stand on certain issues. For example, several apolitical students said they were so only because the current students' union was speaking out against the current government. In many instances, apolitical students supported the union on campus. Of course, there is a category of apolitical students, disinterested in politics itself both inside and outside campus and do not support students' union. This, in turn, gives the State a chance to wield control over the universities, as resistance and dissent do not find active supporters. For students' union to be effective and popular among students, it needs to be politically articulate and aware, critical of the government, ready to mobilize but also ensure that it does not become the very thing it is opposing.

Entrenched Hierarchies
Caste and Gender

Higher education in a democracy should be a messenger of liberal values and equality for the society. In this, it should be the torchbearer for breaking down the barriers that exist in society, be it in terms of hierarchy, access to resources or differential treatment on the basis of caste and gender. However, educational institutions, in most cases, mirror the society and in that perpetuate the same hierarchies and inequalities. In the introductory chapter, it was mentioned that during the interviews with the students, certain questions were asked regarding admission rules and rules within the campus that the students feel are discriminatory.

Gendered hostel rules serve as excellent example of how socialization works in higher educational institution. In almost all the universities and engineering institutes, students mentioned that hostel rules were always made in favour of the boys. The girls were subjected to a lot more rules and control than their male counterparts. During the fieldwork, students of a few universities did speak of unfair hostel rules and protests that have taken place against the rules.

Students were also questioned if they felt that certain groups were under-represented in their university or institute. Teachers were asked in greater detail about this as, unlike students who leave the university after a few years, teachers in most cases stay on long enough to analyse the change in the gender–caste–class composition of students. This question was also posed about a similar composition of the faculty. In addition to this, teachers were asked their opinion about the impact of reservation on the education system in general and in the classroom. This chapter analyses the findings from the field on these key issues of building an inclusive and gender-equal education system.

This first section of this chapter explores the role of socialization in educational institutions and institutionalization of behaviour through the prism of social control and socialization. How does socialization takes place through education? Jane Elliot,[1] an educator, conducted a blue-eyes/brown-eyes experiment in her third-grade classroom following the assassination of Martin Luther King. She announced in class that all those with blue eyes were superior, more intelligent and privileged than those children with brown eyes. Those with brown eyes had to wear a collar, got less time at recess and were denied some other privileges given to blue-eyed people. Soon enough, the blue-eyed children stopped talking to brown-eyed children, mistreated them and, in turn, brown-eyed children started feeling inferior and distressed. Next day, the experiment was reversed with the brown-eyed children being the more privileged group. Ms Elliot remarked that she was astounded to see how children quickly adapted to the idea of being inferior or superior. She said, a group of children who were friends probably an hour ago became mean, vicious and nasty towards their friends. When she asked the brown-eyed children why they didn't perform well when they were said to be inferior, they said the collar they wore stopped them from thinking. Discrimination and differential rules visibly disturbed children and adults alike (when the same exercise was conducted among adults); while the children did not express their distress, the adults lost their temper and started reacting within minutes.

Elliot used this to teach the children about racism and how non-White people felt when they were looked down upon or segregated in society. This experiment could be conducted by replacing race with the social roles and statues assigned by gender and caste based on a system of hierarchy, and the results would be similar. The experiment yet again reiterates the important role education can play in breaking down the barriers built by socialization within family and society in general. It is for this reason that the role of schools and education

---

[1] Jane Elliot speaks out against racism and appeared on *Oprah Winfrey* show in 1992 to expose how inherently racist people are, and this is due to socialization. She has conducted this experiment even among adult men and women; videos are available on YouTube.

in socialization has been theorized from several perspectives. The emphasis on children has been for the reason that most of the cognitive development takes place during the early years of childhood. However, the process of socialization takes place during one's lifetime; this is because people continuously learn about social norms and the right behaviour in different circumstances. This was central to Erikson's theory (1980) on identity development.

Universally, socialization has been accepted as the primary function of education. The kind of socialization has been debated, but it cannot be denied that it is a part of the process of education. Parsons (1959) in his treatise on sociology of families says that the two functions of a family are primary socialization and stabilization of adult personalities. Secondary socialization takes place through agencies other than the family, such as school, media and so on. During this phase, children learn universalistic values as opposed to primary socialization, where children learn family- and community-specific norms. Parsons was criticized for his gendered perspective on socialization. He wrote that boys are instrumental while women are expressive, which creates a clear division of labour where men are in charge of discipline and earning a livelihood and women are nurturers. The social role theory is based on gender norms, setting expectations of feminine and masculine behaviour. According to psychoanalysts, 'gender is something that becomes deeply embedded in our personality structures very early on in our development' (Ryle 2012, 136). This has found its way into education in several ways, from the entry of women into the education system to the subjects they chose to study (science versus humanities) and the attention they receive from teachers. Gender also finds its way in the content of what is taught in school through text and images. The feminist movement has made a concerted effort to change the highly gendered content in textbooks in school, so that in their crucial formative years, children are not socialized into highly gendered and segregated social roles and norms.

According to psychologist Kohlberg, children develop their ability to think and act over several stages, namely pre-conventional, conventional and post-conventional stages. As each stage progresses, children learn about societal rules and morality, starting from avoiding punishment as kids to following rules set by parents, and because they recognize it as morally right, in the final post-conventional stage, there is a conflict regarding moral standards. An individual may feel that the society does not match up to his/her own moral standards, leading to mental conflict which may also lead to a rebellion.

Mead (1934), well known for his work '*Mind, Self and Society*', believed that the self has two parts, the 'I' and the 'me'. The 'I' is the creative, spontaneous part, while the 'me' is the more passive part of the self based on the internalized expectations of the larger society. 'I' and 'me' complement each other, as society needs both creativity and conformity. Cooley (1902) developed the concept of the 'looking-glass self', in which he said that we constantly imagine how we appear to others and how others are evaluating us. This, in turn, becomes the looking glass through which we develop a perception about ourselves which could be both negative and positive.

Functionalists believe that education is essential in maintaining social order. Education performs certain manifest and certain latent functions. Among the manifest functions, central is social control and conformity. Through authority and discipline, in student–teacher relationship or administration–student relationship, social control is reinforced through rules and regulations and punishment for those who do not adhere to the rules. This prepares the child for his/her future interactions in the workplace or elsewhere, as they know how to interact with those in the position of authority. As Berger and Luckmann put it, 'The more conduct is institutionalized, the more predictable and thus the more controlled it becomes if socialization into the institutions has been effective outright coercive measures can be applied economically and selectively' (Berger and Luckmann 1967 62). One of the examples of discipline and social control is the attendance rule in most colleges and universities. In school, children cannot be absent from school without adequate explanation or letter from the guardian. One of the attractions of joining colleges and universities is the anticipation of enjoying some degree of freedom. But teachers and administration wield control over students in several ways and attendance is one of them. There is a sense of power over students, and elaborate rules are chalked out with regard to when a student can be excused (extracurricular activities, letter from another teacher), making it more and more complicated.

Latent functions of education include creating networks and relationships. Students learn to interact with people other than their family/immediate circle. They also widen their network; of course, today, the social media has widened the scope of creating networks beyond the school and workplace. In universities and, sometimes, in school, students also learn how to work in small groups (through group projects/seminars). Another vital latent function that universities perform is to acquaint students with social issues facing the society. 'Education is deeply implicated in the processes of transmitting key messages as to knowledge, personal and social realities' (Davies 2012, 8).

One of the arguments by phenomenologists and symbolic interactionists has been that of a status quoist, structural-functionalist system producing 'over regulated' and 'over socialized' members of society. 'This view of socialization tends to be one of a passive actor being socialized into a consensual institutional framework rather than one which allows the actor to participate in his own conceptual construction of the world and his own fate as a project' (Sharp, Lewis and, Green, 2017, Introduction). This has given rise to the debate of free will, individualism and determinism. Are all social actions predetermined by social norms instilled by socialization? 'Men's 'freedom' does not spring from the absence of control but depends both quantitatively and qualitatively upon both those controls built into and those exerted around him for its type' (Davies 2012, 19).

Conflict theorists do not believe that public schools reduce social inequality, rather they perpetuate it in the guise of maintaining social order. They see educational institutions as arenas where the social inequalities due to race, gender and class (add caste in the context of India) are present in the society. Conflict theorists are more critical of the role of education and, to some extent, even have a negative view of it. This is where French sociologist Pierre Bourdieu comes in. Conflict theorists say that the functionalist approach of education benefits the upper class as it ensures that they continue to dominate the discourse and the lower class in the quest for maintaining status quo and are pushed into obedience. Students belonging to the low socio-economic class do not have the same advantages as the upper-class students. They do not have access to the same opportunities even if they have the ability and desire to learn, and in addition to this, the upper-class students enjoy the advantage of generations of access to education. Bourdieu writes that the upper class are better equipped to negotiate the classroom and the education system, which he calls the cultural capital or cultural knowledge. Members of the upper and middle classes have more cultural capital than families of lower-class status.

Everett in the first *Encyclopaedia of the Social Sciences* (1937) wrote, 'Education is probably the most powerful tool of social control but it works for militarists and class conscious snobs as well as for the humanitarians and for men of vision' (Everett 1937, 347, as quoted in Davies 2012, 14). Davies in turn writes,

> Education is the more or less systematic pursuit of normalcy in all societies which practice it. It always involves making people more similar as well as more different but which people, in what degree and to what end depends upon the nature of a particular society's hierarchy. (Davies 2012, 8)

The recent introduction of the compulsory attendance rule of 75 per cent was mentioned in all the universities by students. Even research scholars pursuing their MPhil/PhD are now required to mark attendance every day. There seemed to be no adverse reaction to it on the whole; most said that they didn't really have an opinion about it, while others were fine with the rule. The high degree of conformity doesn't come as a surprise, since most students are used to adherence to rules from school days. A handful of students questioned the need for such stringent attendance rules. It is ironical that the voting age stands at 18, which means youth plays a role in deciding the fate of governments but cannot be trusted with attending classes of their volition.

Among the few students who did express unhappiness about attendance rules were—one in Pondicherry University, because the attendance sheet is shared with parents and if any student bunked a class the parents would immediately come to know about it. Another student mentioned the university doesn't treat them like adults. In Calicut university, respondents had a lot to say about the attendance rule, unlike other universities. A PhD (male, OBC) student mentioned, 'A couple of years ago, the university made attendance compulsory for research scholars. But we found it unscientific for research and protested, and the university had to withdraw the order. But marking attendance has been more strict now.' Another PhD student expressed his apprehensions about a new legislation. 'The admission rules must be changed according to the recent legislations earmarking 10 per cent reservation for the economically disadvantaged among the upper-caste section. This might have resulted in effectively reducing the opportunities of the socio-economically backward/SC/ST communities. Attendance rules of research scholars have been made stringent.' A few teachers also remarked that research scholars should not be expected to mark attendance every day as they may need to visit libraries or go for fieldwork and so on. At the level of MPhil/PhD, when students are almost in their mid-20s and involved in research, it is absurd to subject them to attendance rules. The idea of discipline cannot and should not control every aspect of education.

Stemming from the idea of social control, university rules restricting women from going out and accessing facilities in the campus act as a deterrent to their development, as students also further the gender hierarchies in a formal, legalized manner, which further indoctrinate expectation and create formal social pressure. The administration, on the basis of its ideological position, can perpetuate entrenched hierarchies of the society. Conservative ideas about gender roles or student as a stakeholder can further restrict the growth and development of the student.

> Institutions imply historicity and control ... institutions always have a history ... institutions also by the very fact of their existence, control human conduct by setting up pre defined patterns of conduct which channel it in one direction as against the many other directions that theoretically be possible. It is important to stress that this controlling character is inherent in institutionalization as such, prior to or apart from any mechanisms of sanctions specifically set up to support an institution ... these mechanisms is generally called a system of social control. (Berger and Luckmann 1967, 54–55)

Historically, women have been denied education, and the very few who managed to read and write were homeschooled. One of the initial roadblocks was the stepping out of young girls and women from upper-caste families from the confines of their homes to attend classes. Interacting with male teachers was another hindrance. Over the years, women slowly started making some space for themselves in the education system. There are several barriers to female education in school such as cost, physical distance, boy–girl intermingling, lack of infrastructure in school, preference to male child and so on. In higher education, some of the barriers continue to be same as in school days, i.e., cost, male students in class and the physical distance. There are also restrictions within the family, sometimes, with regard to the subject women should study and how much they can study. Since gender norms of society do not give primacy to women as bread winners of the family, families are hesitant to invest in their education. Also, stereotyping and bias slots women in humanities and liberal arts, and in many families, women are discouraged from taking up science subjects. Some research also suggests that often teachers neglect the female students in science classes and allow boys to dominate classroom discussions, so much so that boys are given preference for computer usage if it is placed in a common area (Acker and Oatley 1993).

India has come a long way, and today, the gap between male and female enrolment has been bridged to a certain extent. Total enrolment in higher education has been estimated to be 37.4 million with 19.2 million males and 18.2 million females. Females constitute 48.6 per cent of the total enrolment (All India Survey on Higher Education [AISHE] 2018–2019). The ratio of male is higher than female in almost all levels of higher education, except MPhil, postgraduate (PG) and certificate courses. Student enrolment at undergraduate (UG) level has 51 per cent males and 49 per cent females. Diploma has a skewed distribution with 66.8 per cent males and 33.2 per cent females. At the PhD level, again, the number of males is higher with 56.18 per cent males and 43.82 per cent females. PG diploma students' enrolment is 54.09 per cent for male students and 45.91 per cent for female students. However, female enrolment in professional courses is lower than male enrolment, which is not surprising, given that boys are still given the preference with regard to planning their professional lives as women are seen to be fulfilling their home and nurturing roles at some point of their lives. Boys do not have to choose between career and marriage/kids, like many women have to.

Young women who do manage to overcome familial hurdles to study subjects of their choice find themselves subject to discriminating rules in universities and institutes. Some higher educational institutes have specific dress codes for women and, sometimes, even men. R.M.D. Engineering College in Chennai, Christ College in Bangalore and Pune's Symbiosis International University prohibit girls from wearing jeans. In a few institutes, men are not allowed to wear T-shirts and have to be formally dressed on campus. In Adarsh Women's College in Haryana, four girls were fined ₹100 each on Friday for defying a 40-year old dress code of the college that bans wearing T-shirts. The management strictly adheres to a dress code for students and staff since 1970. The girls must wear white salwar kameez every Monday and any colour salwar kameez the rest of the days. The women staff must come dressed in saris, while formal trousers and shirt is the dress code for the male staff. Lately, women have been allowed to wear jeans, but they are not to be paired with T-shirts. The directorate of collegiate education, which is in charge of all arts and science colleges in Tamil Nadu (1 September 2013), passed an order that male students are barred from wearing T-shirts and women are prohibited from wearing jeans and sleeveless clothing.

Young women also find their movements, even in the campus, subject to rules and regulations. Over the past few years, there have been lot of protests against discriminatory hostel rules against women/girls. While the other university rules are neutral, hostel rules, in many cases, are seen to be restrictive where girls are concerned. Almost all the universities have rules for girls' hostels such as specific entry and exit timings and for allowing visitors, while the boys' hostels had no such rules, and in case of any rule, the boys did not follow it strictly. In Gulbarga University, students spoke of differential hostel rules, where girls were supposed to sign in by 6:30 PM; they are not allowed to go outside the hostel after that; also, boys cannot enter the girl's hostel. Both girls and boys were aware of the rules and see no reason to protest regarding these rules.

In Calicut University, it was apparent from the comments that there are discriminatory rules with regard to hostels for girls and boys. Several of the respondents across gender, caste and education commented on the restrictive rules for girls in hostel. But in comparison to the timings that were mentioned by respondents in other universities, in Calicut, the girl students were more liberal, as girls needed to be back 10 PM (in most other universities, girls have to report to the hostels by 6 PM); boys had no such restriction. A PhD student in Calicut University mentioned that, 'I have heard girl students raising their complaints regarding the discriminatory hostel rules, while attending the meetings of the Research Scholars Association. Those were mainly about staying back at late hours in the central library. Reportedly, they were not allowed to visit the library or walk through the university campus during night.' One MA student (male) pointed out that there have been protests by girls, but the administration has not taken a decision citing moral and security reasons; the protests were mentioned by three more respondents.

In most of the universities, while the students were aware of the different rules for boys and girls in the hostels, there didn't seem to be much of a reaction to this discrimination, rather there was a sense of acceptance. Most of the respondents did not recall any discussion revolving around hostel rules, expressing any discontentment over the hostel rules. But almost everyone did comment that apart from hostel rules and, sometimes, rules regarding accessing the library after a certain time, there weren't any other rules that were different for girls. The reason for the acceptance might have been that over the years, safety of women has been a point of concern, and this was seen in the light of welfare for women. Also, most women are used to such rules at home dictated, in turn, by the norms of society that seek to control movement of women in the name of safety and honour of the family. The university seems to be an extension of the same. The conformity and the obedience to authority is more ingrained in women through socialization in families and schools and continues in universities. 'Social order exists only as a result of human activity ... and all human activity is subject to habitualisation' (Berger and Luckmann 1967, 52–53). Berger and Luckmann point out that there is a pattern to human behaviour, even if an individual is living all alone.

In Bangalore University, surprisingly, very few students were aware that the rules were different for girls and boys in hostels. Only four students said that girl's hostels had different rules from that of boy's hostel. A female respondent said, 'There is a fixed time to enter the hostel and are not allowed to go out late nights or they have to pay fine. And visiting hours for the visitors are also fixed by the hostel authority.' A PhD student (a male respondent belonging to the SC community) gave a detailed reply to this: 'Dress code should be maintained in the hostel. Girls are not permitted to wear short dresses. Hostel gates will be closed by 7 PM. No outsiders will be allowed inside the rooms for any reason, unless they show ID cards.' In spite of such stringent rules and control, hardly a few said that they disliked the rules. In Kashmir University, too, strict rules are in place for women. A roll call is taken every day in the evening to ensure that everyone is back in the hostel. One rule which men mentioned was that they were not allowed to wear sherwani (formal attire for men) in the university.

In a conversation with two young law students, a different matter came to light. The two students expressed their unhappiness with the way moot courts were organized. 'Every year, the third year batch of the college organizes All India Moot Court Camp, and a committee is formed for the same, positions are decided not on the basis of merits, talent and capability but gender, money and muscle power. These are some of the rules which have been made to undermine capabilities of girls. It is widely prevalent' (LLB Honours, female, General). Another respondent also spoke of the gendered practices in the moot court, for example, 'general practice with respect to the selections of the members to the Moot Court Committee' (male, General, BA, LLB). The two respondents expressed their anger regarding the way the moot courts were organized but said the administration was ignoring it, even though it has been bought to their notice. The female respondent also spoke out against the general attitude of the administration towards women. The understanding of gender sensitization, privacy and other related concepts is extremely bad among many members of administration and teachers' body. The handling of cases related to harassment is not dealt in the best very possible. Victim blaming bringing racism, regionalism can be seen.' All this seems to suggest the prevalence of a deeply patriarchal attitude among teachers and administrative staff in Bangalore University, and to a certain extent, the same had been internalized by the students. In JNU, a few students commented on the gender sensitization committee against sexual harassment (GSCASH) being replaced by the Internal Complaints Committee (ICC) and the administration not handling cases of sexual harassment in a proper manner.

The students of DU mentioned the Pinjra Tod movement and also spoke of moral policing in the name of hostel rules. The Pinjra Tod movement started in DU in 2015 against restrictive rules that influenced many other protests across the country, though not all have been success stories. Women students at Ajmer submitted a list of demands asking for basic hostel amenities, ambulance service, change in entry–exit timings and to be allowed to meet visitors without seeking permission from authorities and so on. 'Women students around the country are drawing strength and inspiration from each other and rising up against discriminatory practices of institutions. Collectively, they are rejecting securitization and surveillance in the name of safety.' Students said that the strict rules regarding hostel timing preventing them from taking part in sports and other extracurricular activities, thus, preventing an all-round development of personality.

A similar protest was seen at the Miranda House, Delhi, when students camped at the hostel gates, refusing to let it shut down. But after all this, the curfew time was extended by only half an hour, from 8:30 PM–9:00 PM. The students have to inform the hostel authorities before availing night out; post the protest, the number of night outs per student increased. Apart from this, none of the other demands of the students were met. In Ambedkar University, protests in 2017 began when the parents of a female student were called in to complain about the student. The protest titled 'University is Our Right, Not a Tool for Blackmail'. The students said that the administration was treating them like schoolchildren rather than the adults that they are. The situation worsened when students were threatened with withdrawal of hostel facilities and timing restrictions were increased. Students narrated several other incidents of moral policing with regard to clothing, so much so that a student lost her seat at the university because of the harassment with regard to her clothing. The students were furthermore made to sign affidavits that they would not participate in protests or they are liable to lose hostel accommodation or even their admission. In Jamia Millia Islamia, too, students were sent a circular that they are not allowed to take part in any protest or signature campaign. The circular also stated that hostel residents were not allowed to step out of the hostel post 9 'o' clock. The students said that these rules and regulations made them feel that in the name of security and safety, they were being stifled and basic freedom was being denied to them. In Jamia Millia Islamia, a massive protest by female hostel residents finally forced the hostel authorities to roll back these decisions.

In BHU, students expressed their unhappiness regarding discriminatory hostel rules. Even the mess operates on different rules for girls and boys. As seen in other hostels, girls were expected to be back by a certain time. In BHU, girls had to be back in the hostel by 10 PM, while there were no such rules for boys. In the mess, boys had a pay-per-diet system, while girls were expected to pay ₹100 per day, even if they do not avail meals at the mess. Girls cannot leave the hostel without permission letters from parents. A female research student said, 'Girls have to pay monthly mess charge (even if they won't eat), while boys don't have to do that. They have to pay as per diet. Girls cannot walk in campus after 10 PM, while there is no such restriction on boys.' One of the respondents in BHU, Institute of Science, mentioned that girls are not served non-vegetarian items. It is distressing that a university seeks to follow the regressive norm of restricting a woman's diet. Most of the respondents said that the hostel rules were gender biased. One may recall the protests that were held by female students followed by police brutalities on students two years ago.

JNU has seen a change in the hostel rules, which were proposed to be introduced in 2019, and this included a dress code, timing restrictions (unheard of in JNU in all these years) and, of course, increased fee hike. Students of Punjab University also mentioned that girls were expected to follow the dress code and girls are not allowed to wear shorts in the hostels. In Pondicherry University, girls are not allowed to wear jeans and leggings to the university. In Kashmir University, the dress code was the reverse: traditional clothes, men are not allowed to wear the sherwani to the library.

In science/engineering institutes, the scenario was the same. In AU, some of the male students were miffed that the female students get the hostel allotment earlier than they do, but they did not say anything about it, while the female students were not allowed to go out post 9 'o' clock, boys had to be in by 10 PM. Women complained that while everyone could enter boys' hostel, in the girls', hostel even their parents and guardians were not allowed inside. These were the typical rules in most of the hostels with only a difference in timings. In certain universities such as Pondicherry University, NEHU and Bangalore University, girls were not allowed to come out of the hostel after 7 PM. In FTII, a respondent mentioned about the power given to security guards to record movement of girls in the hostel corridors. In another context, students of SPPU remarked that the guards would look out for girls and boys hanging out together and threaten to inform authorities and even parents. Similarly, in Kashmir University, the proctor had made some rules regarding interaction with the opposite sexes. Universities are places where, apart from gaining knowledge, one prepares for a life as a professional; controlling interaction between men and women is definitely not the way to do so. On the contrary, this is the place where men and women should learn to have a healthy interaction and respect each other's space and opinion.

In SPPU, boys were allowed to be in the reading room till 12 PM, while girls were allowed to be in the reading room only till 9:30 PM, and the girls' hostel would shut its gate by 10 PM. Guwahati University has installed closed-circuit television (CCTV) cameras in girls' hostels. In NEHU, a male respondent pursuing his MSc said that the administration comes down more strongly on girls for misdemeanour than on boys. He said, 'Strict security for female students. Unruly moral behaviours paid less attention in terms of male students in particular.'

In the conversations with students, some respondents expressed anger and dislike against the discriminatory rules; majority of respondents seemed resigned to the situation. But some also felt that it was necessary for safety, and as one respondent remarked in Bangalore University, it helps girls concentrate on studies; hence, she was happy about the strict rules. In Punjab University, interestingly, while the girls in sciences and humanities had to follow the same rules, the students of humanities were vocal against the discriminatory rules. They also mentioned that the students' union had fought against the entry and exit timings of girls and got it changed. Several of the respondents remarked that the students' union has been actively engaged in making the university more democratic. There have been several tiffs with the administration regarding fee hike and hostel rules for girls. The students have been fighting a battle to keep the girls' hostel open throughout like the boys' hostel.

Apart from universities where the research was conducted, there were reports of several other protests from universities and engineering/medical institutes regarding hostel rules. Some of them will be illustrated here. The female students at the College of Engineering Trivandrum, Kerala, protested against the timings in the hostel, and what was the breaking point was that no fire exit has been provided so as to protect the honour of the girl students. The girls started a massive campaign from street plays to cycle rallies to #Breakthecurfew and #responsiblyfree, till the rules were rolled back. Kottayam Medical College also saw protests by students which saw a successful end with the principal agreeing to change the entry timings to 9:30 PM from the earlier 7:30 PM.

In Rajasthan University, a protest that started with female PhD students against the unfair surveillance rules of the women's hostel soon gathered support from male and UG women students. The administration reached out to the students, but no consensus could be reached. This was not the first time that students had protested; they had spoken out against the inaccessibility to the library after 10 PM, the biometric system of attendance, the installation of cameras inside the campus including the corridors, women could not move around in the campus between 10 PM to 6 AM and the harassment by hostel guards. The hostel guards started sending text messages to parents/guardians regarding the movements of their children/wards and also interrogating the students, too. Instead of trying to understand and rectify the situation, the administration started harassing the protestors and even banned the entry of male protestors into the hostel. They started naming and shaming the women protestors on campus and also banned use of social media.

A similar protest was seen in the Regional Institute of Education, Bhopal and Ajmer. The female students protested against the stringent entry–exit timings and moral policing on campus. They refused to enter the hostels and stayed up all night in the basketball court as a mark of protest. The administration threatened to cut off the electricity and impose more restrictions. When the women turned to the police for help, instead of helping them, the police sided with the administration. It was after a long struggle that some of the demands were met. In University of Mumbai, when the library was open round the clock, the women could not access it due to hostel rules which prevented them from stepping out after 11:30 PM. The female students are demanding that the rules for access to campus facilities should be the same for both men and women.

The reaction to the different rules regarding reading-room usages, dress code or hostel timings for men and women or even interaction between the opposite sexes were very often surprising. In the interviews with the respondents, there seemed to be a sense of acceptance, be it out of fear of authority or merely because the rules have been in existence for a while, or the internalization of the argument of safety of women by enforcing strict rules only for men. It is this that Berger and Luckmann refer to as internalization that can be seen in the process of habitualization and institutionalization. Rules such as these give a sense of social order for the authorities and teachers and, to a certain extent, to the parents. They are assured that the university is not trying to bring in a change, rather it is perpetuating the same norms as dictated by society with regard to women with no attempt to bring about a change in the narrative.

CULTURAL CAPITAL: INCLUSIVE EDUCATION AND RESERVATION

Mannheim writes,

> From a sociological point of view, the decisive fact of the modern times in contrast with the situation during the middle ages, is that this monopoly of the ecclesiastical interpretation of the world which was held by the priestly class is broken and the place of a closed and thoroughly organized stratum of intellectuals a free intelligentsia has arisen. (Mannheim 1955, 10)

He further explains that education becomes a common bond between intellectuals, and this has the potential to overcome the differences that arise due to one's status, wealth and so on. But he also points that education cannot guarantee that all the differences will melt away due to education.

Education creates the grounds for cultural capital by endorsing certain forms of knowledge, behaviour, learning, mannerisms, clothing and so on. This is what distinguishes those who have had access to education from those who hadn't. In India, education was a medium of perpetuating status quo by limiting its access to certain groups of people, incidentally upper castes and upper class. Bourdieu spoke of cultural capital among the elite in France, but this could well be extended to not only the class but also the caste elites. In most cases, caste and class elites may overlap, but this may be true for the dominant castes and not necessarily in the traditional caste hierarchy. It has been established that post Independence, education became more accessible to the poor and was not just the privilege of the dominant castes. With the changing nature of education from a status quoist system to an agency of social change, the composition of students on campus started changing over time. As Mannheim rightly points out that this does not imply that education does away with the inherent hierarchies in society instantly, but it does become a leveller of sorts.

The reader may recall Altbach's argument about the decline of student politics and activism due to the changing composition of students in the campus. But the way the fee hike situation is building up, it could reverse the trend. One of points of conflict that has emerged over the years has been discriminatory hostel rules. On being asked whether there has been any change in the caste/class/rural/urban composition of the campus, majority of the respondents said they don't know. But it is noteworthy that in all the campuses where research was conducted, at least two to four students remarked that the number of SC/ST students or rural students has gone down; also, the campus now has more rich and urban students. We will give more examples as we move on. In Gulbarga and OU, students said that there were fewer girls now. Else in other universities like DU, the general opinion was that there are fewer SC/ST and more rich students than before.

The teachers were asked similar questions but from the perspective of the changes in the composition of both faculty and students that have taken place over the last few years. The answers to this would be incomplete without a reference to the role of reservation in education. It may be pointed out here that enormous literature exists on reservation and caste representation in India, and this work does not intend to delve into that. What it seeks to do is to capture the observations of students and teachers about their colleagues and classrooms in terms of caste and place it in the context of cultural capital. There were certain universities where caste seemed to loom large over relationship with students and teachers and in recruitment. AU and BHU are two such examples. Faculty spoke of the caste divisions that exists in the campus and manifest in several ways in everyday life and interaction on campus.

In India, reservation in education and jobs was envisaged as one of the ways to overcome the differences. In the lines of Mannheim's vision but not necessarily influenced by it, education was seen as an agent of social change. In the introductory chapter, some of the ideas pertaining to education as an agency of social change have been discussed. Over the years, successive plans and expenditure on education have yielded some results. SC students' enrolment is 14.89 per cent of the total enrolment and the male–female ratio is more or less similar to the all categories. On the other hand, students belonging to ST category constitute only 5.53 per cent of the total student enrolment and the male–female ratio is similar to All Categories.[2] 36.34 per cent of the total students belong to OBC with 50.83 per cent of male OBC students. Estimated gross enrolment ratio (GER) for SCs is 23 per cent and for STs is 17.2 per cent. GER for male population at all-India level is 26.3 per cent, whereas for SC males it is 22.7 per cent and 17.9 per cent for ST males.[3] Similarly, GER for female population at all-India

---

[2] The AISHE, in its survey of 2018–2019, states that the total estimated student enrolment was 37,399,388, out of which nearly 51.36 per cent were male and rest 48.64 per cent were female students.

[3] Estimated GER in higher education in India is 26.3 per cent, which is calculated for 18–23 years of age group.

level is 26.4 per cent, whereas for SC females, it is 23.3 per cent and for ST females, it is 16.5 per cent. While considerable progress has been made in making education system inclusive, but STs representation has a long way to go.

Tables 4.1 and 4.2 give a quick overview of the growing literacy rate among the SCs and STs.

On the teachers' front, at All-India level, teachers belonging to the General category are more than half, that is, 56.7 per cent of the total number of teachers in India; OBC follows with 32.1 per cent; while SC and ST with 8.8 per cent and 2.36 per cent, respectively. About 5.4 per cent teachers come from Muslim minority group and 9.2 per cent are 20 from other minority groups.[4] The student composition has seen a considerable change in comparison to the faculty positions. Of course, the faculty positions are limited and fewer in number.

In the field, the students were asked whether they felt that the composition of the campus is changing. In almost all the universities, out of 20 students, at least 4 or 5 students mentioned that the campus is now more urban, rich and there are fewer SCs and STs. Similar question was posed to the teachers about their observations regarding the changing caste composition of students in the classroom and faculty. The teachers were also asked about their opinion on reservation and how it has impacted education according to them. The notes from the field are substantiated with data from annual reports of as many universities as was available in the common domain (data was unavailable for universities like Punjab, Guwahati, Bangalore, Calicut and SPPU). The number of General, OBC, SC and ST teachers in the universities is based on an answer to a parliamentary question on the central university caste data.

---

[4] Among various levels of posts, majority of teachers are of the level of assistant professor, followed by associate professor. The number of total teachers at university level is around 1.90 lakh, out of which 63.35 per cent are males and 36.65 per cent are females. At college level, the number of teachers is 10.72 lakh with 56.81 per cent male teachers.

Table 4.1 Literacy Rate for SCs

Year	Rural			Urban			Combined		
	Female	Male	Total	Female	Male	Total	Female	Male	Total
1961	2.52	15.06	8.89	10.04	32.21	21.81	3.29	16.96	10.27
1971	5.06	20.04	12.77	16.09	38.93	28.65	6.44	22.36	14.67
1981	8.45	27.91	18.48	24.34	47.54	36.60	10.93	31.12	21.38
1991	19.45	45.95	33.25	42.29	66.90	55.11	23.76	49.91	37.41
2001	37.84	63.66	51.16	57.49	77.93	68.12	41.90	54.69	34.76
2011	52.60	72.60	62.80	68.60	83.30	76.20	56.50	75.20	66.10
% increase (2001–2011)	39	14	23	19	7	12	35	38	90

Source: Ministry of Statistics and Programme Implementation, http://mospi.nic.in/sites/default/files/reports_and_publication/statistical_publication/social_statistics/WM17Chapter3.pdf, Pg 48; mospi.nic.in.

Table 4.2 Literacy Rates for STs

Year	Rural			Urban			Combined		
	Female	Male	Total	Female	Male	Total	Female	Male	Total
1961	2.90	13.37	8.16	13.45	37.09	22.41	3.16	13.83	8.53
1971	4.36	16.92	10.68	19.64	37.09	28.84	4.85	17.63	11.30
1981	6.81	22.94	14.92	27.32	47.60	37.93	8.04	24.52	16.35
1991	16.02	38.45	27.38	45.66	66.56	56.60	18.19	40.65	29.60
2001	32.44	57.39	45.02	59.87	77.77	69.09	34.76	59.17	47.10
2011	46.90	66.80	56.90	70.30	83.20	76.80	49.35	68.53	58.96
% increase 2001–2011	44.57	16.40	26.39	17.42	6.98	11.16	41.97	15.82	25.18

Source: Ministry of Statistics and Programme Implementation, http://mospi.nic.in/sites/default/files/reports_and_publication/statistical_publication/social_statistics/WM17Chapter3.pdf, Pg 48; mospi.nic.in.

Central University Data on Teachers' Posts

Name of University	Category of Staff	General			OBC			SC			ST		
		Sanctioned Posts	Existing Posts	Vacant Posts	Sanctioned Posts	Existing Posts	Vacant Posts	Sanctioned Posts	Existing Posts	Vacant Posts	Sanctioned Posts	Existing Posts	Vacant Posts
DU	Professsor	198	105	93	0	0	0	39	3	36	19	1	18
DU	Associate	484	235	249	0	0	0	97	8	89	48	2	46
DU	Assistant	379	276	103	214	42	172	119	55	64	59	24	35
Jamia Millia Islamia	Professsor	125	73	52	0	0	0	1	1	0	0	0	0
Jamia Millia Islamia	Associate	200	165	35	0	0	0	0	0	0	0	0	0
Jamia Millia Islamia	Assistant	407	372	35	0	0	0	67	67	0	20	20	0
JNU	Professsor	148	85	63	0	0	0	29	11	18	14	0	14
JNU	Associate	274	215	59	0	0	0	54	17	37	27	5	22
JNU	Assistant	161	163	-2	90	31	59	50	31	19	25	12	13
Pondicherry University	Professsor	53	24	29	0	0	0	9	1	8	4	0	4
Pondicherry University	Associate	109	79	30	0	0	0	21	15	6	10	0	10

Pondicherry University	Assistant	161	141	20	46	34	12	41	33	8	20	17	3
BHU	Professsor	194	136	58	0	0	0	37	2	35	18	0	
BHU	Associate	404	335	69	0	0	0	76	13	63	37	1	
BHU	Assistant	572	608	-36	305	107	198	170	131	39	85	49	
AU	Professsor	60	12	48	0	0	0	11	0	11	5	0	
AU	Associate	150	40	110	0	0	0	30	1	29	15	0	
AU	Assistant	275	179	96	154	36	118	85	25	60	42	7	
Central University of Kashmir	Professsor	17	8	9	0	0	0	3	0	3	1	0	
Central University of Kashmir	Associate	32	3	29	0	0	0	6	0	6	3	0	
Central University of Kashmir	Assistant	46	29	17	24	11	13	13	9	4	6	4	
Central University of Punjab	Professsor	17	6	11	0	0	0	3	0	3	1	0	
Central University of Punjab	Associate	32	17	15	0	0	0	6	0	6	3	0	

Name of University	Category of Staff	General			OBC			SC			ST		
		Sanctioned Posts	Existing Posts	Vacant Posts	Sanctioned Posts	Existing Posts	Vacant Posts	Sanctioned Posts	Existing Posts	Vacant Posts	Sanctioned Posts	Existing Posts	Vacant Posts
Central University of Punjab	Assistant	42	39	3	22	14	8	12	12	0	6	2	
NEHU	Professsor	83	48	35	0	0	0	6	1	5	3	1	
NEHU	Associate	130	85	45	0	0	0	10	1	9	6	5	
NEHU	Assistant	141	131	10	21	19	2	25	21	4	16	15	
Central University of Tamil Nadu	Professor	18	6	12	0	0	0	3	0	3	1	0	
Central University of Tamil Nadu	Associate	37	14	23	0	0	0	7	0	7	4	0	
Central University of Tamil Nadu	Assistant	47	22	25	26	10	16	14	7	7	7	2	

Source: Ministry of Human Resource Development, Lok Sabha, Starred Question 212, answered on 8 July 2019, 'Central Universities: Caste Details and Vacancies'. Question by Nihal Chand Chauhan and Prabhubhai Nagarbhai Vasava, reply by Shri Ramesh Pohkriyal Nishank. http://loksabhaph.nic.in/Questions/questionlist.aspx (accessed on 17 June 2021).

Table 4.3 *Composition of Students: Periyar University*

Year	General	OBC	ST	SC	Physically Handicapped (PH)	Total	Male	Female
2017–2018	97	1,568	39	409	3	2,113	777	1,336
2016–2017	60	1,327	31	418		1,836		
2014–2015	34	383	11	172		1,136		

Source: Periyar University Website (UG and PG).

1. Periyar University

The data on student composition in Periyar University clearly shows that OBCs and SCs are in considerable number, in fact more than the General students. There has been a steady increase in students from OBC and SC since 2017, much more than the increase in General and ST (Table 4.3).

2. Pondicherry University

The data released by Pondicherry University shows a considerable increase in the number of OBC and SC students, but majority of the students seem to be General students. However, the gap between the number of General students, Scheduled castes and OBC continues to be substantial when analysed from the perspective of admissions per year (see Table 4.5A). From a cumulative perspective, as Table 4.5B suggests, the gap between the number of students from SC/ST communities and the General/OBC students is wider. The number of physically handicapped students is also higher in Pondicherry University in comparison to other universities mentioned in this section. Even among the faculty, there has been a huge jump in the number of SC and ST teachers (see Table 4.6). When asked about the same, most of the teachers said that it was representative faculty, while one said it consisted largely of SC/ST/OBC. Among the science teachers who were interviewed, one of the teachers belonged to the SC category and expressed unhappiness with the current situation. He came in through reservation but has not been promoted as per UGC rules. He also added that there is no proper representation for SC/ST as the roster system is not followed. The two SC teachers interviewed were unhappy with the situation in the university. They said they needed

Table 4.4 *Composition of Students: Pondicherry University*

	2006–2007	2007–2008	2008–2009	2009–2010	2010–2011
ST	28	36	61	75	131 (5%)
OBC		311	632	775	860 (32%)
SC	171	208	324	356	453 (17%)

Source: Pondicherry University, 25th year Annual Report.

Table 4.5A *Pondicherry University: Students Strength (Admitted) for 2017–2018; Courses: Ph.D./M.Tech./M.A/M.Sc/M.Sc (Int)/M.B.A/M.C.A/ Others*

Year	General	OBC	ST	SC	Ph	Foreign Students (FS)	Total
2017–2018	1,264	740	187	375	57	8	2,631

Source: Pondicherry University Website, pondiuni.edu.in, https://www.pondiuni.edu.in/wp-content/uploads/2020/05/32-Annual-Report-2017-18-English.pdf, Pg 2.

Table 4.5B *Pondicherry University: Students Strength (on the Rolls) for 2017–2018; Courses: Ph.D./M.Tech./M.A/M.Sc/M.Sc (Int)/M.B.A/M.C.A/ Others*

Year	General	OBC	SC	ST	Ph	Foreign Students (FS)	Total
2017–2018	2,648	2,336	894	402	63	26	6,353

Source: https://www.pondiuni.edu.in/wp-content/uploads/2020/05/32-Annual-Report-2017-18-English.pdf

an SC/ST cell, as they were victims of a sort of untouchability; they were not being given promotion on time; for some, even confirmation letters were delayed if they were SC/ST (Table 4.4).

The teachers in Pondicherry University agreed that the student community in the university was representative of all groups. One said that while all caste groups were there, but it was more urban. Opinions were mixed on whether reservation had a role to play in making education more inclusive, thus, leading to a diverse student population. As in many universities, teachers said that low-cost education is responsible for making education inclusive rather than reservation. Others pointed that sometimes UGC rules are not being followed during admission.

Table 4.6 Faculty Profile—Pondicherry University

Category	Total		SC		ST		Women	
	2016–2017	2015–2016	2016–2017	2015–2016	2016–2017	2015–2016	2016–2017	2015–2016
Professor	82	66	12	6	0	0	12	10
Associate	80	98	17	22	0	0	21	25
Assistant	195	199	30	31	18	18	65	65
Total	357	363	59	59	18	18	98	100

Source: Pondicherry University Annual Reports: 2015–2017.

Another said, 'Yes, but reservation is for namesake only; most of the SC/ST students are not getting any government scholarships, so their education is discontinued.' Some felt that merely caste-based reservation will not help; other kind of support also needs to be provided.

3. BHU

One may recall that teachers in BHU and AU felt that the faculty has strong caste associations even though it may not be overt. The student composition data of BHU shows that General category students are in the majority and the intake of SC/ST students has improved but marginally. According to a professor in Sciences in BHU, there has been a considerable change in student composition. 'Yes. Because now you see students from SCs and STs who are doing much better, if you compare it from 15 years ago, when representation was very less. These students are competing and doing very nice. Some are even topping the class.'

In both humanities and sciences, teachers in BHU agreed that the students were now representative of caste and class. But the representation of faculty opinion was divided. Those from SC and OBC communities felt that it was not representative of all castes, with some departments having not more than one or two faculty from the OBC or SC/ST community. Similarly, in sciences, while most teachers said that there is caste representation in faculty, one disagreed and remarked he is the only OBC and others are General (Table 4.7).

About reservation, in humanities, most of the teachers in BHU said that reservation made education more inclusive. One said that the reservation has led to a diverse classroom in terms of caste and class. 'Indeed, reservation is must. It always provides a level playing field as great enabler.' Another pointed that reservation has made education

Table 4.7 *Composition of Students: BHU*

Year	General	OBC	ST	SC	Total	Male	Female
2017–2018	15,270	9,603	1,556	3,912	30,828	19,186	11,639
2016–2017	15,391	9,859	1,559	3,861	31,201		
2011–2012	13,375	7,545	1,379	3,644	27,223		

Source: BHU Annual Reports: 2016–2018 (across all courses).

more inclusive, there is no denying. But he added that 'although questions can be raised about the process and how it should not benefit more than one generation, but reservation as a whole cannot be denied.'

Even among sciences, representation of different caste has increased in the past 10 years. Another teacher added, 'In our department, we have people from all castes. It can be seen that people from OBC are coming in large numbers which was less before. Minorities are less in higher education. There are many reasons for that. Reservation is one which is bringing people who were on margin to the forefront.'

4. AU

In AU, teachers agreed that the student community was more representative of all caste groups than the teachers. Reservation was to be credited in making the student community diverse and inclusive. But like in BHU, in AU, some of the faculty hinted at friendships or groupism in the faculty on the basis of caste; there was also a preference for students belonging to the same caste as the teachers (Table 4.8).

As with most universities, among caste groups, STs are the least in number among both students and faculty. In AU, the composition was different from that of BHU with OBC dominating in numbers. The overall opinion was that post reservation, there was representation across castes among the faculty. But a few teachers mentioned that in spite of recruitment, many teachers belonging to the SC/ST category left their jobs for better prospects. At least two teachers mentioned that even though faculty was being recruited on the basis of caste, several of them decided to quit soon after. The underlying tone being that the lack of representation was not due to the recruitment process but because of several SC/ST teachers opting out.

Table 4.8 *Composition of Students: AU*

Year	General	OBC	ST	SC	Total	Male	Female
2018–2019	7,154	10,004	459	4,533	22,150	14,933	7,217
2017–2018	7,159	10,009	459	4,535	22,162	14,983	7,179
2016–2017	7,676	10,665	514	4,851	23,703	17,099	6,604

Source: Allahabad University Annual Reports: 2016–2019 (across all courses)

In the sciences too, majority of teachers in AU agreed that reservation has helped make education inclusive. Apart from reservation, low-cost education and scholarship for low-income category groups were instrumental in making education inclusive. In both BHU and AU, caste seemed to be a big factor. In AU, one teacher mentioned that while many may not accept but some teachers do look at students from the caste lens, though they maintain a 'secular look outwardly'.

5. OU

In a shift from the trend of admissions in other universities, Osmania University shows a higher number of admissions of students from SC and STs communities (see Table 4.9). In the other universities covered in this study, number of admissions of SC/ST students is limited to say 300–400 students. In contrast, Osmania University has admitted about 2000 scheduled castes students. Secondly, in contrast to the trend in other universities covered in this study, the OBC students outnumber the General students. The number of ST students also is substantially higher in comparison to other universities but continues to be under represented. If one looks at the larger picture of the caste wise student representation in universities, OU breaks the norms in several ways. In OU, teachers agreed that the faculty is representative of caste. But there was no consensus on the timelines; some suggested that OU had always been inclusive while others said it has happened in the past few years due to reservation. With regard to students, most teachers said that there is adequate presentation from all groups; only one teacher mentioned that certain tribes are not represented like the Chenchus. In most universities, STs (other than in NEHU) were least represented among students and teachers. A science teacher in OU remarked, 'Up to year 2000, more of other castes were taking admission. After 2000,

Table 4.9 *Composition of Students: OU*

Year	General	SC	ST	OBC	Ph	Total
2016–2017	3,093	2,105	876	5,476	69	11,619
2015–2016	3,169	2,157	898	5,611	69	11,904

Source: Osmania University Annual Reports: 2015–2017.

more from backward castes are taking admission. Composition of other castes has decreased. This may be due to the diversified courses they are choosing.'

The science teachers were clearly not in favour of reservation, but it found a few supporters from among the humanities faculty. A teacher said that it is because of reservation that more Muslim students could come in through OBC quota. With regard to faculty both in sciences and humanities, it felt that the faculty is representative of all caste members. Those against reservation remarked that merit is more important than reservation. Those in favour of it said that it made education more inclusive, and those against it mentioned that it was benefitting the same set of people and that it was not reaching out to other people who need it. 'Is reservation at all necessary for the education system? People who have taken advantage of reservation are also encouraging their children to use it.'

6. DU

In DU, teachers agreed that reservation did bring in students from across castes; however, merely reservation is not enough. This was pointed in some other universities where teachers mentioned that scholarship and other kind of help is necessary for the students who come in through reservation. Often, the lack of help leads to students dropping out after admission. A senior professor remarked that while it is a matter of great pride that DU has students coming in across castes, classes and regions, it is troubling that the collapse of State universities puts pressure on DU and JNU as the only options. She also said that the State is failing those students who are unable to get into universities of quality if they do not get admission in DU. She said we need to ask where these students go (Table 4.10).

Table 4.10 *SC/ST Intake: DU*

Year	ST	SC
2016–2017	8,641	31,707

Source: Delhi University Annual Reports: 2016–2017 (for UG, PG and PhD courses).

A senior professor explained in great detail, 'With time, the situation has become better. SC/ST reservation started in 1997 and OBC started in 2007. The UGC guideline of treating the entire university as a unit when it comes to reservation was implemented as late as 2013. We, at Delhi University Teachers' Association, fought for it. We also fought against the statement by UGC chairman to treat department as a unit. With 200-point roster, we are confident that the situation is bound to improve. On the whole, we are representative at least at the assistant professor level. At associate and professor level, we still have a lot of ground to cover.' DU has one of the highest intakes of SC students. Some of the teachers in DU felt that the faculty is largely upper caste.

7. Jadavpur University (JU)

The JU data suggests that General and OBCs are in majority, but the number of SC students has almost doubled. One may also note, JU is one of the few universities with more number of STs than SCs. Both science and humanities faculty said students are from across caste and class groups (Table 4.11).

In JU (sciences), on the question of how reservation has helped in education, the question of merit came up. Most teachers spoke in favour of reservation. One of the teachers remarked that discrimination did take place in West Bengal against backward classes (meant caste), while another said that reservation is necessary for compensation to the backward caste, it should be seen as their due. But there should be other ways other than reservation.

8. NEHU

In NEHU, the teachers had a lot to say about the student and faculty composition. Regional caste composition played an important role in determining the student composition. NEHU saw a reversal in the

Table 4.11 *Composition of Students: JU*

Year	General	OBC	ST	SC	Ph	Total	Male	Female
2016–2017	7,359	2,240	452	412	134	10,463	7,302	3,161
2015–2016	7,580	2,300	482	223	149	10,734		

Source: IQAC, Jadavpur University 2017 (across all courses).

Table 4.12 *Composition of Students: NEHU*

Year	Gen	OBC	ST	SC	Total	Male	Female
2017–2018	1,090	159	3,686	192	5,127	2,278	2,849
2013–2014	1,056	207	3,396	197	4,856	2,212	2,644

Source: NEHU Annual Reports: 2013–2014 and 2017–2018 (across all courses).

trend observed so far in other universities with regard to the faculty. In NEHU, the faculty is more representative of caste, class and region than the students. 'One teacher remarked that the faculty is more representative class wise. This mixture is new; earlier, it was mostly upper class; gradually, other sections also came.' The students in the university were from the home state or nearby states, mostly from Northeast (Table 4.12).

A senior professor pointed out, 'There is a good population from all regions in terms of teachers. There is also mixture of different caste and class groups. But students now are mostly from Northeast. The ratio between girls and boys is also uneven. The number of girls is higher than boys to a great extent.'

In the context of other questions too, some of the teachers spoke of regional politics and conflict being played out on campus. There is a pressure to appoint locals or press for some appointments. As a result, the faculty is less diverse than earlier, but not all the demands regarding appointment are heeded to. Those who have studied in the state or nearby (in Northeast) prefer to come to NEHU. But in spite of all this, the representation of faculty is good as it is across caste, class and region.

In NEHU, a professor of biochemistry said that while the department is a good mix of all caste groups, the reservation policy has not helped in this regard. He pointed that in NEHU, local recruitment has meant majority of ST and some SC. The presence of OBC and General categories has gone down. He felt that 50 per cent reservation is too much and it is depriving General caste category candidates of jobs. This, he felt, was not particular to NEHU but all over the country. A chemistry professor said that the caste presentation among teachers in NEHU is the best, other than, probably, Hyderabad. (All teachers said that NEHU has a good representation of teachers across caste groups, but certain caste groups were losing out.)

With regard to representation of students, teachers were happy about the increasing number of girls in the university and agreed that NEHU is very inclusive. But almost all the teachers said that most of the students were from Northeast; thus, representation from Northeast has increased but lacks diversity from outside the regions. This was because of a rule made. 'More than 10 years ago, it was made a rule that the students of NEHU get an additional 15 points. The 15 points was later reduced to 10 points. Therefore, it becomes very difficult for the students from outside NEHU to make through the entrance.' A few more teachers also pointed out to this point system which builds in a preference for students from the Northeast region. According to a professor, the quality of the students and thereby the reputation of the university has also improved over the years. Several students studied in JNU and have come back to NEHU. Students who have passed out from the university are doing very well, thus, adding to the reputation of the university.

Reservation has had different implications in NEHU. A senior professor said, 'Yes, reservations definitely played an important role and a step forward. In fact, NEHU also gives quota to the people of regions whose literacy rate is below the national average. That way, the people (students) from very poor and weak backgrounds can also come to the university. Also, things in Northeast is much about tribes issue rather than caste. But students from all different tribes of Northeast are present in the campus. If there is no reservation, Kanhaiya would not reach where he is.' NEHU is an example of how admission criteria can block out certain communities from accessing education.

In the context of reservation, a professor in NEHU said, 'Reservation did good, but it only allowed people to enter. From there onwards, they have not been taken care of. We still need to take care of people from remote areas. Another reason of inclusivity is low-cost education, but that is in limited courses and colleges and the competition is high.' Not only in NEHU, similar opinions were expressed by professors in other universities. Another associate professor added, 'University in hill areas cannot be that inclusive. Within the Northeast, the groups are all represented but not outside because the reservation is 50 per cent here. Now, ST students also come in the General category; hence, 97 per cent of students are ST, hardly anyone is General or OBC.' The idea of a limited number of people benefitting from reservation came up here, too, along with the issue of merit and quality. According to an associate professor, while reservation has helped in education, only certain groups have benefitted from it. He also pointed that many of the students who have got through SC/ST quota are actually General category students. A suggestion for economic criteria for reservation came in from many science faculties across universities.

According to one professor in the science faculty, reservation for students from SCs and OBCs were losing out as they were put in the same block as STs; instead they should be given a different quota. He added that reservation is very important, and it has made education more inclusive and people more aware. We may recall here that many Bangalore University professors were in favour of reservation on economic grounds rather than caste. This has been a very popular stand especially among the upper castes, who challenge the notion that all upper castes are also upper class. Teachers credited increasing the number of universities and low-cost education for creating a more inclusive education. As one associate professor pointed out, while reservation has made education inclusive, this may be undone by privatization of education (Table 4.13).

9. Jamia Millia Islamia
Jamia Millia Islamia is probably one of the few universities with a high intake of Muslim students. But it needs to be noted that the number of Muslim women is far less in comparison to women from other religion.

10. Gulbarga University
Data on student composition was not available on the Gulbarga University website. However, quality assessment report states that there are violations made in the admission and reservation procedure in colleges under Gulbarga University. Twelve colleges converted unfulfilled reserved seats to management quota. Many colleges have not followed reservation procedures under 370(J), the 50 per cent quota by admitting more out-of-state students. Some colleges have admitted students even after the date mentioned in the circular.

Table 4.13 Composition of Students: Jamia Millia Islamia

Year	General		Muslim			Ph		M-OBC		Total		
	M	F	M	F	MW	M	F	M	F	M	F	T
2017–2018	2,669	1,303	1,681	467	748	77	24	647	146	5,074	2,688	7,762

MW: Muslim Women
M-OBC: Muslim OBC
Source: Jamia Millia Islamia.

One may recall that teachers in Gulbarga University spoke of caste being a divisive factor among the faculty. When asked about the role of reservation in education and the changing composition of the classroom, teachers said that reservation has played an important role in building a more inclusive education system. While another teacher from the women's studies department pointed out that more rural students have joined in the university. It was observed from the background details of some professors (including guest lecturers) that some came in from a rural background and were now teaching at Gulbarga.

A senior professor, who has been teaching since 1987, also said that the faculty consists of teachers across different caste groups. She mentioned that all caste groups are given admission as per the roster system. This was mentioned by teachers in other universities too. She said that while she was not against the reservation as such, but she felt that it has pulled down the standards of education. She said that over the years, the number of SC/ST and OBC students has increased in the classrooms. According to an associate professor (education department), the number of SCs has increased in the faculty over the past few years.

11. Calicut University

In Calicut, one of the teachers interviewed identified himself not only as an assistant professor but also a Dalit activist. This was the first time during the course of the research that a teacher had openly identified himself as an activist. He made an interesting point when he said that education also creates barriers—gender, caste and class barriers. He said that although systemic changes have been made, it has not yielded adequate results, and as a result, the faculty is not representative of all caste groups. According to him, 'Reservation is a reason, but also economic stability.' As per another assistant professor, who is a guest lecturer, reservation has played an important role in ensuring representation of different castes in classroom and faculty, but STs lack representation in the faculty. An associate professor, too, said that apart from reservation, scholarship and increase in number of colleges has made education more accessible. He said that in the past few years, more students are coming in from backward classes and regions. Overall, the teachers felt that there are adequate caste and class representation among both students and teachers.

12. Bangalore University

In Bangalore University, both science and humanities professors said that the faculty and student community is representative of all caste groups and reservation has played an important role in this. While some said it has always been so, others said it is a recent phenomenon; there were some complaints of increasing casteism among faculty. Professors of political science and history said that reservation is very necessary in education and more so for girl students. She said that the caste composition is a recent phenomenon post 1994 after the SC/ST recruitments were made. Reservation has broken barriers of caste; education, too, in turn has brought in change. The teacher here implied that education too has brought in social mobility.

In Bangalore University (sciences), a few teachers expressed that a class-based reservation is more beneficial than caste based. Several teachers in IIT and NIT also spoke of merit. A professor in Bangalore University expressed the opinion that reservation is not important in education, nor has it led to building a more exclusive education system. She felt that it was better if poor students were given opportunity to study. Another guest lecturer also mentioned the need for scholarship beyond caste as all groups have poor people. Apart from reservation, low-cost education can create an inclusive society was a common view.

The roster system was mentioned in several universities, and here too, two of the teachers said that the roster system, which is being followed strictly, ensures that different caste groups get a chance. He said that faculty was a mix of different castes, and he credited the roster system for this. He supported reservation and said that it was necessary in education but added a cryptic statement, 'The importance of it is known by giving reservation to upper caste.' This roster system is under the scanner now; a more detailed discussion will ensue later in the chapter.

13. JNU

In JNU, which is known for its class, caste and regional representation, the low-cost fee structure has played a key role in making education inclusive. Apart from this, the unique deprivation point system where students are given extra points during the entrance exams—for gender, and for those from backward regions—plays a key role. As a result, more number of women, especially from backward regions, get a chance to study in JNU. There is a talk of UGC scrapping the deprivation point system in JNU, which could disturb the balance that has been achieved in terms of the student composition. But as an assistant professor pointed out, 'Yes. For higher courses like MPhil and PhD, numbers of students are lower, and there have been accusations against faculty members for discrimination.'

With regard to the faculty, during the interviews, one of the teachers remarked, 'Overall, the representation in SC/ST as well as OBC category is very low in JNU. The fact sheets are available in the public domain of all the central universities, and JNU is not an exception in that case. It can be slightly better than DU and other universities, but number wise, it is a very insignificant number. For example, we have zero professors and associate professors. SC and ST have never crossed more than 4 per cent. So, it is definitely under-represented. OBC representation is minimal, and SC/ST representation is insignificant. There are multiple reasons for this.' He added that whatever increase there has been in representation has been in the past 10 years. A senior professor said that, 'Reservation does have a role here. There also has to be a conscious effort to make places more inclusive, through its structure. Inclusivity has actually led to excellence. There cannot be excellence without inclusivity. Excellence also does not have any link with privatization. If a public university is functioning well, the government wants to privatize them or to make them autonomous.'

14. Punjab University

In Punjab University, one of the teachers said that changes have crept in the past in last 12–13 years when the first reserved category teacher was appointed in 2001. Other than two teachers, all others said that the departments are representative. The one who disagreed said that there are fewer number of SC/ST, while another said, 'No, they are not representing the true multicultural society of India. Most are inborn, as their mothers and fathers were teachers here. You will hardly find any OBC, SC/ST teachers. This section of society is deprived of jobs in the university.' He said that this is how it has been from the very beginning. Not only among students is the idea of cultural capital applicable, but it is so even among teachers. Academics form a close-knit community with clear preferences for certain students, and many a times, children of professors get preference at interviews. The children, in turn, have a cultural understanding of the university system, recruitment and interviews in addition to the network which gives them an advantage over others.

While most of the teachers were not against the principle of reservation but said that now it goes against the General candidates. One of the oft-repeated arguments across universities was one that was benefitting only certain groups of people. There have been demands to include the creamy-layer concept among SC/STs like it is done for OBCs. Others have made the merit argument, and in certain universities, like NEHU, there is a demand for restructuring the reservation for STs. In Punjab University too, similar arguments were made with regard to creamy layer among SC/STs and the decreasing number of students from the General category. To give one such example, 'Yes, reservation does help the needy to join that educational race which might be difficult for them to enter. But it should be noted that the benefit of reservation goes only to needy, not to the creamy-layer people.'

In the sciences, the faculty composition differed from department to department. For example, the IT and electrical department teachers said that they do have a representative from all caste groups, but the forensic and library science department teachers said that it consists of teachers from the General category and one said that an SC post has been lying vacant. One of the assistant professors from forensic science said that while representation of SC/ST might be low, it better than what it was earlier; he had pointed out that there is no teacher belonging to the SC/ST/OBC community in his department.

Speaking of reservation making education accessible, quite a few teachers said yes, it has helped students. When further asked if the caste composition of students has changed, most teachers said yes, there has been a positive change with classrooms consisting of children from different caste groups and one added even religion, but most of the teachers said that they cannot say that it is representative of class. One teacher added that the cost of living and other expenditure is high, so it prevents poor students from joining.

According to a senior professor in Punjab University, 'No, reservation has only been a hurdle in the development of education system;

low cost of education and more alternatives can be attributed to improvement.' Similar thoughts were echoed by others. 'No, reservation is not helpful, low cost of education is a better way to make it inclusive.'

15. IIT Delhi

IIT Delhi teachers said that the faculty is not representative, especially because the SC/ST quota for the teachers does not apply. 'In all the old IITs, we have a few SC/STs,' a professor mentioned. One teacher added that sometimes, there is a special drive to include those from certain categories. There was a strong sentiment against reservation among teachers. The focus, most teachers said, should be on quality of education and not on reservation. The poor and underprivileged, irrespective of caste, should be given scholarships and free coaching. Some teachers pointed that those who come in through reservation are unable to cope up with the others and often drop out. He pointed out that students who come in through quota often drop out as they do not get adequate attention from teachers post their admission. There have been several instances of students speaking of discrimination against students who have come in through reservations. As one professor said, reservation can only help students get in but cannot prevent them from dropping out. An associate professor went so far as to say, 'Reservation has degraded the institution; all reservations should be removed.'

On student composition, a retired professor from IIT Delhi made a harsh statement, 'If looked deeply, the quality has only increased. Different sections have entered, but the deprived ones are still on the road selling stuff.' Most of the teachers said that there hasn't been any overwhelming change in the caste composition. Apart from those who come in through reservation, rest are all General category students. One teacher remarked, 'The quality of SC, ST is relatively lower than the General candidates.'

16. NIT Warangal, SPPU, IIT Chennai, NIT Kashmir, Guwahati University

In contrast to the teachers in IIT Delhi, IIT Chennai and NIT Kashmir, most of the teachers said that reservation has made education more inclusive. In NIT Kashmir, the teachers said that low-cost education and reservation both have attracted students towards education, thereby making it more inclusive. While in NIT Kashmir, the teachers said that the faculty is a good mix of different castes and communities, in IIT Chennai, the teachers gave credit to the systematic recruitment policy at IIT Chennai in particular. The responses indicated a lack of uniformity in the actual recruitment practices, inspite of a common policy on paper.

Similarly in NIT Warangal, on faculty being representative, all of them said yes, it is—one teacher even pointed that he is from OBC himself; another teacher said UGC rules are followed and it has been so for a while now. With regard to reservation, all the teachers supported the idea of reservation and said that it helped people access education. But here too, teachers mentioned increase in number of universities and low-cost education as a catalyst.

In SPPU, everyone agreed that reservation created a more inclusive education, and that the faculty is a representative of all castes. The teachers said that UGC norms were followed, which made faculty representative across castes. In Guwahati University too, an assistant professor commented on the lack of ST teachers, but apart from that, the faculty could be said to be a representative, and this is due to reservation. But another teacher added that the teachers are mostly upper class. Similar sentiments were echoed in Punjab University. A professor from Guwahati University said that the students in Guwahati University are representatives of caste and class. A number of factors have contributed to this—reservation, fee waiver, scholarships and also other socio-economic factors. These detailed points made from several universities were made to illustrate that it cannot be denied that reservation has ensured that those belonging to the marginalized communities (SC/ST/OBC) have an entry point into the education system. But this accessibility was aided not only by reservation but due to other factors too. A low-cost education model further made education accessible to thousands who otherwise would have been out of the education system, not only due to caste but also due to poverty. A few pointed out the changing socio-economic status which also helped families to get their children into the education system starting from the school level. It is interesting to note that the teachers spoke about how economic-social mobility has been one of the factors for more and more children and youth enrolling in education. This same argument of increasing ability to spend on education was used by the Birla–Ambani report to push for privatization of education. They argued that when people have the ability to pay, why shouldn't they? What they didn't understand is that people who had moved up the economic-social ladder could now afford what the public universities were charging; the jump has not been that drastic that they can pay for the kind of fees proposed by the report. In fact, the protests against the fee hikes that have taken place in several universities and institutes are a proof of this. All the achievements of the past could be undone with the current move to increase the fees in universities. This could offset the building of cultural capital that has been achieved through a combination of reservation, low-cost education and scholarships.

ISSUES IN RESERVATION AND RECRUITMENT: CURRENT CONTROVERSIES

Even a casual conversation with teachers, whether at the college level or university level, will tell of delayed promotions and payments, paperwork, internal assessments and so on. This is especially the case in colleges where teachers, who were recruited even while enrolled for their PhDs, are yet to get promoted to associate professors even after 15–20 years of teaching. This obviously means that they get the salary of an assistant professor even when they are in their 40s and should be associate professors and, in an ideal world, ready to get promoted to the next level. In addition to this are the ad hoc positions which are fraught with uncertainty, and several years may go by before permanent positions are offered to them. As reported in a news portal, teachers were caught unawares by the new UGC rule on reservation and in interviews with the reporter spoke of the mental trauma and hardships they have to go through which includes even postponing marriage or having children. Added to this is the new rule which denies pension to all those who have been recruited post 2014. In universities, the situation is slightly better, but promotions depend on publications and research work. During the course of the interviews, teachers pointed out their frustration with the new rules regarding publication and research.

One is the lack of opportunities in State universities and, second, the uncertainty of being given permanent positions. Added to their woes is the new rule on reservations. The implication of this could be both reverse social mobility for some and thereby closing down one of the avenues of social mobility for many others. When we speak of education as an agency of social change, reservation has played an important role by opening up education to those it was otherwise denied—the marginalized sections of society—and also creating job opportunities for the same groups. Teachers in several universities remarked that reservation has opened the door to education for many first-generation learners, thus, making education more inclusive. It is not the only reason but an important one.

None of the teachers, during the interviews, mentioned a recent rule by UGC which invited controversy and protests across universities. On the announcement of this rule, several teachers boycotted the evaluation of examination papers. The reservation for SCs and STs for faculty positions is 15 per cent and 7.5 per cent, respectively, and the recent AISHE report shows that the numbers from reserved category fall short of the sanctioned posts. As per a notification by UGC, all Centrally funded universities and State universities are to consider departments as a unit instead of the whole universities for recruiting teachers for reserved posts. This decision will adversely impact the number of SC, ST and OBC teachers recruited in universities. In BHU, the Centre has stated that the seats for SCs, STs and OBCs will be reduced by 50 per cent, 80 per cent and 30 per cent, respectively. Recruitment has been hit in several universities like JNU and *Indira Gandhi National Open University* (IGNOU), where number of posts have been left vacant, and also, the number of teachers recruited under the reservation policy has gone down drastically; like in IGNOU, from the seven seats that would have been filled in for SCs, there were none under the new rule.

For the faculty, too, reservation has been a point of contention. Data shows that the number of SC/ST and OBC at the associate professor and professor level are negligible. The roster system was mentioned by several teachers during the course of interviews as the reason why there was some representation across castes. But the government is now introducing a change in this system. As of now, the 200-point roster system is being followed; the government plans to replace it with a 13-point roster system. In simple terms, this means that instead of the university being a unit, the department is taken as a unit that implements the recruitment and reservation policy for teachers. Under the 200-point roster system, 99 seats were reserved for the SC, ST and OBC communities and 101 posts were for the unreserved. In case of a deficit of reserved seats in one department, it could be compensated by recruiting more teachers in other departments in the university from the reserved communities in the university. The 13-point roster system does not leave this scope since each department is treated as a unit.

According to the new system proposed, every first, second, third, fifth, and sixth posts will be unreserved in a department. The 7th post and 14th posts will be reserved for SCs and STs, respectively, and the 8th and 12th for OBCs. The 9th, 10th and 11th posts will be unreserved. The main problem here is that since several of the departments in many universities are very small, there may not be recruitment opportunities for those from the reserved communities. So, if a department has only five posts, there could be an opportunity for an OBC reservation (fourth post is reserved for OBC) but none for SC/ST. For the reservation system to be applied in totality, there needs to be at least 14 posts in the department. In BHU, this would mean a 30 per cent, 80 per cent and 50 per cent reduction in OBC, ST and SC teachers, respectively, as stated by the Centre, through its Special Leave Petition in the Supreme Court. Repercussions were seen in JNU, where only 600 out of 900 advertised posts could be filled. In Indira Gandhi National Tribal University, 52 posts for the teachers have been advertised, out of which, only 1 was reserved for the OBC category and none for SC/ST as per new policy. Recruitment on the basis of old norms would have meant that OBC, SC and ST would have got 14 seats, 7 seats and 4 seats, respectively. The protests from students and teachers are on the grounds that this would take back the education system to being controlled by dominant castes.

Giroux points, in reference to cultural capital, that educational institutes 'reproduce the dominant society and also as sites where the culture of the dominant society is learned and where students express the differences between those status and class distinctions that that exist in larger society.' (Giroux 1998, 5–6) The suicide of Rohit Vemula was a pointer at the caste discrimination of the society, which was played out in the university as well. Giroux further points out that the traditional idea of an educational institute is that of reproduction of knowledge based on ideas of a common culture, that is passed down and consumed by students. He writes that the class divisions in society are, therefore, ignored and not questioned (in the case of India, class and caste divisions). 'Teachers and those interested in education must come to understand how the dominant culture functions at all levels of schooling to disconfirm the cultural experiences of the excluded minorities. Teachers should examine their own cultural capital and how it either benefits or victimized students' (Giroux 1998, 7). He is of the view and correctly so that the teachers need to be aware of how class, gender and race impact their thinking and action.

Those from OBC or SC/ST background themselves speak of caste-based discrimination, as seen in BHU, AU and Pondicherry University. On the other spectrum, there have been instances of teachers who said they have never thought of reservation or even looked at the faculty from the angle of reservation. This was an indicator of how the teachers were isolated from each other and from the larger debates of education or, at least, would like to be so. Of course, one cannot rule out the possibility of teachers presenting a non-casteist image during the interview. This again brings to mind what Jane Elliot pointed that several White people tend to say that they don't 'see' colour (in human beings, not otherwise). She says this is just a denial or just pretending to oneself; the truth is that everyone has a view about people who are 'different'. Colour is as apparent as height or gender. Similarly, teachers remark they are not aware of caste of teachers but the surnames of teachers and students may give an indication of the caste. Sometimes, the teachers are well aware of the teachers and students who have come in through reservation. Ending on a positive note, teachers in most universities categorically denied that caste influenced their relationship with other teachers or with students.

Issues in Higher Education

If one were to put together books and articles written on issues facing higher education in India, it would fill up libraries. In that respect, a review of literature of the same would be a tough task and, at the same time, merely repetitive of what several academicians have already expressed. Issues facing higher education was a conversation point in the interviews held with teachers, but not the central one due to the very reason mentioned above. But no research on higher education can ignore this aspect. The teachers were asked what, according to them, were the recurring and the new problems facing higher education. There is extensive literature on recurring problems, and while new problems are emerging, old ones refuse to go away. The oft-repeated issues plaguing higher education are lack of funds, which impact infrastructure, research and salaries. These are concerns not only in India but in most of the developing countries in Asia, Africa and Latin America. After an initial burst of development in the education sector, most of the developing countries witnessed a decline in quality in teaching and infrastructure, inadequate staffing, lack of facilities for students, libraries and equipment (Salmi 1992). In India, the 1950s and a few decades there on saw adequate growth of universities across regions. It was towards the late 1980s and 1990s that the State started withdrawing from the education sector, leaving the space for private sector to stake claim. This brought with it increasing privatization of education and, consequently, higher cost of education, increase in self-financing courses and seats. All this further led to limiting access to education.

At the time of Independence, there were barely 3 universities, 17 State universities and about 500 colleges. As per the *MHRD–AISHE*

Report for 2018–2019, there are now 799 universities and 39,071 colleges. India has 307 universities in rural areas alone. It cannot be denied that this is a considerable progress, considering that at the time of Independence, and thereafter, the nation had scarce economic resources, troubled relations with neighbours and barely any infrastructure to speak of. However, the expenditure on education has not reached the desired levels. In comparison to developed countries, the percentage expenditure on education in India in relation to the gross domestic product (GDP) increased from 1 per cent in 1951–1952 to around 4 per cent since 2000. The percentage expenditure of GDP on higher education in 2018–2019 was around 1.47.[1] The GER in higher education is 34.6 million with 18.6 million boys and 16 million girls. But the GER is at 20.4, which is nowhere near to the percentage of children in higher education in developed countries, say, for example, France and the UK.

With literacy being a concern at the time of Independence, it was important to draft out a vision of education that was inclusive of all sections of society. The Indian system of education differentiated between primary education and higher (collegiate education) since 1882. While the government was responsible for primary education, higher education (college and universities) was to be largely private aided. It was during the national movement that the idea of a national system of education was proposed. The British government had issued orders that students should refrain from participating in any antigovernment activities, political meetings, demonstrations and antipartition movements. The Indian National Congress at this juncture came up with a resolution that they would set up a national system of education which would promote, 'literary, scientific and technical education suited for the requirements of the country, on national lines under national control and directed towards recognising a national destiny' (Ayyar 2017).

---

[1] 2.33 per cent in 1972–1973, declining to 2.15 per cent in 1973–1974, increasing to 3.07 per cent in 1979–1980, declining to 2.83 per cent in 1981–1982 and hovering around 4 per cent between 2000 and 2005. The expenditure on university and higher education to GDP has not been impressive too. It declined from 0.77 per cent in 1990–1991 to 0.62 per cent in 1997–1998 and 0.37 per cent in 2003–2004 (Das 2007, 53).

Back in 1944, the *Sargent Report* on the status of education recommended that the Central government should take over more of the financial responsibility of universities and professional education. It was the very same *Sargent Report* which suggested that the Central Indian UGC be set up, which would function as a regulatory body for all the universities. However, the report also states clearly that the UGC should not interfere in the autonomy of the provincial universities. Based on this, the UGC was set up through an executive order passed in 1945. Similar suggestions were made regarding technical universities, following which the All India Council for Technical Education (AICTE) was set up in 1946 to 'stimulate, coordinate, control the provisions of the technical education facilities' (*Sargent Committee Reports*, 93).

Several subsequent reports, post Independence, pointed out the need for quality of education and access to education, especially in the rural and semi-urban areas. Radhakrishnan Commission was the first commission to be set up after Independence under the chairmanship of Dr S. Radhakrishnan, the eminent educationist who later became president of India. Control of education was a matter of much debate, whether it was to be included in the Union or State List. The states were not ready to concede to the demand of the Centre to make education a Union subject. The result of series of debates and discussion was that education was placed in the Concurrent List, which would ensure that the states ensure a minimum standard of education and, at the same time, there would be joint collaboration with the Centre with regard to policies and addressing gaps and preventing duplication. It was this commission which gave the UGC power to allocate grant within limits, rather than going through the circuitous route of submitting proposals to the Finance Ministry for approval. It was a result of the recommendation of the Radhakrishnan Committee that the UGC was reconstituted as a statutory body in 1956.

Maulana Abul Kalam Azad, Minister of Education, was in favour of education being added to the Union List, as he was of the opinion that there should be uniformity in how the intellectuals think, and this could be achieved if the Centre was in charge of education. He also wanted that the Centre be in charge of planning and standard of education. But this idea was opposed by the states. The result of the discussion was that the Central universities and research institutes were placed in the Union List. The Union was also in charge of maintaining standard of higher education and oversee the performance of the states with regard to education.

In 1966, the Kothari Commission suggested that India should spend at least 6 per cent of the GDP on education. It was between 1950–1951 and 1965–1966 that the number of universities and technical institutes saw a visible jump. It was during this time that the All India Institute Of Medical Science, IITs and Regional Engineering College (RECs) were established. The universities increased from 27 to 64; the number of art and science colleges increased from 370 to 1,536; enrolment in higher education and professional education increased to 13 lakhs from 3.6 lakhs. Over the years, the number of institutions and universities increased, but this came at a cost—that of quality. In his work titled *The History of Education Policy Making in India: 1946–2016,* Ayyar (2017) writes that Central and State government policies are meant to ensure equal access to education. According to Ayyar, the idea of free and compulsory primary education may be hard to achieve 'due to both administrative and financial reasons'.

In 1999, when Shri Atal Bihari Vajpayee was the prime minister, leading the then National Democratic Alliance government, the Prime Minister's Council on Trade and Industry established a Special Subject Group on Policy Framework for Private Investment in Education, Health and Rural Development. The report was given in April 2000. It submitted a *Report on a Policy Framework for Reforms in Education* written by Reliance Industries Limited chief Mukesh Ambani (convenor) and Aditya Birla Group head Kumar Mangalam Birla (member). Many of the reforms happening now are reminiscent of the recommendations of the *Ambani–Birla Report* presented two decades ago. The *Ambani–Birla Report* (2000) made a push for government investment in primary education but not higher education. The report speaks of 'investment' in market friendly and market-oriented courses. Maya John (2013) writes that the problem with involving corporates in education reform is that the recommendations are more aligned to the labour market and promote certain courses and specialization. These reports also pressurize the State to remove subsidies, change existing syllabi and system in a way that it facilitates early entry of students in the labour market. She further writes,

> Recommendations made by the several education commissions were to bridge gap between education and labour market. Indian state has come to purposively envisage and bring into force an education structure though which education can be easily diversified in response to the requirement of segmented job market. (John 2013, 52)

The reports showed that private education has doubled and was projected to become a 180 billion industry by 2020.

More and more private players are looking at education as a money-making venture and students as mere 'consumers'. Nandita Narain, Associate Professor at DU, said that report makes 'education not a right but a luxury.' John also echoes this when she writes that the current system of admission and regulation has restricted education to largely the upper middle-class youth. In the first place, there are only few universities which provide quality education, and these, in turn, are accessible to the more privileged section of society. 'Many youth belonging to lower middle class are denied entry into mainstream academic education and are pushed into lower grade colleges. Education reproduces existing inequalities in society' (John 2013, 53). This inequality is perpetuated, she writes, when a large section of the society that has access to only basic education is part of subsistence work. Only a small section gets into research and other high-end jobs. She adds that many reports speak of gap between quality of students and job requirements, but the issue is not that of 'skill gap' but rather the inadequacy of high-end or even middle-rung professional jobs for graduates. As a result, most of the graduates end up being underemployed. This point is in contrast to the point made elsewhere about unemployability of youth citing the example of master's students in economics, who were found to be lacking in skills and knowledge.

MHRD has been asking universities to raise 30 per cent of their funds. The implications of fundraising is that the donor may get to decide on courses (Giroux and many others have pointed this out in the American system of education) which would inevitably be industry oriented and, also, dictate other terms and conditions like the *Birla–Ambani Report* does. The report clearly says that there will not be a students' union on campus, no political activity or relation with any political party. In short, a sanitized campus which does not promote critical thinking or analysis or provide a democratic space. The sentiments of the *Ambani–Birla Report* are echoed by many who question the 'utility' of education from a market perspective.

It cannot be denied that both quality and employability are central to education but so is access to education. Access to education can be impacted by location/distance and the cost of education to the students. In the previous chapter, it was well established that the composition of students changed over the years and the factors which led to this change were, namely socio-economic mobility (class mobility), reservation, low-cost education and rapid increase in the number of universities and institutes. In the past two years, cost of education has been under attack and one of the reasons for students' protest. Almost all the engineering institutes and universities have seen a fee hike with a difference in the percentage increase. It is no wonder that in response, the country witnessed several protests with regard to fee hike across the country.

FEE HIKE IN UNIVERSITIES AND ENGINEERING/TECHNICAL INSTITUTES: RESPONSE AND IMPACT

Among the universities and engineering institutes included in the study, Gulbarga University, Periyar University and JU have been the only exceptions with no fee hike. JNU has been in the news in the past few months (mid of 2019 onwards) for their protests regarding the fee hike. The JNU protests have taken centre stage in the debate regarding fee hike, and a parallel conversation on different aspects of cost of education and the larger vision of education has been revived. The two key points raised in the issue of fee hike is that of access to education and quality of education. The fee hike has been justified by the JNU administration due to fund deficit of ₹45 crores. The administration proposed the following new fee structure (Table 5.1).

Table 5.1 *JNU—Original Fee Hike*

	Existing Charges	Revised Charges Approved by IHA
Mess bill	As per actual	As per actual
Establishment charge	1,100 per semester	1,100 per semester
Crockery, utensils	250 per year	250 per year
Newspaper	50 per year	50 per year
Room rent (single)	20 per month	600 per month
Room rent (double)	10 per month	300 per month
Utility charges (water and electricity charges)	Nil	As per actual
Service charge (mess services, sanitation services, supporting staff)	Nil	1,700 per month
Refundable mess (security)	5,500	12,000

IHA: Inter Hostel Administration
Source: https://www.bbc.com/hindi/india-50469921

A student of JNU remarked, 'We cannot let this happen; if we let this go, then there is no coming back.' Students' protest march took place within and outside the campus. Inside the campus, they went to each centre and shouted slogans and did not permit entry to teachers or students at that time. Posters were made on the spot, informing others of the proposed fee hike, its implications and details. Added to the issue of fee hike especially in hostels, there was another point of contention—that of dress codes in hostels. A student who was shouting slogans said, 'There are many in my class who cannot afford these fees, and that is what the government wants. They want to change the character of JNU, and we will not let it happen.'

Subsequently, many editorials and articles were written by professors and students alike on how their life and life experience changed after studying and teaching at JNU. This was because it gave equal opportunity to the poorest to study. Speaking in this context, two professors, one retired and one associate, were in favour of the students' protest. A retired professor, looking at the students going from centre to centre, said, 'This is JNU culture—people don't understand it. They think if a student is involved in a protest, s/he won't study. But that's not true. This has been JNU culture from the 70's, when we were students here. You will see that the same students who are marching now will go and study in the library in a little while.' Another professor said, 'the students were being pushed to the wall and there was no way of this but to protest.' It was evident that the teachers were sympathetic to the cause of the students.

With the VC of JNU ignoring the genuine demands of the students, the students staged a protest in front of the MHRD, and after many days of struggle, a 50 per cent roll back was announced. But the students think that this roll back is not sufficient. The protest against fee hike has taken a turn for the worse with teachers and students, who have been speaking out against the fee hike and other positions taken by the administration, being attacked by students belonging to right-wing political outfits. The students' union has issued a long letter stating that they will continue to protest against the fee hike, fund cut, seat cut and the revised entrance-exam rules. The JNU Teachers Association has written to the President of India, Ram Nath Kovind, stating that the very fact that the administration has chosen to target those who were protesting against the fee hike, 'let's the cat out of the bag'.

Table 5.2 shows the revised fee structure post the roll back.

Apart from the tuition fees, an increased hostel fees poses a huge problem for those who cannot afford to take up accommodation in metro cities. This further acts as a deterrent for not only the students who are struggling with finances but also for women who face opposition from their families on staying outside the campus. Kanupriya, a student leader of Punjab University asked, 'Is education a commodity like onion that it should become expensive?'

Engineering institutes have seen a steady increase in fee structure over the years. In November 2012, the IIT council recommended an 80 per cent hike in UG courses, which would amount to ₹90,000 per year. It came into effect in 2013. The HRD ministry justified the increase by citing that the expenditure on every student is around

Table 5.2 JNU—Revised Fee Hike

	Revised for All, Including BPL[a] with Scholarship	For BPL Category Without Scholarship
Mess bill	As per actual	As per actual
Establishment charge	1,100 per semester	1,100 per semester
Crockery, utensils	250 per year	250 per year
Newspaper	50 per year	50 per year
Room rent (single)	600 per month	300 per month
Room rent (double)	300 per month	150 per month
Utility charges (water and electricity charges)	As per actual	50% as per actual
Service charge (sanitation services, supporting staff)	As per actual	50% as per actual
Refundable mess (security)	Dropped down to 5,500	Dropped down to 5,500

Source: https://www.bbc.com/hindi/india-50469921
Note: [a]Below Poverty Line.

2.25 lakhs. The government quoted the *Anil Kakodkar Report* recommendation that the IITs need to become financially independent. The only exception was the fee waivers given to SC, ST and disabled students. Keeping in line with this, in 2016, the fees of MTech in IIT was increased from –90,000 to 2 lakh rupees.

The NITs saw a similar fee hike after a proposal was sent by the NIT council. The fees increased from ₹70,000 to ₹1.25 lakh per annum. There were protests against the rise. A student from NIT Patna said that apart from the fee hike, the withdrawing of scholarship also caused anger in the community. The boy stated that he received scholarship for two years but not the final year. As a result, students who are unable to afford the fees once the scholarship has been withdrawn are forced to drop out. On the other hand, the fees also increased from ₹73,000 to ₹120,000 per year from 2016. What has made life difficult for students is that the national scholarship scheme, as it has resulted in additional paperwork and administrative procedures. The scholarship has been reduced to half and students have to run from one office to another. Similar concerns of scholarship amounts being reduced to half were voiced by students (SC/ST/OBC) of Nilamber Pitamber University in Jharkhand. In addition to this, students are subjected to demand for bribes and also humiliated (Sengupta 2017). A respondent from NIT Warangal added a different dimension, 'They mentioned that we will provide fee waiver for SC/ST student like other NITs, so I didn't pay the fee as per their instruction. Later, when I was collecting no dues, they asked me to pay the fee and they stopped my consolidated grade reports.' If the SC/ST waiver is not honoured by NIT, then it would mean that many more students will be forced to drop out and also prove to be a deterrent for many to seek higher education. This is a harbinger of things to come, how students and their families have to face the brunt of increasing cost of education. In the following section, we will see more examples and details of fee hike taking place in several universities.

SPPU saw a substantial rise in the course fees of Master's in Social Work. The hostel fees are also increased by a substantial amount. Students of Mahatma Gandhi Antarrashtriya Hindi Vishwavidyalaya (MGAMVV) protested against a fee hike in 2015. Most of the students of MGAMVV belong to the SC/ST/OBC categories, and hence, a fee hike would mean dropouts among those belonging to these categories. Similarly in Lucknow University, fees have seen a constant hike since 2005, and it is even more problematic for students as, very often, the fees are raised during the course which catches students and their families off guard. Students pursuing the MBA course were asked to pay ₹45,000 more as the fee had increased to ₹75,000 for the students. They were paying ₹30,000 in the earlier semesters. Fees of some courses which were earlier ₹1,400 are now ₹36,000, and other courses have seen a rise from ₹1,260 to ₹24,000 (Sengupta 2017).

Universities are being pressurized to raise their own funds rather than seek or depend on government funding. In 2016 and 2017, fee hikes were proposed in Jamia Milia Islamia. Both the times, the fee hike was rolled back due to student protests. The reasons cited for the increase refers to the MHRD's expectation that university should mobilize resource internally. In 2019, hostel fees were hiked by ₹1,300, apart from the nominal increase made every semester. The students were successful getting the decision of fee hike rolled back. Tata Institute of Social Sciences (TISS) has been asked to raise its own funds. TISS started in Mumbai and now has campuses in Gauhati (2012) and Hyderabad (2013) and has got new affiliated centres in Patna and Tuljapur also. The 180 ad hoc faculties are funded by private agencies like TATA trust and no reservation has been implemented during recruitment. Since 2013, TISS is being asked to fund itself and raise 30 per cent of its own expense. This forced the institute to hike its fees by 46 per cent and in some cases up to 100 per cent. Fees went up to ₹61,000 for OBC students per year and the SC/ST students also pay need to pay ₹60,000. The repercussions are already there to see; the OBC student community is seeing an increasing dropout rate, the SC/ST may soon follow.

The students of Presidency College in West Bengal met with success when the counselling fees were increased to ₹500 and then brought down to ₹100 following protests by students. In 2019, Visva Bharati students spoke up when the fees for General students doubled and that of the South Asian Association for Regional Cooperation students increased by 10 times. The fees increased by 20 per cent –30 per cent. In 2016, there were protests in Calicut University as the fees for examination-related services were increased by 20 per cent. The protests led the university to rethink, and the university decided to roll back the fees. All India Students Federation opposed fee hike in engineering courses and law courses in OU and Hyderabad University saying that the norms of the Telangana Admission and Fee Regulatory Committee (TFRC) have not been followed. The TFRC is also in charge of fixing fees for the unaided professional colleges in Telangana for 2019–2022.

Indian Institute of Science Education and Research (IISER) too has been subjected to fee hikes since 2016 by MHRD. MHRD minister said that the fees of IISER are very low and need to be increased progressively. In May 2017, a council represented by the IIT and IISER chaired by HRD minister Mr Javadekar decided that the fees should be hiked by 10 per cent every year. The fees were increased from ₹2,500 to ₹3,500 in 2016. The fee for PhD was increased from ₹700 to ₹2,400, against which the students protested. A fee revision example in IISER amounted to ₹14,000 from ₹7,000 six months ago, which has now again increased to ₹24,000.

In Delhi, several colleges under the DU have seen a steep fee hike. Among other universities which have raised fees and witnessed protests is Indian Institute of Mass Communication (IIMC). In December 2019, IIMC students protested against the unaffordable fee hike and administration's turning a blind eye to the problems that students would face. English journalism would cost ₹168,500 for a 10-month course besides the mess dues, which is unaffordable for many. Hostel and mess fees are around ₹4,800 for men and ₹6,500 for women. Ambedkar University, too, has been in the news for similar reasons. There were protests against the alleged 10 per cent fee hike in Ambedkar University that takes place with every new batch. The administration of the university denied the claim.

Not all fee hikes have met with protests; in some universities, it has been slipped in quietly or the students have accepted it as part of the process. For example, in NEHU, fees were revised for all the courses and published in 2018. There is an official notification on the university website to this effect. Bangalore University syndicate approved the increase of fees of its affiliated colleges in order to manage the revenue crunch. A fee hike of 5 per cent to 10 per cent in all categories was announced. The fund crunch happened mostly due to the trifurcation of the university. Two new universities were formed from the parent university. Even open universities catering largely to the unprivileged sections have also seen a fee hike. For a total of 163 courses in IGNOU, a fee hike of 10–20 per cent has been proposed. This is the result of reduction in funds for the Central varsities. In Himachal Pradesh University, students taking up BEd degree course would be compelled to spend ₹16,000 more, from ₹84,870 to ₹98,000, in 2019–2021. Besides tuition fees, students would be charged an additional 7 per cent on the current fee, which would amount to ₹5,880 and pay ₹10,000 for other expenses.

It is clear from the examples shared in this section that almost every government-funded university and institute is headed for a fee hike. What are the implications of a fee hike for the students and the nation?

The mushrooming of private institutions was repeatedly pointed out as part of the problem by several teachers during the fieldwork, which is an indication of how 'lucrative' education is as a business model. The *Sargent Report*, in one of its recommendations, stated that the government's role and expenditure on education should increase with time. Unfortunately, with the progress of time, the government is slowly withdrawing from the field of education. This is evident from the share allocated to education in the budget, a mere 3.7 per cent. The *Comptroller and Auditor General Report* of February 2019 states that ₹94,036 crore of the secondary and higher education cess and ₹7,298 crore from the research and development cess remained unutilized.

It is indeed problematic when a government decides that it is not responsible for education of its youth. After Independence, several educational institutes were set up to shape the minds of young men and women. The youth was seen as crucial in nation-building and education was the first step towards that. Let us take the example of the IISER, established in 2006 by the government. The IISER website says, 'An overarching goal of the IISERs is to enable students to shape the nation by inventing and implementing sustainable solutions for societal problems through research in science.' Yet, we found that most of the dropouts from higher-education institutions belong to the disadvantaged groups of the SC/ST. Fee waivers or fee subsidies in government-aided technical institutes are essential for students from economically and socially deprived groups. Education at these institutions can ensure social mobility for the families. Fee hikes, on the contrary, push them back into the poverty cycle. The other question that arises is whether the employment opportunities justify the fee hike. In most cases, the youth do not get a high-compensation job immediately after they finish their degree. It is even more difficult for those who take education loans, as most of their salary is spent in repaying these loans.

Here is the dichotomy that is presented when one looks at education as merely 'utilitarian' versus something that shapes your mind and life beyond textbooks and jobs; it is a step towards equality, dignity and diversity. The testimonials that came out when the JNU fee hike was announced spoke of children of vegetable sellers, manual scavengers and poor farmers getting an opportunity to study and without any discrimination by teachers or students. These children went on to become teachers, administrative officers and professionals, thereby changing the lives of their families for ever. Fee hikes will change all this, the high enrolment in higher education will be replaced by dropouts or, worse still, close the doors of education for the poor and, perhaps, affect even women. Families hesitant to spend on education of girls will refuse to do so in the face of exorbitant fees, thus, reducing the chances of women pursuing higher education.

OTHER ISSUES WITHIN THE SYSTEM

The decades of 1950s–1960s saw a flurry of activity with regional universities and institutes being set up, and these boasted of world-class faculty. But this growth soon unravelled in the face of challenges like internal politics, interference of the government and lack of credible leadership. The core issues facing higher education have been a topic of discussion for decades. In the introductory chapter, some of the salient points included under the umbrella of crisis facing education and, in particular, higher education have been briefly discussed. Academicians and researchers have written on lack of quality and infrastructure, teacher–student ratio, privatization, dropout rates more so in the context of caste and gender, employability and so on. The *Sargent Report* of 1944 on status of education may well be talking of the problems being faced by the higher education system today.

> There has been a general lack of planning in university education and both Central and Provincial Governments have yielded to popular pressure in bringing universities into existence without providing the necessary resources to enable them to function on sound lines...Moreover the universities have been handicapped by the fact that the education given in most high schools have been very inadequate preparation for a university career. (*Sargent Report* 1944)

Tilak, in his article (1997) assessing five decades of education in India, makes a few pertinent points. He writes that on mapping the trend of expenditure on education over the years may appear to be a big leap—from ₹55 crores to ₹25,000 crores (updated figure in 2018 is ₹85,010 crores), but considering the increase in population and thereby the numbers of students and the rising costs, the government expenditure is not adequate. Taking the argument further and placing it in today's context (the article is nearly two decades old), the percentage of GDP spent on education is a clear marker of the priority given to education by the government. *The Economic Survey of India for 2018–2019* said that the Government of India has reduced expenditure on education, and it has spent only 3 per cent of its GDP on education, while the minister for education claimed that the government had spent 4.6 per cent of the GDP on education. At the time of Independence, India was spending about 1 per cent of the GDP on education. Tilak, in this analysis of the decadal trends (1997, 2239) in real rates of growth in public expenditure on education, notes that the 1950s and 1960s saw a rapid growth in total expenditure on education, mirrored in many developing and developed countries of the world. The 1970s were marked by a 'great setback' for the growth in public expenditure in education in many Third-world countries, including India. The author attributes this to the 'global disenchantment with education' due to growing educated unemployment at the empirical level and 'the emergence of screening and credentialism theses on the role of education' on the theoretical level. The 1980s saw a marked increase in expenditure as compared to the preceding decade. The decade was characterized by a global 'revival of faith in education,' with 'human resource development' becoming a key slogan. In the 1990s, there were concerted efforts to increase allocation confronted by economic reform policies that focus on programmes of 'stabilization' and 'structural adjustment'. The decade is that of 'containment' for public financing of education in India.

Education in India started on a shaky footing with high rates of illiteracy and inadequate number of schools and universities. Added to this were the barriers of caste, gender and poverty. In the years following freedom from the colonial rule, education in terms of both content and infrastructure has come a long way as the MHRD reports prove. However, there are several issues which need to be addressed, and considerable scholarship exists on this, considering that every decade has seen its share of problems (some mentioned earlier). In the past few years, some drastic measures have been announced by the government; ideological battles are being fought on content and curriculum in education, and the relationship between administration, students and teachers is going downhill.

Employability

Several reports such as the most recent *National Employability Report for Engineers: 2019* or the *National Association of Software and Service Companies–McKinsey Report of 2009* have spoken of the unemployability of engineers, given the mushrooming of private technical institutes, going so far as to say that 90 per cent of the engineers are not fit to be employed. We see an echo of this in Ayyar's work in which he points out the problem of 'unemployability' of most of the college graduates and the wasteful chasing of degrees and diplomas in the hope that prospects of employment would thereby improve. Similar ideas mark the articles of Mishra and Singh (2015) and Sahni and Shankar (2015). In 2015, Shankar and Sahni, in their article based on a research of economics graduate students, argue that most of the social science graduates are unemployable, and hence, their employability is to be linked to the abysmal school education. Many of their conclusions were drawn from the *Annual Status of Education Report* that is based on school education. They point that the social scientists form a considerable part of the educated unemployed. A rebuttal was published by Mishra and Singh a few months later that, 'the higher education system reproduces the learning deficits of schools, but rather it adds to them and closes opportunities for academic growth even of those students who could do well' (Mishra and Singh 2015). They further point out that it is the lack of ethics and quality among teachers in universities that has led to this situation. The question of employability of graduates from higher education institutions remains an issue. Several reports point that while enrolment and number of students may well have increased but the employability of the youth remains a concern, and this we can link back to the unplanned growth of educational institutions leading to a lack of quality thereby affecting employability.

Privatization

Kapur and Mehta refer to the problems of higher education as the 'trilemma' of Indian higher education. They write that the Indian higher education faces a 'trilemma' in trying to address scale, cost and quality issues simultaneously. India has addressed this by focusing on scale and costs, with the quality inevitable casualty (Kapur and Mehta 2019, 7). The 'massification' of higher education was made possible by establishing several new private colleges with a bulk of them in technical and professional education. Little is known about the quality and outcome of teachings of these institutions. The cost challenge was met by shifting the burden of expansion to private-sector providers and thereby to students, who in turn were granted ample loans by the financial system (Kapur and Mehta 2019, 7). This point is echoed by several teachers in the conversations with them.

The general consensus is that the higher-education sector saw a drastic change post economic liberalization, post which there was a steady withdrawal of the 'welfare state'. As Das puts it,

> The presence of the state in public welfare activities suffered a severe erosion once in the late 1980s the Indian State subjected itself to the force of globalisation and adopted the Structural Adjustment Programme. This breakdown of consensus around the viability of the welfare state meant the triumph of neoliberalism and increased privatization of social & services, particularly health, housing and education. (Das 2007, 53)

Das places some of the blame of the crisis in education, especially with regard to expenditure on the acceptance of the World Bank terms which categorized education as a non-merit good. He quotes from the *World Bank Report* (1994) which states, 'Indeed it is arguable that higher education should not have the highest priority claim on incremental public resources available for education in many developing countries, especially those that have not yet achieved adequate access, equity and quality at the primary and secondary levels' (Das 2007, 54).[2] Following

---

[2] Cited by Das in his article from *World Bank Report of 1994 Higher Education: The Lessons of Experience*.

this, in 1997, a discussion paper was released by the government questioning the subsidies on education.[3]

Upadhyaya (2007), speaking on the same issue, elaborates that the government in 1997 categorized social and economic services into public, merit goods and non-merit goods. It was further proposed that the non-merit goods no longer be subsidized. While elementary education was in the category of merit good, secondary and higher education was in the non-merit good category, and it was proposed that the subsidies on higher education be cut back by as much as 50 per cent. She ties it up with the 1991 New Economic Policy, which states that public expenditure in the social sector should be reduced and privatization should be encouraged. This included education, as policymakers, at that time, were of the opinion that people were capable and ready to pay for quality education. The *Birla–Ambani Report* further endorsed the move by the government to make higher education complete for profit endeavour and privatize it. As per the *AISHE Report 2018–2019*, about 77.8 per cent colleges are privately managed; 64.3 per cent are private unaided and 13.5 per cent private aided. Andhra Pradesh and Uttar Pradesh (UP) have the largest number of private colleges with about 88 per cent private-unaided colleges and Tamil Nadu comes a close second with 87 per cent private-unaided colleges. It is no wonder that almost all the teachers were concerned about the rate of privatization of education.

Bhushan (2013) refers to the 12th Plan as a shift towards education as a 'for profit' sector. He writes that the Plan mentions several proposals to raise private capital. These include: (a) enabling more and liberal financing options for the sector, for example, by allowing private institutions to raise funds through public offerings of bonds or shares; (b) change the legal status of the sector to attract more investors, for example, by allowing all types of institutions to be established as Section 25 companies and allowing existing trusts and societies to convert to Section 25 companies (the Companies Act did not allow it

---

[3] In May 1997, the Government of India issued a discussion paper on 'Government Subsidies in India.' It is difficult to justify subsidies on items like electricity, diesel, fertilizer and higher education, since there are normally no significant differences between private and social valuations in these areas (Das 2007).

earlier, as profit might lead to reinvesting in surplus) (c) give priority recognition to the sector, for example, by providing it 'infrastructure' status with similar, financial and tax treatment, this might lead to commercialization of higher sector.

Quality and Quality Control

One of the oft-repeated complaints against higher education is the lack of quality control in universities and colleges. Batabyal, in his expansive work on JNU, also writes about the decline of State universities and the reasons for the same. He writes that not only in India but across the world, especially in Europe, the nature and composition of the classroom began changing sometime during the 1960s. There were more number of students who were entering the education system which put pressure on the existing infrastructure, which hitherto had been only for limited number of elites. Classrooms, libraries and hostels were crowded like never before. This put enormous strain on existing resources, thus compromising on the quality.

In addition to this, there were other factors working in India which set the path for the decline of universities. One key reason, according to Batabyal, was the introduction of vernacular languages in higher education. Gujarat, Uttar Pradesh, Madhya Pradesh (MP), Rajasthan and Maharashtra were among the first to adopt vernacular languages, and this impacted the quality of education in the universities leading to their decline. Maharashtra and Rajasthan universities, at one point of time, had some of the finest faculty lost out after a sudden shift to regional languages as a medium of learning. University of Rajasthan was a premier institute in 1964–1965 with the best departments in sociology, economics, philosophy, etc., and was easily among the top-three universities in the country. But the anti-English movement initiated in the 1960s by the Jana Sangh and socialists, which demanded that English be replaced by Hindi, heralded the downward slide. This movement gathered steam in several Hindi-speaking states—Haryana, MP, UP and Himachal Pradesh. Soon, RSS and the Jana Sangh joined hands and propagated the idea that English had no place in the Indian democratic state through the Hindi Sena and Hindi Sainiks. The agitation against English as a medium of education took a violent turn in 1967. Adding fuel to the fire were the political class and local publishing houses. Both saw an opportunity in the agitation and decided to put their weight and money, respectively, in this agitation, leading to a hasty shift from English to Hindi.

Other factors like caste alignments, political movements and student protests further led to the deterioration of education, especially in the states. On the issue of declining quality of State universities, Gudavarthy writes,

> There has been an erosion in the quality of state universities and institutions in comparison with the central universities. In the 1970s the best of scholars who returned with degrees from foreign returned to their home states and contributed to their growth. Last few decades, state universities—Allahabad, Osmania, Madras, BHU have witnessed a decline due to migration of faculty to Delhi Universities, poor funding from State government. State universities collapsed into sites of inbreeding, networking and kinship based recruitment. (Gudavarthy 2019, 34)

On a similar note, Batabyal (2014, 380) also points out the role of caste, politics inside and outside the campus and religion that slowly but steadily eroded fine institutions. Citing examples from across the country, he writes that in Bihar, the Magadh University saw a Bhumihar versus Rajput caste politics and Ranchi University saw a tribal versus non-tribal conflict. Universities in Bihar became centres of political power play. Visva Bharati and Calcutta University were controlled by communist politics. Aligarh Muslim University (AMU), Osmania and BHU had lost their sheen by the 1980s. In AMU and BHU, faculty-recruitment policies based on religion and caste played havoc with the quality. This was particularly visible when there was an attempt to change the name of BHU in 1964–1965. RSS, along with the complicity of the VC, incited students to agitate against any attempt to not only change the name of BHU but also to modernize it. National politics also encouraged caste and religion-based politics in universities, further worsening the situation. Caste dominates the narrative of problems facing the universities, both among students and faculty, even today, as we have the conversations with teachers in Gulbarga University, AU and BHU.

The question often asked is that India now has 700 odd universities, as per MHRD statistics, then why is it that very few are known internationally or even make it to the global ranking of universities. 'Quality and work ethic have been a long-term problem in India's higher education. The best of our institutions and scholarship is comparable to global standards, and our worst is as worst as that of any lesser-developed nations. The problem is posed by the middle-level institutions; while they maintain a bare threshold level in the US and Europe, our institutions fare rather poorly. The primary reason for having a poor average has been both poor infrastructure and even poorer work ethic' (Gudavarthy 2019, 33). As a senior professor in Gulbarga put it, 'A value crisis is what the education system is facing today. There is a lack of quality of education; not only teachers but the students, too, don't work up to the expectation.' Gudavarthy points out,

> UGC order[4] recognises the gap between the quality of education provided by the different universities. In recognising this gap, UGC is promulgating graded autonomy, which in effect will also mean providing graded funding to the differentially located universities that would end up exacerbating those differences. In essence what the current government intends to do is to phase out public funded universities that way state owned industries, airways, railways etc have gradually been shrinking. (Gudavarthy 2019, 35)

Batabyal says that many universities placed the blame of their declining standards on both the State and the student politics. The students were perceived to have lost interest in studies and were more focused on political activities within and outside the campus. The situation was similar in India with universities witnessing declining standards. Many universities felt the strain of state policies, protest movements and student violence. 'This created a discussion on how Indian universities were declining because there were now supposed to be infested

---

[4] As per the UGC (categorization of universities for Grant of Graded Autonomy) Regulations, 2017, it is stated that 'commission may have different provisions for different categories of institutions as defined in clause 3.1 with the objective of giving higher levels of autonomy to institutions under category I compared to its institutions under categories II and III, 4.2 while framing any regulations the commission may also sub-categorise any of the categories in that regulation to give a differentiated autonomy under the specific regulation to institutions within that category'.

with youth interested only in politics. RSS gained entry through the back door amidst all this. The decline of universities was but a reflection of the new class structure emerging in India which would try and establish its hegemony in post-Nehru Delhi. Power emanated from proximity to the new ruling class combined with capitalist class, which was assisting in stabilizing the State. Power rested in the hands of bureaucracy, business aristocracy, erstwhile landed aristocracy and personalities from media, culture and politics' (Batabyal 2014, 63).

There is no dearth of literature on the problems facing higher education, some already referred to in the first chapter. During the fieldwork, teachers were asked to speak about recurring issues in education. What are the problems they have been facing over the years and the new issues that have cropped up (if any)? There was hesitancy in holding an open conversation about the new issues, in particular, as it was perceived as speaking out against the policies of the current regime. Some found a way out of it by saying that the problems have remained the same over the years, there is nothing much to add. But the question on recurring or old issues established clearly that there can be no hiding away from the fact that successive governments, irrespective of ideological positions and political party, did not treat education with the urgency and sincerity it deserves.

FROM THE FIELD: POLITICAL INTERFERENCE, RECRUITMENT, ACADEMIC PERFORMANCE INDICATOR (API), SCHOLARSHIPS, RESEARCH, INFRASTRUCTURE

In Punjab University, teachers were quite vocal about the problems facing higher education. Syllabus, plagiarism, funding, preference to private institutions, fake certificates and shortage of teachers were mentioned. In most of the universities, the private-versus-public debate, more so in relation to funding, was discussed. Of late, the push for private universities at the cost of public universities has become apparent. In Gauhati University, a teacher spoke out against the system of ranking. According to him, the MHRD took about a crore from each university for the Institutes of Eminence (IoE) tag. But very often, a

State university is not able to fulfil the criteria for the ranking, which then affects the fund flow. In BHU, almost all the teachers mentioned autonomy as a major issue. They said that institutes are becoming an extension of the government and academic leadership is now aligned with right-wing politics.

The mushrooming of private universities have opened up opportunities for those who are unable to get through public universities and can afford it, but there has been an indiscriminate growth which has impacted quality of education. There have been numerous cases of fraudulent universities' courses and certificates which is probably what one of the teachers was referring to. A number of teachers spoke out against the API system. The API was introduced in 2010 in order to assess the quality of the teaching staff and also links teacher selection and promotion to their achievements like teaching, learning and evaluation. It includes publication, research and so on. As per the rules, to become an associate professor, an assistant needs 300 API points, and for a professor to be an associate professor needs 400 points. This system has come under scanner because it led to the mushrooming of pay-per-article journals and even journals with fake credentials. Clearly, there was unhappiness with this system which seemed to favour 'quantity' over quality as one teacher put it. Another point that was raised was that of research. Dissatisfaction was expressed about research being forced on teachers. To quote an associate professor, 'Not all teachers can be researchers and not all researchers can be teachers.'

An assistant professor in JNU said that crisis in higher education is at several levels—representation, scholarship, infrastructure, fellowship and student politics. Above all was a disregard for social sciences (on the same lines of Giroux), 'But the current regime hardly cares for social science; they care for technical education. They care for professional education; they think education is an investment and market-oriented facility. Social science is about making you a better person and socially conscious being and a good citizen. They do not care about that.' In AU too, teachers voiced their concern over the declining standards of social sciences and the neglect of social sciences itself as it is deemed inferior. Seats in social sciences have seen a decline in many universities.

Issues of autonomy, saffronization (increasing elements of right-wing ideology), political interference and control over higher education, being market oriented (arguments were made against privatization and fee hike) were concerns that were voiced. A professor from NEHU specifically mentioned 'end of scientific thinking' linking it to saffronization. In JU, a teacher mentioned that rationality has been replaced by superstition today. In Gauhati University, teachers were unhappy with political diktats on the research topic that were to be pursued by teachers and the rewriting of history books. Even in Bangalore University, the teachers were not happy with the trend of rewriting history books and increasing political interference.

The political control was being exercised through executive council, placing vice chancellors who would toe the political line of the current regime and by banning unions on campus. 'The government is unnecessarily interfering and curtailing economic freedom in the name of different development. Now, it seems like the government doesn't want to fund public universities and seems to promote private universities. In addition to this, students and teachers are being branded anti-national and syllabus is being changed on religious and political lines.' In Gulbarga University too, political interference was listed as a major issue. According to a senior professor from department of social work, political interference in education was a key issue. He said that political parties should stay away from higher education as 'too much of political influence is disturbing the faculty, student community and destroying the administration.'

Lack of permanent teachers and reliance on ad hoc/guest lecturers was a common complaint. In most universities, recruitment took place almost seven to eight years ago. The implications of ad hoc/guest lecturers have been discussed in great detail earlier in the section in rules and recruitment. Lack of employment opportunities for students was mentioned more by science teachers than humanities. Some universities had specific problems. For example, in Periyar University, teachers do not have the freedom to speak about politics and ideology, students' union has been banned by the Tamil Nadu government, scholarships have been scrapped and, in addition to all this, there is no SC/ST cell to address the problems of the faculty or students from the community. Fee hike was mentioned as a problem, though not in all universities, in spite of the fact that nearly all universities barring Gulbarga and JU had seen a hike in fees, but teachers and students mentioned it, particularly, in OU, NIT Warangal and Pondicherry University.

In AU, a teacher said, 'Student politics has criminalized. In the meetings of Allahabad University Teachers' Association (AUTA), only selected people are invited. The semester system is not right. It does not have holistic approach. Because of reservation, there is distance between students of different categories. Posts of faculty members are vacant, and therefore, number of guest faculty has increased, but it impacts the quality of education. Infrastructure in the department is old and there is a lack of basic facilities.' In NEHU, teachers spoke out against digitization without adequate preparation. According to a biochemistry professor, there was an excessive focus on 'show off, for example, the Swayam digitization (digital initiative by the government to make education available to students from Class 9 to PG online, video lectures by teachers, etc.) was introduced even when the basic infrastructure was not available. Digitization of education is not good.'

The science teachers also mentioned lack of infrastructure and funds. Many mentioned that new equipment could not be purchased due to lack of funds. Laboratories do not have required equipment to function. In addition to this, a professor in DU said that there is a tedious procedure for buying equipment. Several professors in NEHU, teaching sciences, said that the 'course designs are more output oriented and structured like business models. Start-up culture should not be encouraged so much.' Another professor added that the focus is now shifting to business-oriented courses, and the universities who do not make this shift face a fund crunch. This approach is confusing the students. Funds for research were also seeing a cut. A retired DU professor on lack of funds said, 'I do not think there is enough funding, and it has multiple consequences. First is the research. You cannot expect universities to be there in top 300 if you do not fund them. You cannot do good research without funds. It also prohibits quality students from enrolling in the course. And hence, the quality of teaching and the profession goes down. Because of this, the infrastructure is not good, the salaries are not that good and the facilities that you get are not the best that you could get. I think the government realises it, but it does not want to put the money.'

In BHU, the science faculty pointed out casteism and autocracy of the administration as new problems that have crept in. There is a continuous pressure on teachers to toe the political line of the current regime. The overall vision for education is missing and students are just preparing to score marks, and multiple-choice questions have worsened the situation. One question that was asked separately from that on issues facing education was regarding the proposal to replace the UGC with HECI. The next section focuses on the developments leading to the proposal to replace UGC and the teachers' opinion about the move.

HECI VERSUS UGC DEBATE

The establishment of UGC was recommended by the Radhakrishnan Commission (1948), the first education commission. The UGC was later established as a statutory body under the UGC Act 1956. However, the making of the UGC Act was a highly contested process, which saw an extensive participation of academics and political leaders. The main focus of the debate was around two issues: autonomy of universities and rights of the State governments, which reflects the overarching spirit of federalism in policymaking (Abrol 2010). In 1951, the Union government moved the Bill for the establishment of UGC, titled Universities (Regulations of Standards) Bill. A majority of VCs and provincial political leaders were opposed to the very idea of UGC, fearing centralization and loss of provincial autonomy. As per the initial draft of Bill, UGC was to be established only for coordination and determination of standards. UGC was opposed by many as they feared excessive control by the State. Patel (2004) points out that the removal of two key provisions from the proposed UGC Act took the teeth out of UGC. The first provision was that no university could be established without the approval of the UGC. Second was that the UGC could derecognize any degree. Unfortunately, both the provisions were removed and 'UGC became merely a coordinating body that invoked standards rather than being a monitoring and regulatory institution leading to unregulated increase in colleges and universities by the State and Central government with subsequent lowering of standards of quality of teaching and learning' (Patel 2004, 2152).

This led to the growth of self-financed universities. The situation was further complicated with separate bodies—AICMR and AICTE—being set up for medicine and sciences. There was an overlap and conflict in the guidelines of the UGC and the AICTE/AICMR. Interestingly, today, many fear that without the UGC, private players will control the education sector.

In a move last year, the government had proposed the dilution of UGC through the IoE regulations which follows the HRD ministry's suggestion to rechristen the UGC as the HECI. The draft Higher Education Commission of India (Repeal of University Grants Commission Act) 2018, which was made public on 27 June and was open for feedback till 7 July, takes away funding powers from the proposed regulator and gives it powers to ensure academic quality and even close down bogus institutions. Bhushan (2018) points out that this power may be used against institutions in rural areas which suffer from lack of resources; similar will be the case with developing institutions which are yet to reach a state that was planned. With HECI in charge of ensuring academic quality in universities and colleges, the HRD ministry, or a different mechanism put in place later, will be responsible for funding universities and colleges.

When asked about the proposal of the government to replace the UGC with HEI, majority of teachers was against the concept of HEI and a few wary of voicing an opinion. It should be noted that since this move impacts teachers from humanities/liberal arts, so teachers from engineering institutes were unaware or did not know much about it. Among those wary of commenting felt that since it was in the conceptual stage, hence, too early to say anything about it. They had adopted a wait-and-watch approach. The ones who were against it thought that there was nothing new in the idea, it was merely a matter of nomenclature. Some feared that it would be disastrous for the future of higher education. For example, 'It will withdraw funds from higher education. Education won't be free for all and be in the interest of few. It will ultimately finish off higher education, and we will see the death of higher education.' (Punjab University). This fear of public universities coming under attack under the HEI was expressed by a few teachers. In JNU, an assistant professor said, 'UGC's role is diluted and changed. This is a direct attempt to privatization and autonomy, but at the end, all of these will lead to an expensive higher education. Higher education is now structured to be catering to the global market. Funding will be given to the institution that caters to the interest of the industry. The higher education will only be funded for market profits rather than to increase inclusivity. The functioning of the UGC was not at the best place, but an institution cannot be replaced by something which is totally against the principles of the original body.' Oft-repeated comments were the HECI was 'just old wine in new bottle'; unless there are structural changes, just changing the names doesn't mean anything. The sentiment regarding UGC was that like every other institution, it had loopholes that could be fixed.

An assistant professor in Bangalore University said, 'Unfortunate one (move towards HECI). UGC has been doing good work. It is like old wine in a new bottle. It really affects research and appointments. This government has made the UGC a very weak statutory body. No notification regarding post doc, major and minor research projects and no grants for seminars, etc. No clarity about promotion. Frequently, they have been changing UGC regulations pertaining to promotion and recruitment condition.' In Calicut University, the teachers voiced that the HEI was a way of letting the RSS control education. An assistant professor saw it as a 'clear move towards neoliberal policies which will destroy the concept of education. It is a ploy to incorporate more RSS people in decision-making bodies.' Similarly, another assistant professor said, 'this will create a highly centralized system of education and the involvement of RSS in higher education will hamper the quality of education.' Those in favour of HECI were very few but those who did so believed that the UGC had outlived its purpose and it was time for reforms to take place. It was placed in the line of reforms that have been carried out by the government. The few who were positive about it said that it would bring in the much-needed changes in syllabus, infrastructure and funding.

Professor Bhushan (2018) writes that the HECI does not address the structural problems of higher education. It emphasizes on monitoring outputs without taking into consideration the constraints many colleges and universities function within like teacher shortage, infrastructure problems or funds. He further adds that the HECI Act permits institutions to commence the academic operation just after the authorization of HECI, which leads to indiscriminate mushrooming of institutes, an already existing problem as flagged by several teachers during the interviews. The new accreditation system proposed seeks to standardize education in a way that the teachers do not have the autonomy to design the curriculum according to the needs of the students. The HEI may also lead to private players going unchecked, since colleges can function and expand without any affiliation to a university and yet enjoy all the privileges of being a university and even grant degrees if approved by the HECI. The new Act treats colleges, universities and deemed universities at par. This allows colleges to have all the privileges of a university, expand at all length and function without being affiliated to any university and also grant degrees provided the HECI allows it too. The State has no say in preventing or allowing institutions.

Compared with the UGC Act 1956, the draft gives the HECI and, in effect, the Central government sweeping powers to control and monitor HEIs. The HECI would effectively increase political interference in the Commission. The UGC Act 1956, under Section 5.2, mandated that the chairman of the Commission 'shall be chosen from among persons who are not officers of the government or any State government'. This was done to maintain the autonomy of the Commission and protect it from any direct interference by governments. However, under Section 3.6 of the HECI draft, this clause has been dropped, thus leaving room for functionaries of the Central and State governments to be appointed as the chairperson of the proposed HECI. This is complemented by providing for the creation of a search-cum-selection-committee to appoint the chairperson of HEC. The Committee will be headed by a cabinet secretary and will also include the secretary of higher education, both of whom are government functionaries. It would also reduce the number of teachers in the Commission to two. The UGC Act, under Section 5.3, mandates that apart from the chairman and vice chairman in the Commission, out of the other 10 members, a minimum of four must be teachers and at least six should be officers of State/Central governments. In the HECI draft, although the total number of members of the proposed HEC has been increased from 10 to 12, the representation of teachers has been reduced to 2. There are also no provisions for ensuring that there is less presence of government functionaries in these 12 members. The UGC Act also had a final proviso that 'not less than one half of the number chosen under this clause shall be from among persons who are not officers of the Central government or of any State government.' This proviso has been entirely dropped from the HECI draft, instead of providing for appointing a 'doyen of industry' in the Commission, with no definition of who constitutes as one. The HECI would also impact fee regulation. The UGC Act has a full section on 'regulation of fees and prohibition of donations in certain cases' (Section 12A). The UGC is empowered to specify by regulation 'the matters in respect of which fees may be charged, and the scale of fees in accordance with which fees shall be charged'. However, the HECI draft dilutes this stringent provision by just providing for the HECI to 'specify norms and processes for fixing of fee' and to merely 'advise' the governments on 'steps to be taken to make education affordable for all' (Section 15.4.1). The draft also does not provide for a prohibition on donations.

India has an advantage that many countries, especially European countries and even China, ARE losing—that of a young population. India's age demographics show that is has 17.79 per cent of the population in the age group of 15–24 years, and 41.24 per cent in the age group of 25–54 years of age. China's one-child policy is beginning to have its repercussions on its population composition rapidly shrinking and ageing population, which, in turn, is going to affect its economic productivity. The advantage of a youthful productive population would work for India only if it invests in its youth, in education and skill development. Low quality of education and lack of access to education will create a population unsuitable for employment and will create social problems rather than solve them. Be it the UGC or the HECI, the main purpose of any such commission would be to address the concerns of teachers and students. The exasperation of teachers was evident during the conversations regarding what ails the education system. The fact is that a new set of problems seem to creep into the system without a resolution of the older, existing ones, and this sets back any progress made over the years.

The Teacher
Roles, Rules and Challenges

Even as this book is taking shape, the known methods of imparting knowledge in schools and HEIs/universities are changing course due to the lockdown imposed by the virus corona. Teachers and students alike are struggling with the new-found 'normal' of teaching and attending classes online. The home is the new classroom, and this is not good for several reasons, but we are left with no choice as of now. After the initial days of struggle, some order of sorts has been established, but problems remain such as availability of computers and interconnection for the economically backward students, limited interaction between teachers and students and the biggest problem of all—conducting examinations. Educational institutions at all levels provide a normative structure which is enabled to a large extent by the physical infrastructure. The manifest and latent functions of education could, well, break down if the classroom experience is replaced by the internet. Socialization, social change, social control, network building and teamwork takes place within the physical structure of school/university and composition of the classroom.

In a previous chapter, the perception about ideology and political affiliations among students in the universities under study was analysed in great detail. In the interviews with teachers, their own political affiliations or ideological positions were not enquired upon directly nor was it a point of enquiry. The research did not intend to point out the number of rightist, leftist or centrist teachers on campus. What the research maps is how ideological leanings impact the relationship between faculty members; does the faculty discuss political ideological positions with each other, and how did they think ideology impacts student–teacher/teacher–teacher relationship and pedagogy itself

There were a few who were politically active in their respective campuses and did not hesitate to mention it. Then there were a few who said that the questions being asked in the interview were too political, pointing out their discomfort in merely talking about how ideology plays out in universities. Teachers were clearly hesitant to speak on this issue, even though the question was asked merely to ascertain the world view the teacher brings with him/her to the classroom, drawing from Berger and Luckmann,

> The distinctiveness of ideology is that the same overall universe is interpreted in different ways depending upon concrete vested interests within the society in question. Ideology is taken by a group because of specific theoretical elements that are conducive to its interests. Ideology generates solidarity, but relationship between a group and ideology is not always logical.' (Berger and Luckmann 1967, 124)

This chapter brings to you some parts of the conversation held with teachers across universities. The conversation with teachers ranged from class–faculty caste composition to ideological positions of teachers to relationship among teachers and between teachers and students. Valuable insights into the functioning of the universities, both past and present, were given by teachers. A stray comment from teachers set off a new direction of research, thereby adding more dimensions.

For the teacher, the classroom can become a site of authority; they can ask students to leave the classroom in case of misbehaviour, prevent the latecomers from entering the classroom, punish students, asking them to stand up when spoken to, control through the marking system and so on. There are myriad ways in which the hierarchy of relationship between the teacher and the taught is established in classrooms. Of course, this also brings forth the question as to whether the teacher–student relationship should be centred on authority and discipline at all. Apart from this, the role of a teacher is crucial in acquainting the student with the social reality of the world and HEIs play an important role in this. By the time students enrol themselves in higher education, they should have (hopefully!) a certain understanding of the world around them, however basic and rudimentary it might be. Teachers can further shape and mould and sharpen the existing world view or even change them. While in school, drawing upon G. H. Mead's idea of significant others, the students are keen to imitate teachers in their manner of speaking or other personality traits, but in colleges and universities, students move on from mere imitation of mannerisms to adapting the world view of the teachers, and this is probably the most crucial role of a teacher.

In the preceding chapters, students were the lens through which the role of ideology and the state in education were brought into focus. The perception of students regarding the idea of a nation, ideology and forming political affiliations or taking political positions is a combination of the content of the education and the experience of being on campus. Central here is the theory of the construction of social reality by Berger and Luckmann. They write that typfication and habitualization make actions 'predictable'. Examples of these are labour, sexuality and territoriality. The key to normalcy and construction of a social reality is the ability to predict and understand each other's actions. One of the roles, among several others, educational institutions play is acquainting a child with the world outside the family, and schools are credited with the first initiation in this process because of which schools, as an agency of socialization, have received considerable sociological attention. However, in universities, socialization is much more complex as the students interact with the institution and, in many instances, the State directly as adults, unlike schools, where parents negotiate that space. As a consequence of this, students engage in activities, such as student union or protests against administrative measures or for better facilities in HEIs and not in schools. In this phase, students learn to navigate the social processes of both conflict and cooperation, not limited to classmates but also outside the classroom with those in a position of hierarchy. The relationship with teachers also undergoes a subtle change in HEIs even though teachers continue to exercise authority over students.

Freire (1993, 2017), in *The Pedagogy of the Oppressed,* closely examines the relationship between the student and the teacher. He strikes at the core of the problem when he points out that the contemporary teaching process is passive with the teacher as the narrator and students as the listener. A teacher cannot hold a one-sided monologue which very often is far removed from reality. Freire writes about teachers,

> He talks about reality as if it were motionless, static, compartmentalised and predictable. Or else he expounds on a topic completely alien to the existential experience of the students. His task is to 'fill' the students with the content of his narration-contents which are detached from reality, disconnected from the totality that engendered them and could give them significance. (Freire 2017, 44)

In this one-sided giver–receiver relationship between the teacher and the student, the less the student questions the knowledge he is receiving, the better s/he is as a student.

The relationship of power that exists between the teacher and the student is expressed through various ways, some mentioned earlier, but Freire dives deeper into the process in which knowledge is shared between teachers and students. As Freire explains, the teacher is seen as a fountainhead of knowledge and the student as ignorant. Hence, the student is a receiver of knowledge and due to his/her ignorance cannot question the knowledge or the teacher. He refers to this as the 'banking' concept of education. He writes,

> In the banking system of education, knowledge is a gift bestowed by those who consider themselves knowledgeable upon those whom they consider to know nothing. Projecting an absolute ignorance onto others, a characteristic of the ideology of oppression, negatives, education and knowledge as processed of inquiry. (Freire 2017, 45)

Here, Freire makes a crucial point that in this process of education, the students are geared towards being amenable rather than critical beings. Critical consciousness, he says, is necessary for transforming the world. The education system is representative of the oppressive society, and suppression of creative and critical thought is the beginning of the control over young minds. Here, one may think of one's own classroom and think of the number of students who would ask questions—not just critically examine what is being taught but also express curiosity. This is also the normalcy in education that Davies spoke of—the normalcy that the education system seeks to maintain and is merely a representation of the hierarchy of the society. Freire too says, 'banking education maintains and even stimulates the contradiction ... which mirror oppressive society as a whole' (Freire 2017, 46).

If one recalls one's current classroom or the days of being a student in the past, both answering questions and asking questions were done by a select few. There would be hardly one or two students who would ask questions and be the 'usual' ones to do so. While most of the times, a teacher would not mind an 'I did not understand' comment, not many would welcome a comment saying that the student disagreed with what the teacher has said or that what the teacher has said is wrong. The basic assumption that works in a classroom is that the teacher is always right. Any student who raises his/her hand to ask a question or point out a mistake is seen as brave or as a mischief maker by the teacher. For example, when the students who were part of the research were asked whether the teachers are friendly or encouraged students to ask questions, in most of the universities, students did say that the teachers are friendly but only few students mentioned that teachers encourage students to ask questions in class. While there might have been a shift from the formal, distant relationship between teachers and students to a more open, friendly relationship but it appeared from the conversations that critical thinking and questioning was not being encouraged as it should be. But a teacher might disagree here and point to the myriad distractions at the disposal of the student today, be it social media, games, phone and so on and say that most view attending classroom lectures as a chore. Teachers mention that today, with the huge number of students in each classroom, personal attention to each is nearly impossible. Added to this, majority of the students are not really interested in learning, which in turn demotivates the teacher too.

An example that comes to mind in this specific context is how students responded to the question on rewriting history. As mentioned in a previous chapter, awareness or even interest in the current trend of rewriting of history from a nationalist perspective instead of a factual and scientific one was very low among students. The few students who did speak about it cited social media sites as their source of information; none of them mentioned that they heard about it from their teachers or discussed it with them. Of course, today information is available at the click of a button and the dependence of the student on the teacher as the only source of knowledge apart from books is far less than it was a decade ago. But as C. Wright Mills points out, there is a difference between information and knowledge. While one may get information on the internet, it does not always translate into knowledge. On the other hand, several teachers during the interviews mentioned that rewriting of history is a matter of concern and even mentioned it as a challenge facing education today. It is indeed strange that teachers did not communicate with the students about what some of them thought was an important issue. It was even more astonishing that the students were unaware of ideological positions that can influence history. These are not active parts of the syllabus, but it is here that the teacher gets an opportunity to acquaint the student with the different world views that exist and how it influences interpretation of facts and analysis. The next section is devoted solely to the concerns of the teacher and are responses to queries on recruitment policies, syllabus designing and engagement in politics among teachers. Apart from the conversations, the minutes of the academic council meetings (ones available on websites) are given to further corroborate the findings.

ACADEMIC FREEDOM: RECRUITMENT, RESEARCH, RULES

As with students, the teacher–State–administration relationship in HEIs/universities is very different from that in schools. Schools leave very little scope for freedom in the content of teaching with a system of centralized syllabus and textbooks at an individual level, and the interaction with the administration is limited and teachers do not form associations or unions. In higher education, the system is much more complex and universities with teachers' union have some room for manoeuvre. The State controls education through content in the syllabi and textbooks, allocating funds for universities, scholarships for students and so on. One of the examples would be the Karnataka Universities Act, 2000, which was based on the premise that since the State funds education, it has the right to control it. The education minister stated that the universities must prepare for the neoliberal market-oriented education system. The governor would appoint the VC from the three names suggested to it by the selection committee, and none of the teachers from the university would be included in the selection panel. Even the registrar would be appointed by the State government and would be from the Indian Civil Services.

It is clear that one of the ways that the State controls the education system in universities and, in turn, the teachers is through the process of recruitment and appointments. The problems with recruitment of teachers in higher education are manifold: tenure, promotions, the process of recruitment itself and its impact on the democratic culture in a university. The problems of tenure and process of recruitment are not specific to India but are universal in nature. But the administrative delays in promotions in India have resulted in assistant and associate professors across colleges and universities awaiting their promotion and arrears for years on end, sometimes, even 20 years. Even in universities, associate professors applying for full professorship with required number of publications are waiting for their due. The State, through the administration, which is more often than not in its control, can discourage teachers from taking anti-establishment stand or participate in political activity by using denial of promotion as a pressure point. It can also wield control over the education system and the teachers by not appointing full-time staff.

Recruitment in Universities

Both students and teachers were asked during the interviews held in the universities and engineering institutes about the adequacy of the number of teachers. Institutes like IIT and NIT seemed to have adequate number of teachers as mentioned by both students and teachers. However, in universities, the humanities students mentioned that only part-time or guest lecturers were being appointed rather than full time. Lack of permanent appointments was pointed out by very few teachers, even though most of the appointments done in universities were of ad-hoc staff. Most of the universities, other than JNU, have not seen any active recruitment for full-time posts in the last four to five years.

There were very few complaints about the number of teachers either by students or teachers, but it was acknowledged that recruitments for full-time teachers in universities was not being actively pursued by the administration on instructions from the government. A professor of DU succinctly put it, 'Last major hiring process was conducted in 2010. After that in 2014–2015, there have been appointments and then in 2017, few appointments took place but largely in departments. But the process was arbitrary. In DU, we have more than 4,500 ad-hoc teachers who have been working for the last 10 years. After the Sixth Pay Commission, some fresh talent did opt for academia as a field to become teachers, but today, their professional lives are marred by instability. Next generation of students do not look towards higher education as a career prospect.'

It was pointed out earlier that the reluctance to appoint full-time professors in universities is not unique to India. This process began in the West at least a decade ago. Giroux (2009) points out that the reasons as to why universities have developed a preference for part-time or ad-hoc faculty. He writes that with the trend of corporatization of universities starting in the 1980s, one of the first steps taken was to reduce, what he calls, 'faculty power'. This was done by systematically removing the idea of full-time faculty and replacing them with part-time or contractual teachers. This is to ensure that the faculty become dependent on the largesse of the administration for the continuation of their contracts and do not oppose the decisions of the administration. This limits the rights of the faculty to speak out against unfair policies and practices, which the full-time faculty can do so without any fear of losing their jobs. The guest/part-time lecturers do not have a role to play in the academic councils and other activities of the university, and in many cases, the guest lecturers are students in the university, thus, making it even easier to control them. Apart from the weakening role of teachers in administrative process and rules that impact both students and teachers, it is also seen as an efficient financial model, with the university not having to pay other benefits usually given to full-time professors. The entire system is now heavily tilted in the favour of the trustees/administrators. Needless to add that while teaching adds to the work experience of an MPhil/PhD student, it may not necessarily add to the intellectual growth of the students being taught or the university itself. Several universities, more often the private universities, have adopted this model. The most important impact according to Giroux is on the democratic culture of university and society. As democratic decision-making in the university dwindles, questions regarding the social responsibility of higher education disappear from public view and both 'the democratization of the university and the democratization of society' are undermined (Angus 2007, 73, cited in Giroux 2009, 119).

What Giroux pointed out in the 1980s and 1990s is coming true for India today. Sundar (2017), in her article on academic freedom, writes much on these lines that in both private and public universities, teachers have to suppress anti-establishment thoughts in order to safeguard their jobs. She writes, echoing Giroux,

> In central and state universities, the higher pay scales go under successive pay commissions, the more permanent faculty are tied to keeping jobs safe and therefore, keeping silent. At the other end of the scale, in what is a global problem, academic freedom is threatened by the increasing precariousness of academic employment, reflected in the rise of contract employees such as *ad hoc* or research associates, and the lack of secure employment and fellowships for young research scholars and recent PhDs. (Sundar 2017, 197)

Giroux speaks of both corporatization (funding of universities and courses) and ideological stance leading to recruitment biases. Unique to India is the additional bias of caste in recruitment and this is not new. Both Batabyal (2014) and Gudavarthy (2018) point out the recruitment bias which often impacts quality. In their respective work, they mention that in the late 1980s, several universities, especially the State universities, witnessed a decline in quality because of a faulty recruitment process. Batabyal writes that by the 1960s disillusionment had set in the academia, and apart from the mismatch between the academic world and the new world order, location of the universities and

> stagnation in economy where the universities were located did not give much hope either. Within the academia, favouritism in the appointment of teachers had become a discouraging but established bias. In the 1950s,

1960s—Structure of universities and position of vice-chancellors remained static. Universities were straitjacketed by administrators and bureaucracy, second of the vice-chancellor were either retired judges or people who had no direct connect with people. (Batabyal 2014, 104–105)

Other than caste and probably religion, ideology and political affiliations play an important role in recruitments in universities. In JNU, in the last two years, several recruitments and promotions that have taken place are being questioned on the grounds of qualifications and experience. It is alleged that most of the recruitments and promotions are being made on the basis of political affiliations. This usually is the death knell of any university as the history of several State universities have already shown us.

Designing and Assigning Courses

One of the most important functions of being a teacher in a university is to design and plan courses and most teachers enjoy this process and look forward to doing so. This was evident during the interviews where teachers either expressed their satisfaction over the existing process of designing and assigning courses or the desire to be a part of it. Older universities usually have a set of core courses in addition to several optional courses, but a teacher might want to include a course based on his/her expertise or in keeping with the contemporary needs and developments. The recruitment and appointment impact the freedom to design and teach courses. This is again another part of the 'educational process', as Giroux puts it, that is slowly being taken away from a large section of teachers.

In the interviews with the teachers in the universities, it was apparent that the control over content and course was in the hands of the senior and permanent staff. Overall, the process of course designing is fairly uniform with the Board of Studies being the approving body consisting of permanent and, usually, senior faculty playing the key role in designing courses and also designating courses to teachers. Universities like JNU and DU have a more elaborate system of teachers presenting and defending the courses they want to introduce in their centres/departments and also getting it peer reviewed. This was mentioned by several teachers during the interviews. The teachers expressed satisfaction with the system where they got an opportunity to design and defend their course/s. Though older universities had a set of core courses that were compulsory, over the years, a number of courses had been added. This limited the scope of fresh courses as the teachers and students were expected to complete the existing number of courses. This was mentioned by a few teachers from JNU and DU.

In most of the universities covered in the study, the younger and temporary staff did not have any say where courses were concerned, be it designing or teaching. When the teachers were asked about their freedom to design courses or speak out openly about their political affiliations or even about issues facing the teachers in most cases, the senior faculty were more forthcoming, while the younger faculty appeared to take a more conformist stand. If one looks at the overall responses from teachers, the senior to mid-senior level teachers spoke of the freedom to decide on courses they want to teach or design. The younger teachers, namely the assistant professors and the ad-hoc teachers were dependent on the decisions made by the seniors. There was an underlying hint of dissatisfaction among them regarding the lack of choice and decision-making. In Gulbarga University, at least two teachers expressed dissatisfaction with the recruitment process. According to one of the teachers, people with merit were often not selected. He suggested that a monitoring or advisory body like an Indian University Service should be there to 'check the appointments'. A young assistant professor in Gulbarga University mentioned casteism in the education system. She was also unhappy with the research work in universities; she felt it was not up to the mark. In addition, she felt the need to change the syllabus. There was a hesitancy in the guest lecturer to speak out too much, but there was a tone of unhappiness with the limited role of guest lecturers. There also seemed to be a sharp divide between permanent lecturers and guest lecturers. The guest lecturers did not have any role in designing courses and nor any representation in the academic council.

The story was similar in Calicut University. Of all the universities, the teachers of Periyar University were most vocal about it. Almost everyone mentioned that they were unhappy with the current system of assigning of courses to teachers. In Punjab University, too, an associate professor mentioned that they are not allowed to choose the courses they want to teach. Not only in humanities, several teachers in sciences (example BHU), mentioned that the course teacher was decided by seniors. There were a few exceptions like NEHU, JNU and DU where professors across levels could introduce new courses and also had a say in what they want to teach. But there were exceptions rather than the norm. Assistant and associate professors expressed unhappiness, directly and indirectly about this rule, but no attempt had been made to challenge or change this. At least there was no mention of it during the interviews. Both tenure and seniority played an important role in decision-making with regard to courses.

Research, Administrative Work and Other Rules

Over the years, the teachers have been unhappy with certain other rules. Rules regarding biometric, teaching and research have not gone down well with some of the teachers. There were complaints about the approach to research and publications. An assistant professor in Bangalore University said that too many rules curb creative and innovation. Several teachers across universities mentioned that they are being burdened with administrative responsibilities, and this is hampering teaching, this was across humanities and sciences. With regard to research, there seemed to be mixed feelings. While some were happy with the emphasis on research, many felt that not all teachers are likely to be interested in research. A senior professor of history in Bangalore University was unhappy regarding rules of research and publication. He said, 'All teachers are not good researchers and vice versa and publishing cannot be the sole criteria for promotion. The administration is literally forcing teachers to publish, and as a result, some teachers are getting promotion.' On the topic of attendance, a teacher remarked that attendance for teachers was not yet in place and said that since it is expected that students' presence in the class be marked, it should be the same for teachers. On the other hand, some teachers were against this, as an assistant professor from BHU remarked that with the increasing administrative and compulsory attendance marking, the teaching profession is becoming more of a clerical job. He added that teachers also needed to spend time on preparing for lectures and going for fieldwork; so they may not be able to mark in their attendance. In NEHU, a few assistant professors (sciences) said that much of their time goes in filling in data sheets for administrative purpose, and the scope for research has been reduced.

On the topic of research, one was the resentment against being forced to pursue research and the other point of dissatisfaction was the recent move by the government to force certain research topics. Some of the teachers mentioned that a directive has been issued by the State that certain pre-decided research topics that pertain to national interests should be given priority. This falls right in the framework of how Gramsci saw the State using its power to push its ideological agenda. Soon after Independence, nation-building was of prime importance for the State and as a subject of study within the academia. There was a push to seek help from all quarters to build a new nation, but there was no State-led agenda to drive only certain kind of research. The topics of 'national interests' that are being foisted on teachers are more a part of the agenda to push for a right-wing nationalistic approach to nation-building.

While on the one hand, some teachers were unhappy with research and research topics being foisted on them, on the other hand, student research programmes have been under constant attack with drastic seat cuts in PhD programmes. This has been particularly severe for JNU, where the academic council passed a move to cut seats in MPhil and PhD courses, as a result of which no admissions were made for PhD courses in several centres in JNU for a year. But many other universities continued to follow the 2009 regulations. Even in Periyar University, a professor mentioned that the research seats have been halved from eight to four. There has been a further move to curtail the number of MPhil/PhD students that a professor can supervise, which has led to a crisis of sorts for both teachers and students with a shortfall of professors who can guide students. A retired professor (science) from DU lamented the lack of attention to research by the current government. 'I do not think there is enough funding, and it has multiple consequences. First is the research. You cannot expect universities to be there in top 300 if you do not fund them. You cannot do good research without funds. It also prohibits quality students from enrolling in the course. And hence, the quality of teaching and the profession goes down. One of the disastrous policies that government started was setting up institute of sciences research and funding them preferentially over the universities, which meant that in experimental disciplines, the universities started getting starved of funds.' It is strange that research is viewed as essential for teachers and denied for students. Of course, as mentioned earlier, in humanities, teachers are being pushed towards particular pre-decided topics. Both the scenarios are not conducive for the intellectual growth of a university. Innovation and creativity are the cornerstones of research, and in the absence of any or both, it is difficult for quality research to thrive. Teachers and students alike should have the freedom and be encouraged to think of new perspectives and alternatives through research. Stifling of research will only exacerbate problems of quality of learning and limiting knowledge to the classroom.

Added to this has been the cut back on scholarships in many universities. In Periyar and NEHU, professors mentioned that the Rajiv Gandhi Fellowship has been discontinued for a few years now, and this has affected several students, especially minorities. In IIT Chennai, two assistant professors mentioned that the numbers of scholarships and the number of students that can avail scholarships have reduced, and this had led to some students dropping the course midway. A reduction in scholarship when paired with the current trend of hiking the fees may prove to be disastrous for students, especially for those from the underprivileged and marginalized sections of the society. In the past one year, there have been several protests against reduction of both seats and scholarships but to no avail. Some of the teachers commented on the new rule whereby even research students had to mark their attendance. Almost all the students across universities mentioned the new rule of compulsory attendance of 75 per cent that has been introduced, and the teachers spoke of the new biometric system in universities to mark attendance of teachers.

McCoy, in her article on impact of education on the working class in Britain, writes that 'compulsory attendance is viewed as normal and defining part of childhood' (McCoy 1998, 106). Plat takes it a step further and writes, 'Compulsory education has become a customary way of regarding childhood and has created a new category of youthful misbehaviour that is truancy' (Plat 1969, 8). In Pondicherry University, the attendance is available online and can be monitored by the parents. Both teachers and parents seek to control students through a compulsory attendance rule. The students attend classes out of fear that they will be denied permission to write exams due to lack of attendance. Different views on this emerged during the course of the fieldwork; a young guest lecturer in Bangalore University (sciences) said that the attendance system was good as 'discipline teaches a person how to behave and work.' In contrast, a teacher in AU (science) said that too many restrictions were not good for the students, adding that if a teacher is good, students will automatically attend classes. Similarly, in JNU, an assistant professor felt that rules such as these attack the very nature of the university. For the uninitiated, JNU historically has never had an attendance system. The premise of this is simple; once out of school, an individual is an adult and is to be given the right to make his/her choices. It is left to the discretion of the student to make informed choices. So, while at the age of 18, one is expected to choose the right candidate to represent the people by exercising the right to vote but is seen to be incompetent to decide whether to attend class or not.

In all the interviews conducted, only one student mentioned that universities should treat students as adults; very few students expressed dissatisfaction with this rule. The rules regarding attendance and biometric was accepted by many on the grounds of discipline. It cannot be denied that both students and teachers need to operate within a system where there is an acceptance of general rules of behaviour: class timings, deadlines for research papers, etc. But the idea that discipline is always imposed from outside by an authority figure is problematic. Disciplining the mind can be an internal process, and discipline doesn't need to become synonymous with rigidity and authoritarian control. Say, a student doesn't attend any class; s/he has to bear the consequences during evaluation. We leave it to the young adult to make a decision about it being cognizant of the consequences. A person sitting in class is not necessarily attentive or interested.

Several universities have issued circulars or teachers have been orally informed by the administration not to speak against the university, be it against its policies or the vice chancellor. A professor from NEHU mentioned, 'Everybody should be given the right to express themselves in their dignified language. Even a labourer should have voice. VC also mentioned subtly that since the professors derive salary from the university, they should not be criticizing the university, which is totally unfair and curtailing the growth of university and a threat to the freedom of academics.' Interestingly, several other teachers from the same university said there was no lack of freedom and that teachers should use freedom 'constructively'. But again, another said, 'Teachers and public intellectuals are sticking to the basic duty of teaching; they have to go beyond that and exercise the freedom and make something good out of it.' Within the same university, teachers had differing views on what constitutes freedom and how it should be exercised. In JNU, an assistant professor said, 'Unnecessary rules and regulations just to get the teachers to attend the administration work. There is no transparency on who is making the rules. There are constraints in context of teaching as the teacher has been made very conscious of the presence of an authority looking through lens. Usually, the classroom used to be very communicative. Now, the teachers are a little conscious that nothing stated should fuel any controversy or taken out of context.'

Teachers were hesitant to speak out openly about the issues facing higher education or even their own university. It did seem strange that none of the teachers mentioned the controversial rule by the UGC to invoke the Civil Services Rules in Centrally funded universities which prevents teachers and other staff from speaking out in public/media. The UGC sent out a circular to 47 universities in May 2018 regarding this. There was a widespread protest, notably by JNU, which resulted in the MHRD revoking the rule that had been clearly an attempt to curtail academic freedom and institutional autonomy. The controversial Central Civil Services (CCS) Rules state that a government servant cannot be a part of any management or conduct or participate in the editing or management of any newspaper or other periodical publication or electronic media. The government servants cannot speak against any government policy or action in public/media. The MHRD said that the CCS Rules were not mandatory, rather it is left to respective universities to decide whether or not to enforce it. In JNU, the VC used the executive council to bring in ordinances which would make it compulsory to comply with the CCS rules. The Jawaharlal Nehru University Teachers' Association (JNUTA) released a statement saying that the CCS was an attempt to:

> Underhandedly stifle criticism against government policies and was an attack on independence of thinking and the freedom to dissent. Under these rules, economics professors can be punished for discussing economic policy, political scientists can be punished for discussing politics, environmental science professors can be punished for discussing environmental policy and scientists can be punished for discussing government science policy. All educationists can be punished for expressing their views on educational policy. The very role that academics are supposed to play in the classrooms and in civil society has become criminalized. (Shuriah 2018)

However, the Federation of Central Universities' Teachers' Associations noted that several Central universities had already enforced the CCS. In Kerala, a teacher had been suspended for criticizing the administration in his Facebook post. A bigger concern was that teachers could not publish any work that could be seen as critical of the policies of the government. The teachers' associations asked for a uniform withdrawal of the CCS from all the universities.

Similarly, the ministry also had to back track on its decision to bring DU under the Essential Services Maintenance Act, thus preventing the teachers from protesting or going on a strike. The ministry alleged that frequent strikes by teachers were disrupting classes and exams. The teachers, however, were protesting against the various policies of the UGC and decisions of the government regarding autonomy, appointment and promotions. The teachers saw this as a deliberate move by the government to prevent teachers from speaking out.

EXECUTIVE COUNCILS AND TEACHERS

The executive councils in universities provide the space for teachers to voice their opinion and grievances and are also used to discuss finance, funding and other issues facing universities. Sometimes referred to as the syndicate or senate, the councils may also include student representatives. The minutes of the meeting of executive councils are required to be posted on the university website, but not all do so, as was evident when the websites of the universities included in the study were scoured for the details of the meetings held by the executive council. Given the important role played by academic councils, in many universities teachers were unaware of the changes taking place in the composition and role of the councils. In BHU, Sciences—most teachers did not know about changes in the academic council. Only one said that 'there was an academic council at the university level. Earlier, all professors were members of that. But 10–12 years ago, the rule was changed and now only the head, dean and directors are member of that. So, the effect of teachers on that is no more.' This upset teachers but no one opposed it openly.

In JU, a professor remarked that the administration had made changes in the executive council and it no longer has any elected representatives. In Gulbarga University, two senior professors expressed unhappiness with the removal of the council. The professor was clearly reluctant to speak about the changes that have taken place in the academic council. 'Earlier there were 3 councils, now there is only one and a syndicate' (Quote by a teacher). In DU, a senior professor said 'Being in older university, we do have teachers' representation in all the councils, but in 2009, 12 new Central universities came up and teachers' representation in those universities is quite low. Even in draft new policy in 2019, there is no clause of teaching representative. They identify the role of the VC as one of following government dictates. The role of teachers is being looked as someone who slows down the processes, and government does not have the time for their suggestion.' A retired professor said, 'In DU, membership of the bodies was mainly by seniority, which included senior professors and HoDs, which meant the membership was always very pro-administration and that does not change. The senior professors will always support whosoever is the VC; the elected representative which forms a small fraction of it, they change politically. There, you might see conflict between the VC and the elected representatives, if they happen to belong to the opposite end of ideological spectrum.'

Similarly, in Gauhati University, professors said that statutory provision is the same. 'But resource selection, in terms of who is to be called as guest or invitee for a lecture, is manipulated. In a few events, the speech was also given from the administration. VC appoints people of his choice in committees. Teachers do not talk about it officially.' In NEHU, too, teachers spoke of lack of experts in the councils. One professor mentioned that esteemed individuals and institutes were supposed to be part of the academic councils, but instead there is politics over it. In West Bengal, too, the executive council has been undergoing several changes resulting in protests.[1]

Most of the teachers were unaware of what was happening in the academic councils; the large number of ad-hoc/guest lecturers being recruited could not even be a part of the academic councils. Hence, these councils which are supposed to act as a forum where decisions regarding the welfare of the university—teachers and students included—are now becoming purely administrative bodies and teachers and students are being alienated from the process. This is yet another outcome of the recruitment policies whereby fewer permanent staff is being recruited, and this is reflected in the fewer number of teachers in the executive councils, which is not a healthy trend.

---

[1] West Bengal Universities and Colleges (Composition, Functions, and Procedures for Election of Student's Council) Rules, 2017—(a) Any student body with whatever name shall be called as student's council; (b) the whole process of nomination and election should be completed within one month and (c) the date and time of election would be decided by the state.

> The composition of the student council of colleges: (a) President, nominated by principal/vice principal;(b) vice president, nominated amongst the teachers by teachers' council; (c) general secretary and assistant general secretary elected by elected class representatives. Every meeting shall be convened under the president or the vice president. In universities, the president and vice president will be appointed by the VC. The election committee consists of VC or the principal and other teachers or faculty members.

West Bengal Universities and Colleges (Administration and Regulation) Act, 2017

> Under the miscellaneous provisions, the State government shall make provision consistent with this Act, and the university or college in bound to apply it. Any difficulty in applying the provision will be removed by the State. In case there is a tussle between the university and the government, the decision of the State government prevails. Available at https://wbxpress.com/west-bengal-universities-colleges-composition-functions-procedure-election-students-council-rules-2017/

One of the examples of either ignorance or feigning ignorance is the case of Bangalore University. The syndicate, as the executive council of Bangalore University is referred to, has seen a lot of turmoil due to the change of governments in 2018. The coalition government, led by H. D. Kumaraswamy, had barely appointed the syndicate members of the 19 universities that come under the aegis of Bangalore University when the government collapsed. The new government immediately withdrew all the nominations to the syndicate by the previous government, in spite of a request by the erstwhile chief minister not to do so. The same practice had been followed by the previous Congress government five years ago. With the news of nominations being withdrawn becoming public, aspirants starting approaching ministers and Member of the Legislative Assembly to be included in the syndicate. Former members of the syndicate and executive council of Gulbarga University came out in the support of the candidature of Mallikarjun Kharge of the Congress Party from the Kalaburagi constituency in 2019.

JNU and FTII academic council meetings have been in the news for all the wrong reasons. In May 2017, the academic council of JNU successfully thwarted an attempt by the VC to change the university admission policies as per the UGC guidelines of 2016. Trouble had been brewing since December 2016 with the VC making attempts to ensure the passage of the new admission policies without any debate. The minutes of the meeting of the 141st academic council meeting held in December 2016 had been misrepresented as the council having approved and passed the new UGC admission guidelines, when, in reality, the council had asked for the UGC to reconsider the new guidelines and make changes. The council raised the issue of erroneous minutes of the meeting in both the 142nd and 143rd council meetings. One of the main concerns voiced by the teachers was with regard to the increased weightage to the marks for viva voce which they believed would be discriminatory against students from deprived backgrounds. The council approved of written exams and viva voce to be 80/20 respectively. The other point of contention was the reduced intake of students in MPhil/PhD programmes, whereas the teachers had suggested an increase in intake. The JNUTA released a press statement stating the actual resolutions and minutes of the meeting.

The FTII protests grabbed headlines with the appointment of Gajendra Chauhan as the chairman in 2015. In September 2019, the heads of various departments were removed from the administrative council. The HoDs represented the interest of students and teachers alike by playing an active role in appointment of faculty, deciding the syllabus and other academic activities. Prior to this, the students had been removed from the councils in 2017. The administrative council consisting of teachers and students had been set up after a struggle in 1974, after it was recommended by the G. D. Khosla Committee. The change in the composition of the administrative council has allowed the governing and administrative council to make rules that curtail freedom of students. The students can no longer schedule a film screening without approval, instead a schedule for the whole semester has to be planned in advance; also, the students are not allowed to access the classroom theatres of respective departments after class hours. The emphasis is more on building infrastructure than to facilitate learning. Students protested against the move to remove HoDs from the meetings, following which FTII Director Bhupendra Kainthola said that a decision had been taken to include only those HoDs whose departments were being discussed in the meetings.

In AU, minutes of the meeting of March 2018 revealed that the registrar had levelled serious allegations against a senior professor of getting a post under the SC/ST quota when he didn't belong to either the SC or ST community. The registrar further alleged that the senior professor had submitted fake medical bills. The registrar was asked to leave the meeting when the matter was being discussed and rejoined only when the resolution was passed by the executive council that the VC would head an enquiry into the allegations made against the senior professor. In 2016, the executive council of AU took the decision that retired professors would be re-employed only in special cases and most of the recruitment would take place only on contract basis and at junior levels ('recruitment of young faculty'), but there would be no further recruitment of guest faculty. The minutes of the meeting of Punjab University, too, reveal the tension between the VC and the teachers over several issues.

As is evident, academic councils that are meant to help facilitate better governance and address issues facing both teachers and students have been sites of politics—both from within and with political interference. VC of universities play an important role in keeping alive the democratic nature of these councils and ensure that councils function as per the mandate with which they were created in the first place. The several examples shared make it evident that the councils are becoming exclusive committees with only a select few included in the councils. Though political influence and interference is nothing new, but the composition of the academic councils has been undergoing a rapid change in the past few years.

As Gudavarthy points out,

> Autonomy of universities granted by the Parliament and the culture of speaking truth to power under Modi seemed to be systematically undermined through various methods-including posting those close to the RSS as heads of administrative positions, removal of grievance mechanisms internal to these institutions, and removal of individual faculty opposed to the viewpoint of the ruling dispensation. BJP does not imagine a university as sites of autonomy where a life of the mind is fostered; instead they see them as citadels of discipline, efficiency, loyalty and standardization. (Gudavarthy 2019, 33)

IDEOLOGY: TEACHERS AND THE TAUGHT

In the opening section, in reference to Freire, the teacher is seen as someone who trains a mind to think, to question and not to blindly accept the world around. The teacher acquaints the student with the reality of the society and provides the student with a lens to view the world, through both socialization and education as a system of inquiry rather than mere passage of knowledge. Mannheim writes that in universities,

> Nothing is more desirable than those intellectuals who have a background of pronounced class interests should, especially in their youth, assimilate this point of view and conception of the whole. Even in such a school it is not to be assumed that the teachers should be partyless. It is not the object of such a school to avoid arriving at political decisions. But there is a profound difference between a teacher who, after careful deliberation addresses

his students, whose minds are not yet made up, from a point of view which has been attained by careful thinking leading to a comprehension of the total situation and a teacher who is exclusively concerned with inculcating a party outlook already firmly established. (Mannheim 1955, 144)

In the debate of universities being apolitical, the focus is on students, but the teachers, too, are expected to not air their ideological viewpoints in classrooms or outside. The university, then, is to comprise of teachers and students who operate within a fenced structure. But the ideological position of the teacher may simply be reflected in the readings suggested, in the approach to a social reality, be it on gender, sexuality, labour, market and so on. When the teacher puts before the student, as Mannheim points out, after due deliberation, his/her position on certain issues, it is a reflection of his/her ideological position, which is then passed on to the students. The student may choose to imbibe the same ideological position or go in a totally different direction. Teachers are also political actors, and often, these two roles may not be divorced from each other. This adds on a dimension in the relationship between teachers, teachers and students and teachers and administration. The teachers are not alone; the State also steps in with ways of spreading its own ideology through educational institutes.

In connection with education, Giroux (1998, 5) writes that ideology is a dynamic construct and

> ways in which meanings are produced, mediated, embodied in knowledge forms, social practices and cultural experiences. Ideology is a set of doctrines as we well medium through which teachers and educators make sense of their own experiences and those of the world in which they find themselves. As a pedagogical tool ideology becomes useful for understanding not only how schools sustain and produce meanings but also how individuals and groups produce negotiate, modify and resists them. How ideology works presents teachers with a heuristic tool to examine how their own views about knowledge, human nature and values and society mediated though the common sense assumptions they use to structure classroom techniques.

The everyday relationship between students and teachers with each other and within their groups in the framework of ideology was one of the core themes of the research. There is a general consensus that more than ever before, political ideological differences are affecting relationships. One may argue that this is an urban-India phenomenon and more so for those who are social-media users of WhatsApp, Twitter and Facebook. One cannot deny that the readiness with which information is available is partly responsible for this. In casual conversations with friends and colleagues, several of them have mentioned that they have opted out of chat groups or blocked people on WhatsApp and Facebook because they could no longer deal with the types of messages and discussions on these social media platforms based on ideological positions. Jokes, memes, fake news, unthinking forwards on political issues and the ensuing conflict between differing viewpoints is ruining many relationships. Some have decided not to air their opinion on social media platforms, while some have decided to take it head-on. The question then is how ideology has impacted relationship between students and teachers.

Four points stood out during the course of research. First was that there was a discomfort with discussing ideology among students and teachers alike. Second was that majority of the students did not want their teachers to be open about their ideological (political and non-political) positions. Third was that most of the teachers wanted to keep ideology out of the classroom. Fourth was that both teachers and students of sciences, with very few exceptions, said that influence of ideology is a matter of concern only for humanities and not for sciences. Ideology and sciences are divorced from each other and so the former does not enter the classroom in any case.

When asked about discussion on ideology among faculty or about political ideological positions of the faculty, majority of teachers answered that they do not discuss it. Let's place it in the context of what Mannheim wrote: 'In every society there are social groups whose special task it is to provide an interpretation of the world for that society. We call these the intelligentsia' (Mannheim 1955, 9). In BHU (sciences), historically politically active, which is the reason also assigned for the decline in quality, almost all the teachers said that the faculty is political and the caste of a person does indicate political ideological positions. BHU science faculty was one of the few who said that yes, teachers are open about their ideological positions and do talk about it with each other. An associate professor said, 'Nowadays everyone is political. If we talk about association with political parties, then I think it's not allowed. But people are associated with other arms of political parties like their cultural wing or something. But political leaning of most of the teachers are clear.' The teachers said that the rightists were dominant among the faculty and, because of this, the leftists were not allowed to voice themselves. Often, speakers with a left-wing inclination were prevented from even entering the campus. The BHU humanities faculty, on the other hand, said that they did not discuss politics or ideology, but the teachers were either associated with the Congress Party or the BJP. In contrast, in AU, which also has a history of political activism, the science faculty said that they are apolitical, but they did have discussions on politics and ideology, and the few who were political were socialists. In NIT Kashmir, teachers said that they do not discuss political affiliations openly.

On the other hand, OU, where students and teachers alike were deeply involved in the fight for the bifurcation of Andhra Pradesh, now claimed to be apolitical. The faculty claimed that rather than political affiliation, caste creates a bias among faculty. A retired professor from IIT Delhi lamented how politics and caste have destroyed several universities. He said, 'Why to even have these things (ideology, politics) inside the campus? Politics has ruined universities. I had recently gone to Lucknow University. It is in a very sorry state. Similar is the case with AU and BHU. There is nothing left due to all the politics. *Ye is caste se hai. Ye us caste se hai* (this person belongs to this caste, that caste). The students there are very bright but teachers are busy in something else.' Several teachers from these universities confirmed the same during interviews. In Gulbarga University, too, more than political ideology, caste as an expression of social ideology seemed to create a divide among teachers. According to an assistant professor, from an SC community, caste played a big role in determining political ideological leanings in the campus. As mentioned in the context of the students' interviews in Gulbarga University, most of the students were OBCs and identified with the right wing.

In NEHU, political–ideological differences were being played out between the administration and the teachers' union. There were ongoing tussles on several issues with regard to recruitment and promotion. In JU, there was a suggestion of opportunism when a teacher said that the ruling party determined the ideological inclination of teachers. There were no open discussions on ideology; a teacher hinted that the teachers were scared to speak out. Some teachers refused to comment while one said he is a leftist. This was seen even among the humanities faculty. Strangely, even the students were scared to speak out about ideology, and one mentioned surveillance by the state. In JU (sciences), a teacher said that the right kind of ideology was important, else it can only cause harm. A science professor in DU, who was politically active, said, 'I believe apolitical means political of convenience. But in DU, we have space for positions on all issues. The degree of discussion might vary. There is a space. Discussion over national issues and university issues are prevalent in our university. It would be sad if we imagine our university spaces devoid of that. Finally, it is for the teachers and students to critically think and evolve your own positions about these things.' She added, 'I would like draw a comparison between JNU and *Delhi University Students Union* (DUSU) to answer this question. The relationship with the administration is directly in synch with your relationship with the government. The administrator is not free to have a relationship with the unions independent of your political ideology. Administration is in direct control of the government and that, therefore, controls the role administration has with the union.'

With regard to student–teacher relationship, it is clear that both students and teachers were apprehensive that if teachers were open about their ideological positions, it may result in students gravitating towards certain teachers or to ingratiate themselves for selfish reasons. The teachers, on the other hand, were wary about students' union-related violence on campus. Faculty in BHU (sciences) said that the intensely political faculty has resulted in favouritism and groupism among students. As a teacher put it, 'There could be favouritism, but it is disguised. Also, teachers who are open about their ideology, some students are associated with them. It increases groupism, no doubt.' This was reiterated in several universities: OU, Punjab University, NEHU, Gulbarga University and Bangalore University. It appeared from the interviews with the science faculty that students of history, political science and sociology were most susceptible to ideological influences of teachers. As a professor of biochemistry put it, 'Ideology impacts teaching only in humanities; for example, in political science and history, where opinions are formed on the basis of what is taught.' On the ideological inclinations of teachers, the overall impression was that the teachers did have discussions on their ideological positions, and some were part of local politics. A chemistry professor in NEHU said, 'University should contribute to the society, and one can do so without taking sides.' He said that ideological leanings do impact teaching. –'Leftists are mostly intellectuals. Common students may not understand and follow properly; they understand only what is convenient for them.' He was vehement that teachers should not let their ideological leanings impact their relationship with students; it is wrong and against the very idea of university. JU was one of the few universities where the teachers, both science and humanities, said that ideological positions do impact the relationship between the teachers. An associate professor from JU said, 'It leads to groupism, which influences relationship, because students who are more friendly towards those teachers get favouritism in every opportunity, for example, marks, rank or employment.' The humanities were more forthcoming on the impact of ideology on teaching and said that teachers should be unbiased.

One of the most nuanced answers among science teachers regarding teaching being influenced by ideology was given by a professor in DU, who said, 'Personally, my involvement in left politics has changed the way I look at issues. I relate to students now. It will impact how I identify the purpose of teaching. My belief in importance of scientific temper in students is part of my politics. The idea that we have about ourselves and our surroundings does have an impact on the teachers we are.' In BHU, all but one teacher among the sciences said that ideology does impact teaching. The one teacher who disagreed said that it depended upon the 'intellectual capacity' of a teacher to deliver a lecture without letting ideology to influence it.

Among humanities faculty, in Gulbarga University, teachers not only discuss political and ideological positions openly but also were divided into camps based on politics and caste. One of the teachers said that he saw no harm in teachers discussing ideology with students, and he saw no negative impact on students. In fact, according to him, teachers should impart knowledge about ideology to students. In Calicut University, the teachers were largely leftist and open about their ideological positions (caste and economic) and political affiliations. But they said that this did not led to groupism of any kind. It was also one of the few universities where the teachers were in favour of ideology being a part of teaching. For example, an assistant professor, too, said that ideological leanings impact teaching and is a very important 'communal version of historical understanding, and teaching of it has serious repercussions'. As per an associate professor of philosophy, 'Strong political leanings build character and strong opinion. This might improve quality of teaching in certain subjects, provided they are open to discussions.' Similar viewpoint was echoed by an associate professor of philosophy, who said, 'Only teachers with strong political leanings can teach properly. Because then, he takes more effort in research.' An associate professor of political science said that while 'ideology impacts teaching, it is a positive thing, as knowledge is essentially political.' A young assistant professor also said 'Strong ideologies won't hamper the quality of education, and it is to be seen as a personal stand of a person.' It doesn't impact the student–teacher relationship. Contrast this with what the humanities faculty said in Bangalore University, the senior professors of education and history, who said, 'Teachers need to be non-propagandist and not influence young minds with ideology. The students should decide for themselves.'

In AU, speaking on the impact of ideology on teaching, teachers said that it does not impact the immediate relationship between teachers or between teachers and students as such, but it may impact the university at large. So, while ideology may not influence the day-to-day relations or life, but the goal and functioning of a university may be impacted by ideology. The relationship between teachers did not seem to be impacted much due to social world view or political inclinations, but a few teachers spoke of the impact it had on teacher and student relationship. Some of the teachers tend to favour student who have similar ideological positions (social and political) as them.

This leads to favouritism and groupism. 'Yes, students get affected by political inclination of teachers. Teachers form relation with students with that political ideology only. Because of internal conflicts among teachers, groupism takes place.'

The fear of groupism and bias is not unwarranted, as Sanyal points out in relation to political–ideological divisions in universities.

> The left dominance over intellectual establishment has roots in the systematic 'ethnic cleansing' of non left thinkers since 1950s, until the failure of the socialist model was accepted with the term Hindu rate of growth. B.R Shenoy who questioned Nehru's economics was a victim of this attitude. However from 1990s, many soviet derived material were removed from the books, but most of them remained. Students are mostly given courses on Amartya Sen and other leftist intellectuals but exposed very limited to thoughts of Friedrich Hayek, Milton Friedman or Jagdish Bhagawati. (Sanyal 2016)

TEACHERS ON ROLE OF STUDENTS' UNION

One potential area of conflict on campus is student activism. Many of those averse to the idea of student politics were apprehensive about it leading to violence on campus. The idea of a non-political students' union was appealing to most students and teachers. Students did see it as a means of putting forward their demands to the administration. When teachers were asked whether they support the idea of students' union, most of the science faculty was opposed to the idea of student union on campus. Those who did want students' union, wanted it to be apolitical and only concentrate on student issues such as hostel, fee hike and so on. Interestingly, BHU, which has a rather tumultuous political past, had teachers supporting the idea of a political student union. One of the main reasons that the teachers usually spoke out against students' union was that it vitiated the campus environment, but in BHU, teachers had something different to say. One of the assistant professors (science) said, 'This impacts positively in the area of social inclusion and gender sensitization.' While another (associate professor) said, 'I think there should be discussion about every kind of ideology in the campus. This leads to learning and an informed opinion about society and issues.' Teachers were more concerned about casteism on campus, both in classroom and among teachers, rather than politics on campus. Among those from humanities, only two answered directly; both the associate teachers and assistant professors, respectively, said that it is necessary for all stakeholders in the university to get an opportunity to speak out. The associate professor mentioned his experiences at Jamia Milia Islamia and AMU and said that he cannot categorically state that he is against the idea, since he has seen both the benefits and problems of a students' union on campus.

The decline of several universities due to student politics driven by violence and manipulations of national parties is a proof of how misguided student politics can harm universities. In OU, one of the teachers mentioned that students' union by itself is not bad 'but should have a positive ideology', while another teacher spoke of morals. She said, 'There should be morality. Morals should be encouraged as values which build the positive nature of the faculty/students.' Among the humanities faculty in OU, none of the teachers supported a students' union. It was unexpected considering that OU has been the nerve of every activity related to the issue of a separate Telangana. The *Srikrishna Commission Report* defined it as 'trouble spots' and 'trouble creators' during agitations (Pathania 2018, 71). In the same campus, a few years ago, teachers encouraged students to take out rallies and organize meetings on a deeply political issue but today, they are not in favour of politics on campus. During the Telangana movement, teachers realized that as government employees, they could not agitate directly against the government. Therefore, they sought the support of the youth and students. The campus politics of OU also started centring around on the issue of Telangana around this time. In 1968, Osmania University Student Union fought on the Telangana issue. There were several forums formed by government employees to spread consciousness about Telangana. Their main focus was university students. OU provided the platform to think and assert the indigenous identity (Pathania 2018, 92). In Warangal NIT, teachers said that students can be represented through the students' union only as long it is not political in nature, as it may 'ruin the environment in the campu'. In Pondicherry University, a few teachers spoke in favour of students being politically active. One may recall that, in contrast, students of the same university were opposed to political activity on campus.

IIT Chennai, in contrast to IIT Delhi, had more teachers speak in favour of student activism. One reason could be the background of the teachers. The teachers who spoke in favour of students' union and political activity on campus were from Kerala, where political activism among students is very high in educational institutes. Interestingly, all the teachers interviewed in JU (sciences and humanities) were in favour of a students' union, and a few said that students should be political, too, as they are the future citizens of the country and they should be aware of the politics in the country. As an assistant professor (humanities) put it, 'I support the idea of students' union; students' participation is very important for evolving thoughts.' Others echoed support and said that it prepares students for a political career. JU has always been politically active, they added, and according to a professor, the recent trend of unemployment, lack of faculty and quality education had further pushed students towards political activism.

In DU, the students' union is highly political and, obviously, the teachers mentioned this during the interviews with them. According to a professor (DU, science), the political nature of the students' union had a definite impact on the relationship with the teachers' union and the administration, as the students' union is largely determined by who is in power at the Centre. She said, 'When UPA–2 (United Progressive Alliance, popularly referred to as the UPA government, which was in power for two successive terms till 2014) was in power, the students' union led by National Students' Union of India could not oppose its parent body (Congress party) at the Centre. Similarly, when the current student union is led by the right wing, they do not participate in any event that is seen as anti-government, as BJP is in power at the Centre. The DUSU, instead of doing something constructive, was busy putting up statues of Savarkar (right-wing ideologue) and Goddess Saraswati on campus.' JNU, too, has a bittersweet relationship with students' union. In 1975, friction between teachers and students' union on establishing a statutory body to prevent victimization by teachers and, also, settle academic disputes of students and teachers led to the closure of the university. The conflict between teachers and students resulted in the university shutting down in order to curb rising tendencies of students to encroach on rights of authorities. While there was resistance to the students' union, it also mobilized younger faculty and showed loyalty of students to the union in spite of its shortcomings.

One of the few among the interviewed science faculty, who spoke in favour of a political students' union, in spite of disagreeing with them on several points, rightly pointed out, 'I fully support the idea of a student union. Private universities may have seminars on unionism and on working rights, but they will never allow unions of teachers and students. In globalization, where our existence has been broken down to individuals, we need to do everything in our capacity to restore, retain and strengthen wherever we have such bodies today. Even in private university, when there is a fee hike, it is only through a collective movement that one can question such moves. The whole idea is to retain public university as a space for healthy debates and discussions on ideas. Activism centred on students' interest will only strengthen the university and will help the country grow overall. You can do path-breaking research only when you question the existing set of beliefs and norms. We need to promote critical thinking. Words like world power do not mean anything if you do not strengthen your university and stop students from questioning.' Not surprisingly, in NIT Kashmir, barring one, all the other teachers were in favour of students' union on campus. JNU presented a similar story, even though the relationship between teachers' union and the students' union has not always been a smooth sailing one. In DU, one of the reasons cited for friction between the teachers' union and students' union was the difference in political affiliation.

In JNU, the students' and teachers' union have been both left oriented (most of the times), yet there is a history of a turbulent relationship, so much so that JNU had to be shut down. In the initial years, after the students' union fought the first election in 1971, one of the core issues picked by the left was admission. Interestingly, the students' union was pitching in its support for reservations based on economic criteria and not caste. Apart from this, the union alleged that JNU was in danger of becoming an elitist university and even spoke against the 1:5 teacher–student ratio, while the national average was 1:20 and the union pushed for 1:10. The friction between teachers' and students' union took place even as early as 1975, regarding establishing a statutory body to prevent victimization by teachers and settle academic disputes of students and teachers. This conflict resulted in university shutting down in order to curb rising tendencies of students to encroach on rights of authorities. The conflict led to opposition to the students' union by some, but at the same time it helped in mobilizing younger faculty who were loyal to the union inspite of its shortcomings (Batabyal 2014, 399/344–347).

The current situation in JNU is lot more complicated with the teachers' union itself divided on political lines. The students' union has its fair share of conflict with the administration and, sometimes, also with teachers. However, the teachers spoke in favour of the students' union, as one teacher put in succinctly, 'I think students are adults when they enter the university; they are above 18. They need to think about politics all the time, since politics governs their future. If they are not political minds, they are half humans. Politics makes them concerned citizens; if they are engaged in politics, it is better for their own development. The student union acts as a force that makes you think not just about your own body but about being a social and political being, and that is a great way of life.' A senior professor made an interesting observation that while political activity may have increased on campus, but the participation of students has declined. Periyar University, where teachers expressed that they are not allowed to discuss ideology, pressed the need for a students' union.

This is not to imply that none of the faculty teaching humanities were opposed to the idea of student s' union. For example, in Gulbarga University, while the teachers were divided on the basis of ideology, both social and political, none were in favour of students' union being politically affiliated to any party. Only one professor from the social work department mentioned that students should be politically active, as it will create a leadership. In contrast was Calicut University, where majority of professors were in favour of students' union said, 'Students' union reflects the commitment to democracy and a lot of its aspects.' As another associate professor put it, 'Politics should be part and parcel of learning. Students can arise though such a union.' She said that while the campus was politically vibrant, it was not violent. In AU, a professor remarked, 'There is always conflict and struggle. Politics is termite for the campus, which is making university hollow.' The teachers were not against the idea of a students' union, as long as it did not become a vehicle for partly politics. A teacher casually (and approvingly) mentioned that the administration and police 'take care' of the situation, if there is any tussle between students' union and administration on campus. The teacher saw nothing wrong in the police being deployed on campus to tackle the students, rather saw it as a welcome move. In contrast, during the course of interviews with the students of AU, some of the students had pointed out that conflict had taken place on campus and the police had been called in and were not in favour of it.

Interestingly, majority of the students did not want a teachers' union on campus, and the ones who did want a teachers' union believed that students and teachers have to put forward a united front. Of the very few who said that a university should have both teachers' and students' union, said that both have to take a clear stand and put forth a united front to fight for the rights of both teachers and students. There was a fear of favouritism by teachers among the students and that of groupism among teachers. The truth is that ideological camps exist in almost all universities. In some universities it is a given that some teachers with similar world views may gravitate towards each other and, unknowingly or deliberately, create an ideological group. These groups are, often, easily identifiable by students and they, in turn, gravitate towards teacher/s in groups, which become power centres due to ideological leanings. The discomfort that students had with openly ideological positions of teachers was rooted in the fear of this 'natural' gravitation of teachers and students which may isolate those who do not wish to overtly identify with such group/s.

The engagement of students in non-political (political in the wider sense of the word, not merely party politics) was seen desirable by many teachers and students alike. As pointed out by Altbach, one of the reasons for the decline of students' movements in India was the shift from the political to the non-political. A 'needs' based relationship between students and the State that took shape was quite different from the political and ideological opposition and engagement that had marked the earlier phases. If the students can further the cause of the State, then politics is encouraged, else students are to focus on cultural- and university-specific issues of infrastructure, hostel amenities, etc. OU is one of the perfect examples of the shifting nature of relationship between students' union and the State. In OU, not only students but teachers and administration were involved in Telangana movement, which, as we know, was based on the demand for a separate state. In 1969, the crucial year of agitation in Telangana movement, under the guidance of OU's VC, Dr Ravada Satyanarayana, teachers of OU organized a convention to debate issues facing Telangana. He argued that intellectuals should play a dynamic role and cautioned them against the consequence of inaction. Teachers not only supported the students but also advised them how to counter the Andhra student lobby (which was opposed to the bifurcation of the state) on campus (Pathania 2018, 78). In the interviews taken with the students and teachers during this research, there were no traces of the strong political positions taken by the students and teachers. Rather teachers were against the students being involved in politics, and the recent steps taken by the state also indicate reluctance of the state to allow student activism on campus, and now that the Telangana state has been formed, there are no immediate political needs that the students' union can help with.

CELEBRATING THE NATION IN UNIVERSITIES

In a previous chapter, using the Gramscian framework of how the State uses education as a tool of propaganda, number of UGC circulars and orders were analysed. However, most of the teachers did not mention these events being celebrated. NEHU faculty was the most vocal on this issue and spoke out against the enforced celebration of Balakot strike. In JNU, teachers mentioned that the administration was planning to install a tank in the campus to instil patriotism among students and remind them of the sacrifices of the army in the wake of the meeting in which the famous '*tukde-tukde*' (tukde is a Hindi word that means pieces) speech took place.

Bangalore University's science faculty was one of the few who supported the celebration of Army Day on campus. A life sciences teacher mentioned that on National Science Day, the achievements of the Indian Army were celebrated. It was a matter of great pride and she supports the Indian army. She added that 'it is good to think about patriotism.' She did not question the reasoning behind celebrating the achievements of army on science day. While science does play a significant role in the development of weaponry and other cutting technology needed for defence purposes, however, science day cannot be reduced to only that aspect. Another engineering professor from Bangalore University said that even though her engineering institute has not celebrated the Army Day or any such day, the students are eager for such events. She said we should think about patriotism as we are Indians, and we should support and be proud of the Indian army. In Punjab University (sciences), while most declined to answer the question, one teacher mentioned that a seminar on Pulwama attack was organized on campus on the directives of MHRD and UGC. Very often, contradictory views were expressed in the same university. Say for example, in NEHU, a biochemistry professor said that there have been no efforts by the government to hold events celebrating army or any other national symbol. This was contradicted by two professors who spoke of circulars/recorded clips sent by the Central government to celebrate surgical strike, Swachh Bharat and so on. One of the professors said that there is a disconnect in the Northeast with the rest of India; while the surgical strike may bring in feeling of national pride, but the current government was using it for electoral gains only. A teacher questioned that this was not done earlier, why is it being done now? He asked, 'Will the army celebrate the universities' success as we celebrate theirs?' Yet another associate professor mentioned that the HRD ministry wants the Indian flag to be put on campus to influence the students.

In Gauhati University, a professor remarked, 'Surgical strike celebration was mandated by UGC and MHRD. These are very unwanted programmes. It was army's duty. We don't have to celebrate it.' Similarly, almost all the teachers in NEHU spoke against the need to celebrate army's achievements on campus. An associate professor remarked, 'As the place is far from Delhi, these things do not reach here; also, these tribal areas have anti-army sentiment. MHRD mandates these events, so they are mechanically done; stupid events, critical perspective lacks, we should not glorify any public institution.' Others implied that teachers attended the events out of force, not choice, just to mark their attendance. The teachers were afraid of getting marked as opposing the current administration. This could lead to them being targeted, as it has been reported to happen in other universities. IIT Chennai teachers mentioned that the national song had become popular on campus, and a new group named 'Vande Mataram' had also been formed.

In the last few years, there has been a definite increase in discussions on patriotism, nationalism and, in this connection, the army. The army was postured as the supreme symbol of sacrifice and patriotism. There could be no questions asked regarding actions of the army, including army excesses in Kashmir or the Armed Forced Special Powers Act, 1958. An extension of this idea has been the recent emphasis to celebrate the victories of the armed forces in universities to inculcate a feeling of pride and unquestioning support in the army. Some have even proposed a compulsory two-year stint in the army for every citizen. History is rife with examples of how unbridled power to the armed forces in governance sounds the death knell for democracy. The police force also works for the protection of the citizens and more visibly so, but it does not invite the same feeling of pride, instead it is constantly questioned, criticized and viewed with suspicion and fear. However, the army is seen to be above corruption and falsehoods, and this is further encouraged with a constant one-sided view of the armed forces. This is a very dangerous precedent and needs to be opposed by students and teachers alike. Else, the result would be narrow-minded, jingoistic students favouring status quo over social change. As a teacher in Punjab University said, 'The Government of India and UGC want to make us more mechanical and less thinkable. They do not want us to engage or ask political questions.'

IDEOLOGY AND SCIENCE

In the context of the impact of ideology on teaching, it did not come as much of a surprise that the science teachers did not really see ideology as a 'problem' they counter while teaching or in their relationship with the students. With the exception of two or three teachers, all the other science teachers mentioned that ideology doesn't have any role to play in the teaching of sciences, nor does it come in the way of relationship among the faculty or the students. Both science teachers and students said, specifically, that ideology does not really matter in sciences; it plays a role in humanities and in that more in certain subjects than others. From a sociological perspective, this brings to mind Karl Popper's and Thomas Kuhn's position on ideology and science. For Popper, the criterion for science was quite clear; anything that could be falsified could not be categorized as science. It is this that separates non-science from science. Progress in science is measured by the falsification of theories, which helps it move closer to the truth. In that ideology is the opposite of science as it is non-falsifiable. 'If ideology is always the conformist, science is seen as critical. Popperian framework demands continuous movement towards truth, hence moving away from ideology. Science needs to be corrected of ideological distortion. What constitutes valid scientific enquiry is socially determined' (Purkayastha 1989, 28).

In almost every era of scientific discoveries, there have been questions of ethics, morality and religion raised. Say for example, the idea of evolution of man is still not accepted by several orthodox Christians and also by Islam and Judaism, as it goes against their religious belief of how God created human beings. Not to be left far behind, the education minister of India, Satya Pal Singh, spoke out against Darwin's theory of evolution at a conference and said that there is no record of any 'person' having 'witnessed ape changing into a man'. Religious beliefs as world view come in conflict with science as one deals with sentiment while the other with facts. One cannot help but recall the imprisonment of Galileo on his theories of a heliocentric solar system which angered the Catholic Church. Before Galileo, Nicolaus Copernicus's book *On the Revolutions of Heavenly Spheres* that was published in 1543, was banned by the church and was allowed to be published only after the disclaimer that it merely is a theoretical conjecture that the earth and other planets revolved around the sun. These are but a few examples of how scientific discoveries are not merely statements of facts or proving a theory but also create ripples of change and discord in the existing religious and social belief systems.

In the 1940s–1950s, there was a shift in the way science was perceived. There was a clear attempt to move away from the then prevalent approach to include in the study of science: the social functions of scientific research, Marxism and interdisciplinary studies. One of the most influential works of this era was by Daniel Bell in 1960s called *The End of Ideology*. He pointed out that campuses were now verging towards a non-ideological positioning in the name of professionalism, scientific rigour and detachment. Kuhn, in his *Structure of Scientific Revolutions*, wrote that while philosophers and scientists have studied scientific revolutions, they did not devote time to understanding its implications on scientific knowledge. According to Kuhn,

> Scientific theory functions as an ideology in scientific communities and in the minds of scientists who belong to them. It directs attention to certain kind of scientific problems. In some ways it even tells the scientists what to think, it dictates preferred techniques of interpretation and discourages creativity and imagination that might lead scientists to think outside their ideological box. (Reisch 2019, xxvii)

Kuhn was of the opinion that politics and science are influenced by ideology and that scientific revolutions were to be seen as ideological revolutions.

> Revolution itself is the replacement of one ideology with another that once again permits professionals to see the world scientifically but which is in significant respects incommensurable with the scientific view of the world that preceded it. While ideology is in place it governs both the activity and evaluation of research and science appears to proceed by accretion. (Reisch 2019, 219)

Kuhn makes another important point that the history of scientific revolutions is rewritten after each revolution and, more often than not, the history is false.

Lynch writes that there are two ways in which ideology can be conceptualized. One is the critical aspect and the other a neutral aspect. The critical concept of ideology distinguishes between ideological and no ideological forms, and in this, ideology is opposed to science. 'Ideology may be distinguished from science by relegating it to social and political realm' (Lynch 1994, 199). Marx, Althusser and Mannheim, all saw ideology as being opposed to science. For Marx, ideology is an

> Inversion in thought corresponding to a contradictory reality. It is the relationship between consciousness and social contradictions. Ideology is conceived as opposed to science and proletarian consciousness. For Althusser too, ideology is opposed to science as it exists outside social history while ideology is present in all social classes and in all societies. (Lynch 1994, 200)

Mannheim provides the genesis for Althusser's position when he says that other than natural science, all other ideas are socially rooted. This he refers to as 'asocial' knowledge.

Most ideologies tend to declare themselves to be scientific and Marxism is no different. Popper's two main contentions with viewing Marxism as scientific were, one, because it is unfalsifiable and, according to him, true scientific theories are falsifiable.

> For Marxists ... all facts verify the theory because the theory has an application for every circumstance. But the consequence of this is that the theory can never be tested because there are no possible facts that could show it to be wrong. But the point about scientific theories Popper insists, is that it can be tested; that is they are so constructed that they exclude certain circumstances which if they are found to obtain, will falsify the theory. (Adams 1989, 47)

The second argument against the scientific validity of Marxism was on methodological grounds of historicism, using the patterns of historical development to predict the future. 'Popper's main objection is a moral and ideological one: belief in historicism leads to a 'closed society with its attendant evils and belief in Poppers own scientific methodology leads to the open society which is the good society' (Adams 1989,

49). While Popper saw physical science as objective knowledge, Kuhn viewed science as rigid, applying knowledge belonging to a particular period and one set of wisdom replaces another. Kuhn went against the then prevailing understanding of science as accumulative knowledge built over the years. In his work, *Structure of Scientific Revolutions*, Kuhn uses the word paradigm and writes that historical and sociological factors help in understanding why certain paradigms are dominant at a particular point of time.

Subjects like history, political science and sociology are viewed as 'subjective' interpretations as a result of which they cannot be taught without bias. This was the overall impression that was conveyed by science teachers. Science is about facts and can easily be taught without it getting 'contaminated' (usage by a teacher during an interview) by ideology. The oft-repeated answer was that science students do not have the time for activism or getting involved in such discussions as social science students do, implying sciences are more time-consuming and demand more attention than social sciences. Not only teachers, students, too, were of the opinion that subjects like law, history and political science presented more of an opportunity for ideologically influencing students through teaching.

Social science students, in nearly all countries, have the most liberal and radical views on social issues (Altbach 1984). But to this, Giroux in the present context adds, 'Currently the fine arts, the social science disciplines and classical languages are not considered as legitimate as those bodies of knowledge found in the sciences or those methods of inquiry associated with the areas of business and management' (Giroux 1998, 4). This was evident to some extent in the subtext of interviews, where science subjects are seen as based on facts and not coloured by subjective views, including ideology. So, science cannot be touched by personal beliefs and positions as it is based entirely on facts that cannot be altered, while history can be interpreted according to one's ideological position and similarly with subjects such as economics and sociology.

Many years ago, Louis Wirth pointed out the danger that is perceived in the evolution of thoughts in social sciences. 'The more secularised social and political theory became and the more thoroughly it dispelled sanctified myths which legitimised the existing political order, the more precarious became the position of the emerging social science' (Wirth XVI). He illustrates through the example of the erstwhile regime in Japan, where any discussion on 'democracy, constitutionalism, the emperor, socialism and host of other subjects as dangerous because knowledge on these topics might subvert the sanctified belief and undermine the existing order' (Wirth XVII).

As pointed out earlier, even those teaching humanities were against teachers approaching their subjects in the classroom through the lens of ideology. Ideology, largely interpreted by teachers as political ideology, is seen as too subjective. Mannheim speaks of the trend in modern intellectualism: 'The most striking fact about it is the complete separation between theory and practice, of the intellectual sphere from the emotional sphere. Modern intellectualism is characterised by its tendency not to tolerate emotionally determined and evaluative thinking' (Mannheim 1955, 109). While not expressing in this manner, the underlying tone when speaking of ideology and its impact on teaching and classroom was exactly this—teaching should be confined to merely transferring of knowledge in a dispassionate and factual manner. Ideology can bring in a personal and emotional aspect that has no place in the classroom. The other aversion to ideology was as Batabyal put it, 'Politically articulate teachers were perceived as spokesperson of the state and statist ideology and considered the adversaries of the students who tried to subvert the penetration of the state's ideological apparatus' (Batabyal 2014, 209). The students were not very comfortable with the idea of teachers being open about their ideological positions. When asked about it, most students said that while most of times they don't really know about the ideological positions of the teachers, they guess it either from their support to certain politicians or from the textbooks they prescribe. Majority of the students said that they were not really sure of whether they would want their teachers to openly declare their ideological positions.

Mannheim presents the opposite viewpoint. He writes that as more and more universities of higher education are established, it would be desirable to have the intellectuals engage in politics. Not only students but also the teachers should also be actively engaged politically. But he also points out,

> But there is a profound difference between a teacher who, after careful deliberation addresses his students, whose minds are not yet made up, from a point of view which has been attained by careful thinking leading to a comprehension of the total situation and a teacher who is exclusively concerned with inculcating a party outlook already firmly established. (Mannheim 1995, 144)

One is aware of how Gramsci viewed the school, church and media as 'hegemonic apparatuses', which are able to organize people on the basis of ideology and, in turn, people become the organizers for propagating certain ideologies. Hegemony is established through this link that is formed between the civil and political society. A symbiotic relationship is formed wherein the political hegemonic leadership uses the hegemonic apparatus of school, media and church to strengthen their leadership.

The teachers view on student activism and give a context to the paradox of student activism. Teachers realize the need for a platform for students to air their grievances and need. They are aware that students have to speak out on many issues, but the teachers want it to be so within a limited framework of activism. They want students to become leaders but are apprehensive of the negative influences and that the unions will go out of hand. Most teachers and even students, for that matter, advocated a limited and restrained activism only on certain issues. There is no doubt that students' union should not become or create manipulative, coercive and violent spaces. Rather students' union should strive to become examples of progressive leadership, but for this, students need to be given the space to form unions and the space to discuss conflicting ideas, liberty to speak on contemporary issues that concern them as citizens of the country and engage in critical thinking.

The university is a complicated space, and it is bound to be so as it is made up of individuals at different stages of their lives. On one hand, we have students who are beginning to give a concrete shape to their world views and negotiating with the world beyond classmates and teachers and, on the other hand, we have teachers who are set in their ways. This leads to a situation which is at once hierarchical, professional and one that has the potential to transform an individual. In this several social processes of conflict, consensus and accommodation come into play and the university continues to provide the latent and manifest functions that began at school but now involve a larger arena.

Conclusion

> *The paradox of education is precisely this—that as one begins to become conscious, one begins to examine the society in which he is being educated.*
>
> —Baldwin (1963)

This book began with the central premise of the role of education in democracy. As stated clearly, the initial idea of this book was triggered by several instances of conflict between the State and HEIs. These conflicts were being largely viewed by academicians and the general populace as a purely political ideological battle between the left wing and the right wing. But a closer look revealed that some of the protests were more than just a political–ideological battle and also a focus on merely political ideology would limit the scope of this book. Consequently, this book moved away from merely documenting and analysing the various causes of political and political–ideological conflicts between the State, teachers and students. In doing so, it stepped into a realm less explored.

The relationship between the three main actors in higher education, namely the State, students and teachers, is a complicated one, as it involves elements of authority, freedom, constraints, policies, employment, access to education and so on. This book takes some of the key questions of contemporary relevance and analyses in the larger framework of the vision and role of liberal education in a democratic country.

This book puts forth the role of HEIs and the family in shaping ideology and the impact of ideology in everyday life in the campus. As already explained in Chapter 2, this book uses ideology as a conceptual category of 'world view', as described by Mannheim, beyond the common understanding of political ideology. By everyday life, this book refers to relationship among students and teachers and within the student and teacher community. Students and teachers spoke candidly about their opinion and experiences with ideology in the classroom and outside. Open discussions on the national anthem and rewriting of history provided an understanding of critical thinking among the student community. Another point of debate for long has been student activism and unions. Rather than looking at the purely political aspect of student activism, this book analysed the level of awareness with regard to student activism across the country and the support to the idea of students'/teachers' union from both students and teachers. It also looks at the relationship between State and student unions, as an example of the State that can control or give space to democratic expressions. Both students and teachers spoke about the role and relevance of students' union in higher education. Similarly, the issues of fee hike and hostel protests were examined as an exercise to the right to protest in a democracy against measures that reinforced ideas of utilitarian view of education and institutionalization of behaviour, respectively. The conversation with teachers revealed the dynamics of State control, academic freedom and their views on reservation and other issues facing education.

The following illustration shows the main points of query.

What is the paradox of education that James Baldwin speaks of in this context? The nature of education itself is a paradox. Education is a complex and contradictory combination of socialization, social and State control, social change, conflict, consensus, freedom and creativity; the last two are desirable but not necessarily present. It is not surprising that these concepts have been at the centre of sociological theorization on education, which further lends to the fact that there are differing and, often, opposing views, not only about the role of education but also its relationship with the State. Each chapter of this book touched upon at least one integral part of education as a social process and as a lived-in experience.

Second paradox is the role of education, the meaning, purpose and process of education. This was discussed at length in the introduction. But as one moved from one element to another in each chapter, it become clear that the purpose of education has been substantially

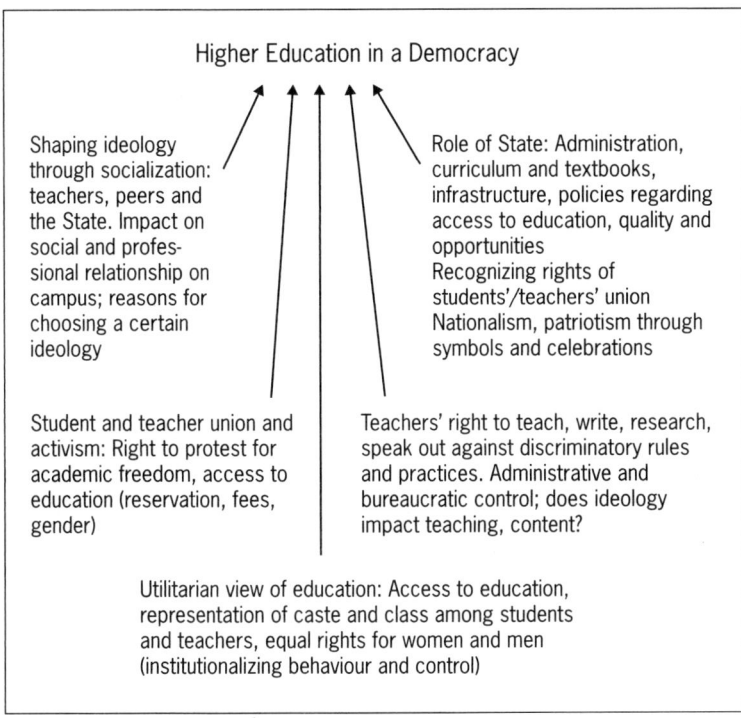

narrowed down with the passage of time. In this, it questions whether education can be understood merely through the prism of functionalism and utilitarianism. In Chapter 5, there were references to several such reports where there is a conscious effort to push a functionalist idea of education based on the idea of consensus and utility rather than conflict and critical thinking. What would be the implications of this? If anything, it would merely contribute to the idea of a status quoist society which doesn't look at education outside its primary function of passing on knowledge, tradition and norms. While within the prism of functionalism, education may be able to create some kind of social mobility in terms of class, providing employment opportunities, but is providing employment the only purpose of education?

> Through functionalism, the nature of education cannot be understood, and education cannot promote social change and innovation. In fact, the functionalist 'old' sociology of education which asserted optimistically

that it could contribute to remedying the crisis of education in the 1960s proved, in effect, to be powerless. For example inequality of educational opportunity cannot be as readily dissolved as the functionalists imagine. (Shimbori 1979, 409–410)

Several academicians have written about limiting the purpose of education to occupation. Giroux speaks of how education today, in schools and universities, is geared towards meeting industrial needs and contributing to the economic activity. He laments the lack of critical pedagogy and a shift towards conformist pedagogy that encourages passivity. Giroux writes that the present neoliberal education system is focused on what he refers to as 'conservative pedagogy that emphasis on technique passivity' rather than 'critical literacy and active citizenship' (Giroux 1998, 1). Pathania too speaks of the impact of neoliberalism on education. Like Giroux, he believes that that the value of higher education is seen from the lens of productivity, efficiency and economic contribution and, as a result, social sciences are not seen economically productive as it does not directly contribute to economic activity.

> The general popular argument about 'wasting of tax-payers money' on social science courses in public universities draws its arguments from this ideology. But what it does not consider is that public university education is not only about personal gain or career development in a competitive age, but also about social justice and creating an intellectually vibrant space. (Pathania 2018, 6)

In India, with the arrival of the neoliberal model in the 1990s, education quickly became a commodity and business, and teachers 'traders of knowledge' (Pathak 2017). A professor in Gauhati University mentioned that the universities of 'eminence' became recipients of funds and autonomy, which were incidentally engineering institutes. In a country where the youth form the majority of the population, access to education is of utmost importance. We speak of population as a resource and yet exclude a large number of the youth from the education process by making in unaffordable. Therefore, it is not surprising that one of the foremost worry that teachers expressed when asked about what plagues higher education in India today, the answer was the increasing cost and privatization of education. Very few students interviewed spoke of higher fees, barring three universities—Gulbarga University, Periyar University and JU; all the other universities included in the study had seen fee hikes. On the other hand, teachers were worried that higher fees would undo the years of work done by affordable education. While the NEP 2020 does talk about making education accessible to disadvantaged groups, there is no mention of regulating fees which is one of the biggest hindrance in providing access to education. The State is shifting its responsibilities to the private sector which problematizes the notion of democracy, which Jessop (2002) calls 'de-statization'. This shift from the public good to private commodity has been impacting the educational institutions in particular and society in general.

The other paradox is the role of the State, which is crucial in shaping education, and it is in here that integration of the values of liberal thought, consensus and conflict come into play. The State also uses education as a tool to indoctrinate young minds as was discussed earlier. The State controls education in various ways but, namely through policies, rules, administration and also through prescribed curriculum, textbooks, courses and even banning books. The State may also pose restrictions on conferences and seminars. The vision of the State is crucial in shaping education and charting out its course through policies. The State also uses education as a tool to create a unified idea of nation. For this purpose, it uses symbols such as the flag, celebration of days of national importance, such as Independence Day, Republic Day and so on. It may also use certain icons to represent the struggle for freedom or freedom from caste oppression and so on. However, this purpose could get problematic if the State pushed for an extreme stand on nationalism and obedience to the State. This position is not restricted to authoritarian regimes but is seen even in democratic countries.

A controversy raged in France, too, over the use of the term 'Islamo-Leftism' ', referring to left-leaning research in academia. Several ministers including the President, Macron, urged researchers not to focus on race, ethnicity or colonialism and move away from such topics. They urged it was time for French universities to come out of the grip of 'ideological excesses' and that the focus on issues of discrimination and race only deepened the divide in the society and also blurred lines between research and activism. In India, topics pertaining to nationalism and the nation are being suggested for research, irrespective of the interests of the teachers. In Hong Kong, the government has mandated that the children should learn about the 7,000-year old Chinese culture. The guidelines state 'a sense of belonging to the country, an affection for Chinese people, a sense of national identity, as well as an awareness of and a sense of responsibility for guarding national security' (Vivian 2021, *Indian Express* Published from *New York Times*). The article suggests that the government is intent on using history as a tool to indoctrinate people and also erase all mention of collaboration with the West. Courses on liberal studies are being reduced, and with it, critical thinking and dissent is actively discouraged. Added to it, students have been asked not to be analytical in their approach, especially with regard to recent political developments.

In Chapter 2, the various examples from the UGC circulars make it apparent that universities are not isolated campuses where the State intervenes only to provide infrastructure or the curricula. It also involves the active engagement of other agencies such as State-owned media, the military to slowly prepare the students for their role as citizens, respecting the armed forces and fighting terrorism, which are examples of such instances. It is apparent that State and education are not two separate binaries; the State constantly uses the education system to influence students and propagate a certain image of the country. One may argue that there is no harm in students going in for exchange programmes or learning about unity and integrity of the country. Indeed there is not. However, when universities become a breeding ground for the kind of nationalism Orwell warns us about, then we need to critically examine the role of the State. In recent times, the emphasis on certain kind of nationalism built on symbols such as compulsorily singing the national anthem or the national song in cinema theatres or the excessive emphasis on the valour and sacrifices of the armed forces, celebrating 'Surgical Strike Day in universities, proposal to place army tanks in universities and so on points to the growth of a dangerous jingoistic nationalism.

Students, irrespective of ideological leanings, said that singing the national anthem is a matter of pride; it binds people together irrespective of caste and community and creates patriotism; this was contrary to the current narrative in the country about the ideological positions on patriotism and nationalism. They said that it reminds citizens of the sacrifices made by the freedom fighters, and also, when the national anthem is sung in the campus, it reinforces the idea that India is not defined by a specific region. There were definitely more instances of critical approach among those studying humanities, but across both streams, there was discontent on the national anthem being made mandatory in public spaces. Rather than a forced nationalism, the students overall viewed the national anthem as a symbol of unity; it reminded them that the students in the campus have come from different parts of the country, and with it they bring regional and cultural differences and need to understand this diversity. It is crucial in a democracy, appreciating the differences rather than forcing a homogenous identity. This is an important paradox to be noted. Education by its very nature encourages uniformity and conformity. But within this system, teachers and students are expected to be critical thinkers, look beyond certain identity, understand diversity and so on. The other important aspect that came through is that contrary to popular linkages between political–ideological positions and nationalism, there were leftists among students who remarked that the national anthem should be sung as it promotes patriotism and there were right-leaning students who spoke of the right to freedom to sing or not sing the national anthem. This is important, as it questions the way we slot people ideologically, it is a positive sign that students from the traditionally orthodox right are speaking of not imposing ideas of nationalism on others.

In India, the past few years have seen similar moves by the State with regard to both rewriting of history and science and mythology. The situation has been further exacerbated by social media and cinema fuelling a false sense of pride by misrepresenting history. Hindi film directors with right-wing inclination and those wanting to cash on the high decibel of nationalism produced films like *Kesari*, *Padmavat* and *Tanhaji*, which not only created a fictionalized history but also used it as a medium to malign certain communities. There is complete disregard for historical fact that India was divided into kingdoms and battles were fought for territorial expansion. These battles were not so much in the name of religion as they were for gaining political supremacy. The fight was for territorial expansion because of which generals, loyalists of the emperors, were not chosen for their religion but their valour and strategic acumen. This narrative has been twisted to give a communal angle. YouTube is flooded with videos made by pseudo historians who claim to have discovered hidden secrets in temples attributing everything from pi to DNA research to Hinduism. Religion is being portrayed as the source of scientific knowledge. The comments on these videos show the dangerous path we are on. Young and old alike are ready to jump on the wagon of denouncing the fact that India is an amalgamation of several cultures, religion and communities. It is in matters such as these that critical thinking becomes very important; else, we will all become victims of propaganda.

Apart from the State, popular opinion, industry and the market also determine the path of education a society may adopt. While public opinion may not always directly influence education policies, but it may find its way into the educational system through representatives in bureaucracy and the market. Two such examples that were discussed here were the issue of fee hike and, second, the presence of students' union in educational institutes. A strong public opinion built up in favour of fee hikes and against students' union. In his thesis on public opinion and liberal principles, Popper (2002, 471–474) warns,

> Public opinion is very powerful ... liberals ought to regard any such power with some degree of suspicion. Owing to its anonymity, public opinion is an irresponsible form of power and therefore dangerous from the liberal point of view. Public opinion often involves propaganda by a group against another group which may be harmful to the latter.

He adds that the view that mistakes of the public opinion will come back to haunt it is a myth.

On liberal principles, Popper (2002, 471–473) begins by saying that the 'State is a necessary evil,' and hence, its powers should be limited. However, the nature and function of the State makes it more powerful than individuals and institutions both public and private. The powers of the State are held in check by other institutions established to counter it. In India, judiciary, at least in theory, is a check against the power of the State. The university can also question the policies and intentions of the State, though it doesn't have the legal power to prevent the State from taking certain decisions. The university has at its disposal the power to critique, question, protests and organize collective action. It is this that the State wants to prevent, hence the attack on autonomy and funding. 'Principles of liberalism may be described as principles of assessing, and if necessary modifying or changing, existing institutions, rather than of replacing existing institutions. One can express this by saying that Liberalism is an evolutionary rather than a revolutionary creed' (Popper 2002, 473). According to Popper, freedom of thought and discussion are the ultimate liberal values and are crucial in the search for truth. Truth, he writes, is reached by trial and error, imagination, critical discussion and also by discovering one's own prejudices.

Liberalism does not assume consensus on everything but hopes for a discussion on varied opinions and growth of new ideas. Rational discussion is critical in liberalism and should be an essential part in politics and government. This involves 'listening to another point of view, the growth of sense of justice; and the readiness to compromise' (Popper 2002, 474). In contemporary India, a public opinion has built up against the funding of higher education. Reactionary public opinion against government funding of higher education has been built as a result of propaganda driven by ultra nationalist agenda and the market. Closely associated with the propaganda of withdrawal of subsidies to universities was the building up of public opinion against certain universities that had an active students' union. There has been a deliberate attempt to rally public opinion against political activism of students in universities funded by the State. This could be related to the anti-establishment stand adopted by the students' union in certain universities. Questions have been raised about the involvement of students in political activity while availing government subsidies. Should a student's life include the right to protest, express dissent or engage in political activism or should they merely prepare themselves to become useful members of a market determined society?

The protests for equality with regard to rules, regulations and access to facilities by young women or the protest against fee hikes should be seen as an exercise of liberal values, not a waste of taxpayers' money. As Freire says, 'Students, as they are increasingly posed with problems relating to themselves in the world and with the world, will feel increasingly challenged and obliged to respond to that challenge' (Freire 2017, 54). This book is peppered with examples of how both State-led commissions and reports by non-state actors' (corporates, industry leaders) public opinion have shaped education policies. The various elements of education, such as pedagogy, curriculum and knowledge, should be constantly under scrutiny by sociologists. Most of the studies in sociology of education focus on schooling, as it is seen as the formative years of personality formation of an individual. The structural functionalist approach ensures that the schools transmit social norms and values. The earlier tradition of sociology placed education in the prism of functionalism. Durkheim credited with creating the theory of sociology of education, analysed how curriculum and educational thought were influenced by the existing social order. He also saw moral education as performing the function of social integration. Weber, on the other hand, examined the varied roles that education performs in societies at different points of time. Mannheim also discussed in great detail, and as mentioned earlier, the emerging intelligentsia, replacing the old guard of knowledge of the priestly class, as one that would play an important role in taking forward the idea of democracy. As Shimbori points out, societies are 'characterized both by conflict and by change' and that functionalism is not adequate as an analytical tool as it, 'insists upon value-free objectivity and ideological neutrality, it serves to maintain the status quo of society.' (Shimbori 1979, 409–410).

In the social phenomenological approach to education, the model of socialization is based on interactions. 'This shifts focus from emphasis on institutional behaviour to focus student interaction with language, social relation and categories of meaning' (Giroux 1998, 25). Giroux points out that the phenomenological approach does not account for social change and consciousness. 'Schools socialize students to accept unquestioningly a set of beliefs, rules and disposition as fundamental to the functioning of the larger society. It stresses on consensus and stability and downplays notions of social conflict' (Giroux 1998, 24).

A few decades ago, sociologists were deeply engaged with the understanding of the school and educational institutes as arenas of socialization and social change. This work revisits this in the context of Berger and Luckmann's *Social Construction of Reality*. As Berger and Luckmann (1966) put it, 'Institutions also by the fact of their existence control human conduct by setting up pre defined patterns of conduct, which channel it to one direction against the many other directions that would theoretically be possible'. Institutions for them imply both historicity and control. Daily life in the campus itself exerts a deep influence over evolving minds. The discriminating rules for men and women in educational spaces have been made in the name of security, but it has been observed that these often become grounds for moral policing and controlling women. The education system, of which the university administration is an inherent part, becomes an agent of control. This point is well illustrated in Chapter 4 on how gender roles are perpetuated by universities and other educational institutes in various ways. From refusal to serve women non-vegetarian food to monitoring their movements on CCTV camera, universities may seek to control women in various ways. Many students expressed unhappiness over differential hostel rules for boys and girls with regard to entry and exit timings for hostels, restricting even guardians from entering girls' hostel, allowing only boys to study in the library after a certain time and so on. During the fieldwork, in some universities, the students mentioned that if they were caught speaking to the opposite sex, they were given a warning by the teachers and administration. In SPPU, the students mentioned that if girls and boys were caught sitting together or talking to each other, the guards would ask them to disperse or threaten to inform their parents. In Gauhati University, a student narrated an episode where she was warned against speaking to boys by her seniors. In many universities, the administration and teachers constantly attempt to use fear as a tool to exercise their control over students. Teachers play a key role using authority to monitor and control behaviour. Fear is used to create obedient, passive and quiet students who unquestioningly follow the terms set by authority.

Last few years have seen several women protesting against discriminatory rules in their campuses, while some have been success stories to tell, some continue to struggle for bringing in change. In many universities, men and women do not question the rules and hardly ever discuss them. The reason being that rules have to been made to ensure safety of women, an idea that has been internalized. As Berger and Luckmann point out, control and habitualization often close mind to alternatives. Hence, internalization of the belief that the only way to ensure safety for women is by controlling their movement is very problematic. Students need to question these rules and not accept them without resistance, as was observed in most of the universities. This provides a fine example of how students learn to first understand the differential behaviour meted out on the basis of gender and then fight this to reclaim their rights. In the beginning of the first chapter, it was stated that democracy and education are interlinked. Fighting for one's rights is one of the pillars of democracy.

One of the biggest challenges before a liberal education is the question of student activism. There have been arguments both for and against it, especially in the wake of the recent controversy in JNU. In the introductory chapter, references were made to conflicts that have taken place in universities and the nature and underlying causes of the same. The instances of conflict were not narrated to present a political view but to rather use it to analyse the fundamentals of the purpose of education and the role of universities. The ideal university is one that embodies liberal values, promotes critical thinking and rationality. As conflicts between State, administration and students/teachers increased, several professors and scholars wrote on various platforms vehemently supporting the right of students and teachers to speak out against the government. Freedom of expression, academicians and students wrote, was an essential part of education. 'Theoretically, the university has the 'onus' or obligation in the training of critically minded students, who can synthesize, see connections, evaluate argumentations and determine the root cause of things' (McLaren 2005). The university and the residential university, in particular, is a site of transformative encounters, with radically different forms of living, food cultures and religious practices. In post-Independence India, the hostel has shed some of its sectarian characteristics, particularly in the public university, and enabled all manners of new opportunities (Nair 2017).

Pathania writes, 'University as a site provides space for ideological activism, which students use to enlarge their space for freedom and autonomy leading to critical thinking, radical ideas, and activism' (Pathania 2018, 8). Scholars have emphasized the relation between society and university as symbiotic (Pant 2008) and 'reciprocal' (Heredia 1996). For Lukacs (1968, 299), it works as the 'form of mediation between theory and practice', where it stands in a close relationship to practical life and to the needs of the State by training the younger generation for practical affairs (as quoted in Humboldt 1970, 248; Giroux 2015). Chomsky defines education as enlightenment, which is to foster the impulse to challenge authority, think and enquire critically (Chomsky 2012).

There is a tendency among the general public to consider university life as far away from reality and in a kind of bubble or utopia (Pathania 2018, 10). But Indiresan (1999) argues, 'campuses cannot remain insensitive to the happenings in society around them.' Campus politics provides a space to understand how mainstream politics works and the working of internal mechanisms and processes involved. That's why it is rare for a student movement to be fully campus based and concerned mainly with university issues (Altbach 1984). Touraine says, 'the university is not a reflection of society; it is society because it is from now on at the centre of society's change' (Touraine 1971). The resistance involved in student politics and activism helps to keep democracy alive. Viswanathan (1998) emphasized the exploration of relationship between the university and liberal democracy. He defines the university as 'the litmus of crisis and democracy'.

Pathak (2020) comments on how role of the students is being redefined and is also reminiscent of the reaction of teachers to politics on campus or students engaging in politics. It was seen as unnecessary and as vitiating the campus environment. Pathak speaks out against this and says that the authoritarian steps taken by the government have only further deepened the resolve of the students not to give in and they are bringing their classroom to the streets by applying what they have been taught to fight against injustice. He sees hope in these students rather than those who are pursuing a narrow vision of the future.

Dasgupta and Singh further write,

> New modes of activism have emerged and found support from students across universities and other institutions of higher education. They have been largely triggered by a new policy thrust of reordering university research, curriculum and administration along the lines of corporate management that cares little for the values of equality and social justice. We are witnessing the political impact of a new economic and administrative adjustment of the function of higher education and of university campuses. If the state is to subordinate their autonomy to business interests and privatise higher education, then critical thinking and political speech must first be neutralised, if necessary, with brutal violence. (Dasgupta and Singh 2019, 73)

Freire, even with reference to schools, says that they do not exist in isolation from the rest of the society, rather they are the manifestation of rules of social relationship.

One of the points made against student activism is that politics should be kept out of campus and students out of politics. In universities and engineering institutes, with or without students' union, students did discuss politics apart from other topics of relevance. The everyday discussions on politics within the campus or outside with peers influence the way political views are formed. Chapter 3 on student activism moved away from a political discussion and focused instead on the need and relevance of students'/teachers' union and support for the same from among students' and teachers. The teachers said that absence of a students' or a teachers' union reduced the chances of conflict on campuses. However, the students and teachers expressed dissatisfaction with the situation as they did not have a platform to voice their opinion and the students were, also, at the mercy of both teachers and administration. Giroux says that the relationship between teachers and administration can be very disabling, as it creates a sharp divide between conception and execution. He strongly advocates that teachers need to align with each other, irrespective of whether there is a union or not.

Several instances of conflict and control have been mentioned in the introduction and elsewhere. However, surprisingly, majority of the students were not aware of incidents taking place in other universities. There was no clear support for the student community in other universities; from among those aware of the incidents, some were ambivalent and some were not sure of exactly what transpired. The responses among the humanities students were different, with more students not only supporting students' unions but a few students wanted teachers and students to work together. Also, the humanities students were more vocal and aware of the events that had taken place in other universities and mentioned about the fake news and propaganda against JNU in general and Kanhaiya Kumar in particular, the case of the missing student Najeeb (JNU) and Rohit Vemula's (HCU) suicide. The students took the names of their own volition and were not prompted by the field researchers. In contrast, a few of the engineering students mentioned the JNU incident and some mentioned Kanhaiya Kumar, however, there was little awareness or no awareness about the Najeeb case or that of Rohit Vemula. Students and teachers had similar apprehensions about politics on campus, that of students being manipulated by political parties. The teachers said that the students would learn the wily ways of the politicians at a young age if political activism was to be encouraged in universities. There were both moral and disciplinary concerns. It was also noticed that universities which had both students' and teachers' union, especially political ones, shared an uneasy relationship often resulting in conflict. Students did not want to see their teachers as 'political', which was reflected in their answers.

Batabyal points out, it was in the late 1950s and 1960s that the students in universities become truly politically active and articulate. The student was no longer merely looking to finish his or her studies and getting into the job market. S/he was a political being in the university. Contemporary student politics in India shows that there is a surge of identity-based and identity-resistance politics, and the earlier model of class-based politics is on the decline. This ongoing resistance should be seen from the viewpoint of marginalized students, where they are challenging narratives of the dominant culture through arguments of counterculture (Pathania 2018, 17).

> Students are often sensitive to the contradictions and needs of their societies. The question of the alienation of student movements from their societies, especially in developing countries, has been a complex one. While Asian student movements are certainly more articulate in political terms than their societies, and often make demands which are not fully understood by the common man, it is hardly true to say that such movements are alienated. (Altbach 1970, 81)

Professor Pathak, in his heartfelt article, questions how teachers and students can remain immune to what is happening in the society.

This study revealed that a very small percentage of students actually translate their ideological leanings (political or otherwise) to political activism. It also became apparent that students may have clear rationale for their ideological stand, but this may not translate into actual politics on campus, or even support for students' unions. In another interesting turn, it was seen that students may categorize themselves as apolitical, but they have strong opinions on criticism of the government, presence of a students' union on campus and so on. Students, very often, interpret being apolitical as not being an active member of politics. Of course, some students claimed absolute disinterest in politics itself both inside and outside campus and did not support students' union. This, in turn, gives the State a chance to wield more control over universities as resistance and dissent do not find active supporters. For students' union to be effective and popular among students, it needs to be politically articulate and aware, critical of the government, ready to mobilize but also ensure that it does not become the very thing it is opposing. There have clearly been instances where students' union have been misled by outside influences, resulting in violence; in some cases, disruptive violence by students' union has gone out of hand to the extent of destroying universities. This is not and cannot be seen as part of liberal values and education. Neither should the State misuse its powers and unleash violence in a campus nor should any students' union indulge in violence. This is, perhaps, the most complicated paradox; HEIs do provide an opportunity and space for future political leadership to take shape, but not many young minds are able to handle the power, authority and responsibility given to them. As they result, situations arise which are able to mould public opinion against student activism. Not only public opinion but the student community, itself, prefers to remain unrepresented than to create something that has the potential to destroy the university itself.

Though this research did reveal that majority of the students were not aware of the current debates on rewriting of history and ideological bias in historical work and books, the few who commented on the issue said they had read about it in the online news portals. None of them mentioned any discussions on it with teachers. But the teachers, on the other hand, mentioned this as an issue facing education. However, the positive aspect was that the few who had read about it were more keen on including histories of what they felt were the marginalized regions, say the Northeast or some southern states. Some wanted history books to include more on the role of Dalit, tribals and local leaders in the freedom struggle. However, the attitude of science studies towards the blurring lines between science and mythology left a lot to be desired. Many expressed the opinion that the 'scientific achievements' of the historical past have not been given their due. What was a cause of worry was not their belief, but that these opinions were not formed on the basis of extensive reading or critical thinking and analysis of historical facts and evidence but through social media and informal discussions. As a result, the students could not really substantiate their answers when asked to explain the reasons for their positions. The situation was similar when students of humanities were asked about the rewriting of history and what they thought about it. Sadly, most of the students were not conversant with the debates regarding the rewriting of history, and the few that did know about it, attributed it to the social media rather than discussion with teachers or fellow students.

The study clearly showed the inadequacy of knowledge and lack of interest of students on these issues. This is not desirable as the State's control over knowledge and inclusion of false knowledge in the education system can prove to be disastrous. Half-baked knowledge and opinions based on fallacious arguments can create deep schisms in society and do not augur well for a democratic society. The Indian higher education system is also accused of following the footsteps of erstwhile colonizers. This was also mentioned by a professor who said, 'We need to come out the need to ape the West.' It cannot be denied that for far too long, we have looked at the Western world to theorize and provide a framework for analysis. But there is also a danger throwing the baby out with the bath water, if one discards all forms of knowledge that come from the West. We may run into the position of extreme parochialism and nationalism that Gandhi, Tagore and Nehru warned us against. The danger is that indigenous ideas and framework run the risk of getting pushed to the other extreme of ultranationalism, which blur the lines between historical facts and myths. It is also inherently against the idea of liberal education and is more in tune with Freire's idea of banking system and one way flow of knowledge. Critical and logical thinking and a scientific temper are crucial to nation-building.

Chapter 2 and Chapter 6 analysed the social impact of ideology. It explored interpersonal and professional relationships with ideology at the crux. It sought to see if campuses were divided on the basis of ideology. It is imperative to point out that, deliberately, focus was shifted from political ideology. As it emerged, students understood ideology as being social, economic and political. The peer group and family emerged as instrumental in shaping ideology. Many students said that they hadn't even heard of the word ideology till they entered the campus; many had not heard of it even after. For some, it was part of the course; so they had studied it, but it did not seem like students were engaged in deep discussions on the subject with the teachers. The fact that many students and teachers mentioned caste as shaping world view and creating divisions more than political ideology, speaks of the deep caste divide inside and outside the education system. In comparison to humanities students, science students were less aware or even inclined towards a discussion on ideology.

No questions on allegiance to any political party or politicians were asked. As a result, students spoke of the ideology of humanism, caste, gender and, of course, political ideology. Those who did speak specifically of being leftist and rightist said that they stood for the core political belief. The students were quite clear about what the different political ideologies meant to them and why they identified with one or with none. Those who shunned any particular political ideology, did so because it was not living up to the original ideals of the ideology. Those who were leftists said, they were so because it stood for helping the poor and the marginalized; those who were rightist said that the rightist ideology was the only one that stood for the interest of the nation above everything else. It was surprising that the right wing was not identified with working for the poor, whereas several right-wing organizations have focused a lot of their energies on working in rural areas and among the lower-middle class, which form the base of their supporters. Right-wing organizations are also aligned with farmers and trade unions. None of the students identified the right wing specifically with the poor, like they did with the left. The students were not conversant with this aspect of the right wing and identified with it only on the lines of hyper nationalism and national security.

Feldman and Newcomb (1970), in their research study, found that social science students were the 'most liberal' with respect to 'politico-economic and social liberalism,' while those in natural or biological sciences fell into the medium category, and engineering students scored the lowest scores on this question. On the question regarding 'liberalism of religious orientation,' the trends were reversed with the social science and humanities students scored within the medium-to-low category and the natural sciences students mostly scored medium to high. Stouffer (1955) and Lipset (1960) researched on support for democratic institutions and conservatism among college students, respectively. Several studies (Kaiser and Lilly 1975; McClintock and Turner 1962) seem to suggest that the more time an individual spends in education, the more liberal his or her thoughts tend to be. However, none of these studies can be generalized; the correlation between the time period of education and sociopolitical and socio-economic attitudes has not been firmly established. With regard to gender and class, some studies have shown that social class does influence the length and course chosen for study. Further, those in vocational studies were found to be more conservative than those in academic courses on social issues irrespective of gender.

While many students may profess to be ideologically inclined to one political group or another, it does not translate into students becoming active political members of campus-based political parties. This was reflected in the interviews, as not many students, among those interviewed, belonged to any political group on the campus. They were clear about their political affiliations and were aware of the reasons why they chose a certain path, but this did not necessarily translate into concrete political activity through political unions on campus. For engineering students (IIT), there wasn't much of an option, as political unions are not allowed on these campuses. The only exceptions were the science and engineering students we spoke to in universities where political unions were allowed. It was encouraging to note that ideological positions had not affected friendships as almost all the students said that ideology would not determine or break friendship. Barring Gulbarga University, there were almost no reports of conflict due to ideology or political affiliations on campuses included in the study.

The discomfort of students with teachers taking clear and open ideological positions was an eye-opener and so was their opposition to teachers organizing themselves into unions. The basis of this was the fear among students that the teachers with strong ideological positions may wield control over them and indulge in favouritism, as a consequence they might be discriminated against or be forced to blindly follow the teacher. Interestingly, a majority of the students did not want a teachers' union on campus, and the ones who did want a teachers' union, believed that students and teachers have to put forward a united front. Very few students were in support of both students' and teachers' unions on campuses. There was a fear of favouritism by teachers among the students and that of groupism among teachers. The truth is that ideological camps exist in almost all universities. In some universities, it is a given that some teachers with similar world views may gravitate towards each other and, unknowingly or deliberately, create an ideological group. These groups are often easily identifiable by students, and they, in turn, gravitate towards teacher/s in groups, which become power centres due to ideological leanings. The discomfort that students had with open ideological positions of teachers was rooted in the fear of this 'natural' gravitation of teachers and students which may isolate those who do not wish to overtly identify with such groups. Even the teachers themselves said that the teacher had to be 'professional' and, therefore, keep subjective opinions outside the classroom. Exceptions to this were the teachers in Periyar University, who were not happy about the ban on students' union. Some teachers were in favour of students being more informed about ideology and politics; they did not want students to be deprived of the political experience that occurs through unions and elections, and also through discussion in classrooms.

Did the teachers think that the ideological positions (caste, gender and maybe even class) and political activity of their colleagues affects their relationship with other teachers and students? Yes, they did; hence, they said that ideology and political activity are personal choices and should be kept out of the profession. This fear is not unfounded, as groups exist in many universities, and many teachers who do not really subscribe to the dominant ideology among the faculty may find themselves isolated. Many teachers in left-dominated universities have also spoken of missing out on promotions due to their non-allegiance to any political ideology; teachers in Gulbarga University and BHU spoke of the divisive force of a caste-centric ideology.

The position taken by teachers interviewed with regard to ideology and education is in complete contrast to that of Gramsci, Freire and Giroux. There was a discomfort with teachers becoming bearers of ideology in teaching. Even in a deeply political campus like JNU, a couple of teachers mentioned that even if they have strong ideological positions, they would not *contaminate* (author's emphasis) their teaching with that, and another teacher said that they were far too professional to allow this to happen. In contrast, in Calicut University, political like JNU, the professors said that it is but natural that the teachers would be influenced and, in turn, influence students through their own ideological beliefs.

As mentioned all along, most of the teachers during fieldwork spoke of the negative influence of ideology in teaching and on social relationships within classroom and faculty. They maintained that teachers have to be professional and objective. Pathak (2020) writes,

> Ironically, there are teachers who seek to retain some sort of abstracted 'objectivism' or 'value-neutrality'. In the name of 'specialisation', quite often they fragment their consciousness .... A teacher has to be necessarily an 'activist'. But then, beyond the 'apolitical/professional' teacher and the 'ideologically charged/activist' teacher lies yet another possibility – a dialogic teacher filled with the poetry of inner conscience, and experiencing the pursuit of knowledge or research not merely as a cognitive skill, but also as an act of awakening.

There were a few instances where teachers admitted that syllabus and course books are influenced by ideology, and the teacher has the freedom to present his or her beliefs and positions to the students, but it is up to the students to make an informed decision.

When the attack on JNU was in the news, JNU alumni from Africa wrote articles narrating their experiences as students in JNU. They wrote that they were aware of the socialist and leftist leanings of the teachers and students in the classroom. As the campus is a diverse one with a considerable section of students from poor and marginalized sections of the society, the teaching pedagogy is sensitive to this fact and is inclusive. The students are made aware of the social ills facing the society, be it the caste system, untouchability or patriarchy. The students write that they were aware of all the political and ideological groups in the campus. There were discussions from all points of view. This also meant that the left was criticized for being authoritarian, especially in countries where it is in power and, also, often stifling freedom of thought. The left has also been accused of caste discrimination, the very thing it fights against. All this happens within the campus with each student entitled to his or her view and also the freedom to express it.

In contrast to this, all the science teachers and students were secure in the knowledge that the study of sciences is outside the ambit of influence of ideological positions. Barring very few, most of them said that social sciences run into the problem of being ideological, not sciences. This was attributed due to the nature of the subject which did not allow the scope for personal beliefs to find space in the content or teaching. This analysis provided a very interesting point of discussion in this book in the context of Thomas Kuhn and Karl Popper in Chapter 6. Several examples from the past have shown how ideology driven by religion has played an important role in shaping scientific knowledge. Be it evolution, shape of the earth, astronomy and several other scientific discoveries, they have been subjected to ideological debates, usually from religious point of view.

Throughout this book, the relationship between State, teachers and students has been explored. The interaction between State and teachers is frequent and direct as evidenced through the issues of recruitment, research, promotion, syllabus, infrastructure, administration and teachers' union. The State and student relationship is defined in both covert and overt ways. Students may come into direct interaction with the State in regard to students' union, admission (especially rules of admission with regard to caste in government-funded universities), scholarship and subsidies, and enforcement of ideas of nationhood and nationalism. Indirectly, the State and students interact through syllabus, textbooks and, sometimes, institutionalization of behaviour. The teachers and students may have overlapping concerns like infrastructure, funds, scholarships, textbooks, political unions and rules.

Teachers expressed a definite reluctance to speak out against the administration or even the problems facing the education. There was a fear among both students and teachers that their answers might be seen as 'political' and they could get into trouble with the administration. This was in spite of the assurance that names of teachers and even departments would be kept confidential, with the exception of those who do not have any objection to names being revealed. In some universities, students made repeated requests that their names should be not revealed in the study as they felt that the State was keeping an eye on them. This sense of fear, of being under constant surveillance, is telling of the times we live in.

Henry Giroux's arguments on bureaucratization of teaching and the impact of privatization and private funding on education and pedagogy ring true even more today, in the scenario of the rules in universities with regard to teachers, cost of education and the increasing influence of the State. Most of the teachers seemed tired of the decades-old problems that keep reappearing regularly and remain unresolved. In almost every humanities university, students and teachers spoke of the need to appoint more teachers. The universities are now following the model of appointment ad hoc or visiting faculty rather than permanent employees. Giroux views this as a means to control the teachers. This was evident when several guest faculties pointed out that they are not a part of the course designing nor can they decide which course to teach. These are reserved for permanent staff. The teachers find themselves devoting more and more time to administrative work, as pointed out by several teachers, and in most universities, they are less and less involved in the planning of the curriculum. This is a result of the recruitment policy of taking in ad hoc or guest lecturers who do not get the chance to either design the curriculum or chose the course they want to teach. This further encourages passivity, referred to earlier on. Giroux points out that teachers need to be aware of the fact that they have a creative role to play and not merely see themselves as mere messengers of the curriculum. They need to exercise control over the process of production of knowledge, to teach children to think critically and, also, engage in the fight for a just society both as an individual and at a collective level.

For Gramsci, analysis of education could only be understood in relation to the existing social and cultural formations and the power relations they imply (Welton 1982). In IIT Chennai, the Ambedkar Study Circle spoke out against communalism and privatization of education. The MHRD swung into action and banned the study circle saying that it was against Hinduism. It is rare for students in science institutes, especially IITs, to indulge in political activity, as any kind of student union and related activities are not permitted on campus. The Ambedkar Students' Association, in HCU, found itself under attack and it resulted in the suicide of a young student. These events are seen as not only the expression of power of the government but also of the caste hierarchies that exist in society. Caste and gender hierarchies are perpetuated by education. This was evident in the stand on reservation, caste-based groupism and favouritism, all of this was substantiated during the course of the research as well. Where the STs were dominant, as in NEHU, there were demands for recruitment of locals (categorized as STs); in certain other universities, the OBCs are dominant and engage with the political parties that support their views.

After Independence, on the matter of academic freedom, Professor Nandini Sundar mentions three reports that sought to define and shape the university space in terms of academic freedom and equal access to education. These reports are the *S. Radhakrishnan Commission Report* (1948–1949), the *Kothari Education Commission Report* (1964–1966) and the *Yashpal Commission Report* (2009). The *S. Radhakrishnan Commission Report* (1948–1949), the first after Independence, made it clear that while the State is obligated to fund and aid universities, this does not imply that it can wield any control over the university, its teachings and positions or faculty. The teachers have the freedom to speak on controversial issues, and this was seen as being important. The report also emphasized on social and cultural activities which would break down the barriers of authority between the teacher and student. It was seen as essential in establishing democracy within the university and, also, teaching the students the ideas of sportsmanship and healthy competition. Not only within the university, but students were also encouraged to take part in the social activities of the region where the university was situated, so that they would become active participants of the social life outside the university. The idea of the university as an isolated unit was not accepted from the very beginning, as is evident. The university was envisaged as an extension of the society.

The Kothari Commission (1966, 275–276), too, stated unequivocally that,

> Dissent was an integral part of the university that it must serve as the 'conscience of the nation', that 'universities are pre-eminently the forum for a critical assessment of society: sympathetic, objective, unafraid, whose partiality and motives cannot be suspected, that the faculty should live by the values they teach, and should resist becoming 'organisation men' eager to suck up to the powers that be. (Sundar 2018, 186–187)

As Nayyar (2017) points out, academic freedom is primary because universities are places for raising doubts and asking questions about everything. 'Exploring ideas, debating issues and thinking independently are essential in the quest for excellence. It would enable universities to be the conscience keepers of economy, polity and society. Hence, the autonomy of this space is sacrosanct. Of course, this cannot suffice where quality is poor or standards are low. That needs reform and change within universities.'

Even as this book was taking shape, NEP 2020 was released, leading to a fresh discussion on education. It is a good opportunity to compare notes on what the teachers had to say about the current crisis in education, research, administrative matters and what the NEP states as the way forward. NEP 2020 states in the introduction that the purpose of the new policy is to change the way in every approach to education. The NEP states,

> Education thus, must move towards less content, and more towards learning about how to think critically and solve problems, how to be creative and multidisciplinary, and how to innovate, adapt, and absorb new material in novel and changing fields. Pedagogy must evolve to make education more experiential, holistic, integrated, inquiry-driven, discovery-oriented, learner-centred, discussion-based, flexible, and, of course, enjoyable. (MHRD, GoI, 3)

It further states, 'Education must build character, enable learners to be ethical, rational, compassionate, and caring, while at the same time prepare them for gainful, fulfilling employment' (MHRD, GoI, 3). The NEP 2020 places the teacher at the centre of the education system and speaks of recognizing the crucial role teachers play. The NEP 2020 professes to move away from long-established methods towards newer ones to make the process of education more holistic, multidisciplinary and aims at both personal and professional development.

Some of the salient features of the NEP 2020 are briefly discussed here. At the institutional level, the policy suggests setting up of a number of national bodies. The policy calls for setting up a National Mission on Foundational Literacy and Numeracy, by the Ministry of Education, a Gender Inclusion Fund and, also, special education zones for disadvantaged regions and groups. In order to encourage research, the NEP 2020 mentions setting up of Multidisciplinary Education and Research Universities across the country following the model of IITs and IIMs. In addition to research-based universities, it mentions the creation of a central body aimed at developing a strong research culture and capacity in higher education. The HECI, which has already been in discussion in the past few years, is to be set up as a single overarching umbrella body for entire higher education. It does not include in its ambit medical and legal education. The reference to the historical legacy of Indian education system finds its way in the setting up of the Indian Institute of Translation and Interpretation, National Institute (or Institutes) for Pali, Persian and Prakrit. There is an emphasis on teaching and learning of Sanskrit. On a contrasting note, it also speaks of the entry of foreign universities in India. The establishment of foreign universities in India has been introduced by previous governments and was marked as an elitist move and another step in the privatization of education. The ongoing COVID pandemic has meant an increased attention to distance learning, online courses, massive open online courses, digital infrastructure and so on. The subject of critical thinking has received much attention in the NEP. It is clear from some of the policy plans mentioned above that several new governance structures are being proposed. However, to encourage critical thinking among students, one needs more than mere governance and administrative changes. Critical thinking cannot take place if students and teachers are not allowed to speak up or given the right to question policies and actions of the State that may be detrimental to education. As Deepak Nayyar, professor emeritus, JNU, points out (19th August 2020) in his article, 'NEP: The Devil Lies in the Implementation', 'The expected transformation cannot take materialize unless we can create more equal socio-economic opportunities in terms of access to education, change the culture of institutions, regulators and governments and end the political intrusions that are so common in every sphere of education.'

Educationists have pointed out that while teachers have been placed at the centre of change, there is no mention of ensuring that teachers in schools, universities and colleges are taken out of the contract system and appointed on permanent tenures. This has been a matter of great concern, and the reasons for the government persisting with the contract system have been discussed in detail in Chapter 6 of this book. According to Henry Giroux, contractual system helps to keep under the check and control of the administration and prevents voices of dissent from emerging in the teacher community. The diminishing number of teachers in academic councils due to the contract system, as only permanent staff is permitted to become part of academic councils, is a point in case of why tenures need to be made permanent for teachers in universities and colleges.

In Chapter 4, on gender and caste in universities, speaking of reservation making education accessible, quite a few teachers agreed that reservation has helped students. When asked if the caste composition of classrooms has changed over the years, most teachers agreed that there has been a positive change, with classrooms consisting of students from different caste groups, but most of the teachers said that they cannot say that is representative of class. A teacher added that the high cost of living and other expenditure prevents poor students from joining universities. These points illustrate the fact that it cannot be denied that reservation has ensured that those belonging to the marginalized communities (SC/ST/OBC) have an entry point into the education system. But this accessibility was aided not only by reservation but several other factors too. One was low-cost education that made education accessible to thousands, who otherwise would have been out of the education system, not only due to caste but also due to poverty. A few pointed out the changing socio-economic status, which also helped families to get their children into the education system starting from the school level. The teachers spoke about how economic social mobility has been one of the factors for an increasing number of children and youth enrolling in education.

Any conversation and research on education is incomplete if does not include the problems and crisis facing education, and this was the focus of Chapter 5. There was a hesitancy, among teachers, to point out the problems that have emerged in the past years. A few teachers mentioned increased political interference, most of the details on this were gathered from the minutes of the meetings of executive councils of the universities. The details that were available on websites of universities have been analysed in the context of these conversations. Even on the issue of UGC versus HECI, teachers were hesitant to speak out against it, even if they were not convinced about the idea. The overall opinion was against setting up the HECI; teachers said that rather than starting something new, could the government not fix the loopholes in the existing governing body. The very teachers in favour of HECI believed that the UGC has outlived its purpose and it was time for reforms. It was categorized along with the other reforms carried out by the government. A few others who were positive about it said that it would bring in the much-needed changes in syllabus, infrastructure and funding. As Professor Nayyar points in his article, entrusting the HECI to perform all the tasks of accreditation, funding, regulation and maintaining quality and standard is way too ambitious, and it is not possible for a single institution to take care of all the aspects.

A lack of employment opportunities for students was mentioned more by science teachers than humanities. The teachers did not complain that the courses do not prepare students for jobs, rather said that there aren't enough and suitable jobs for students. This is what Mary John speaks of (refer to Chapter 5 on issues with higher education today) that contrary to what industry and market claim, underemployment is the key problem. The market seems to suggest that the education system is not producing 'employable' students. With very few universities and institutes of quality available to students, it is but inevitable that several graduates both from sciences and humanities would not meet the industry standards. Surprisingly, only JU students mentioned that they had frequent discussions on employment with friends.

Students and teachers were asked during the interviews about the adequacy and quality of teachers. Students expressed satisfaction when asked about the quality of teachers in their departments and universities; very few students said that the quality of teachers was bad. Most of the students were satisfied with the quality of teaching. However, when asked if the teachers encouraged debates and questions, very few said they did. This brings us to Freire's concept of education and the process itself. The answers given by students seem to suggest a shift from a strict authoritarian figure to a friendly one, but as Freire said, the education process seemed to inherently imply that the teachers are the source of knowledge and students, mere receivers. Since the students did not possess knowledge, they could not question the teachers. He referred to this process as 'banking', where teachers view themselves as the depositors of knowledge. The impression one gets is that this hasn't changed much. Most of the students said that they were happy with their teachers, and institutes like IIT and NIT seemed to have adequate number of teachers.

In Chapter 6, it was noted that the humanities students mentioned that only part-time or guest lecturers were being appointed rather than full time. A lack of permanent teachers and reliance on ad hoc and guest lecturers was a common complaint. In most universities, recruitment for full-time teachers took place almost seven to eight years ago. The implications of ad hoc and guest lecturers have been discussed in great detail earlier on, in the section on rules and recruitment. A lack of permanent appointments was pointed out by very few teachers, even though most of the appointments done in universities were of ad-hoc staff. Most of the universities, other than JNU, have not seen any active recruitment for full-time posts in the last four to five years. There were very few complaints about the number of teachers, either by students or teachers, but it was acknowledged that recruitments for full-time teachers in universities was not being actively pursued by the administration on instructions from the government. In most of the universities covered in the study, the younger and temporary staff did not have any say regarding courses, be it designing or teaching. When the teachers were asked about their freedom to design courses or speak out openly about their political affiliations or even about issues facing the teachers, in most cases, the senior faculty were more forthcoming, while the younger faculty appeared to take a more conformist position. If one looks at the overall responses from teachers, the senior to mid-senior level teachers spoke of the freedom to decide on courses they want to teach or design. On the topic of research, one of the resentments was being forced to pursue research and the other point of dissatisfaction was the recent move by the government to force certain research topics. Some of the teachers mentioned that the State issued directives to universities on the kind of research that is expected from teachers. There was clear preference for research topics that pertain to national interests. Several universities have issued circulars or teachers have been orally instructed by the administration not to speak against the university, its policies or the VC. Universities across India have witnessed increasing interference of the State in HCU, JU, BHU, DU, etc. During this study, even in universities with no instances of conflict to speak of, teachers mentioned political interference as an increasing problem in higher education today.

As far as problems facing higher education goes, there are some broad-ranging issues common across universities. But some universities had specific problems. For example, in Periyar University, teachers did not have the freedom to speak about politics and ideology; students' union has been banned by the Government of Tamil Nadu; scholarships have been scrapped and, in addition to all this, there is no SC/ST cell to address the problems of the faculty or students from the community. The issue of fee hikes was mentioned in OU, NIT Warangal and Pondicherry University.

Four points stood out during the course of this study. First, there was a discomfort with discussing ideology among students and teachers alike. Second, majority of the students did not want their teachers to be open about their ideological positions, political or otherwise. Third, most of the teachers wanted to keep ideology out of the classrooms. Fourth, both teachers and students of sciences, with very few exceptions, said that influence of ideology is a matter of concern only for humanities, not for sciences. Ideology and sciences are divorced from each other, and so, the former does not enter the classroom in any case.

A liberal education system is essential for the survival of any democracy. This includes liberty to speak out, protest against injustices, freedom to teach and the right to political and ideological positions. The State uses textbooks, syllabus and administration as a direct means to control education, but there are several other more subtle ways in which ideas of the dominant hierarchies and symbols of the State are passed on through generations. Fundamentally, this book explored the ideas of liberty and the kind of future citizens that our universities are creating. It brings to light the face of active political views and the pursuit of ideological beliefs. Further, it locates the thread of ideological beliefs that defines relationships among students, between teachers and students and the administration that take place in everyday life.

The presence of political activity on campuses makes students aware of the kind of politics they want. They learn to organize themselves to demand better facilities, infrastructure and fight injustices. The students develop a greater clarity on the undesirable elements of politics. This experience is necessary for students to be able to stand up for what is right and fight for a space for liberal values, principles and ideas opposed to their own. One of the latent functions of education is to teach the student the ability to take these experiences to their workplace, their family and other relationships.

The global world that we live in today demands that we move to different countries and work with people from varied cultural and regional backgrounds. Most of the companies and organizations, today, are not only aiming at diversity and inclusion but are looking for people who can think laterally, work in and with a team and learn to adapt to changing circumstances. Those who can think on their feet and have unique ideas move faster in the professional world. If the education system teaches us only to read certain books, follow unquestioningly and blind submission, it is creating only misfits. Just as an Indian would not like a 'know-all, I-am-superior-in-all-aspects American or European,' the reverse is also true. This describes the paradox of homogeneity that was discussed in detail. India has a rich cultural and historical heritage. Our historical monuments, be it the Brihadeshwara Temple or the Qutub Minar, speak of the tremendous knowledge of science and architecture. We don't need to resort to false narratives to create a sense of cultural superiority and achievements. Our historical achievements are a result of heterogeneity and diversity, and that is our advantage in a global world. No country in the world can lay claim to the 'original inhabitant' theory. There is no 'pure' caste, pure race or even pure culture. Even the cultural practices that we so zealously want to protect have changed and evolved over centuries.

Education by its very nature is political; one cannot run away from this. This also implies that education is not limited to classrooms. It involves a journey that begins when one steps into the campus and continues long after one has left the campus. By the time students enter the higher-education system, a fair degree of socialization has taken place within the school and the family. Students are well aware of the ideological positioning and political affiliation of his or her family and even extended family members. In recent times, social media plays an important role in providing a platform for airing views. The campus, on the other hand, provides or should provide a space where the student learns—to make choices and decisions, regarding courses, to which rules to oppose and about ideology and activism.

Campuses and teachers provide lessons for life, and many of us may subconsciously lead lives in accordance with these lessons. The principles of liberty, justice and equality taught in a campus may find its way in our daily lives long after we cease to be students. This could be reflected in how we treat those who work for us, whether we treat men and women equally in the family or in our workspaces, fighting for what is just and so on. It is not necessary that political activism or beliefs always result in direct participation in the electoral process. However, these beliefs find their way in other aspects of our lives. A parochial and closed approach to ourselves as citizens of a nation and, subsequently, education will only create the proverbial frogs in the well, initially happy to hear their own voices till they turn against one another. Education has the potential to create a vibrant democracy by creating generations of citizens who are more informed, aware, critical and questioning of existing social order, and every society needs to realize this.

BIBLIOGRAPHY

Abrol, Dinesh. 2010. 'Governance of Indian Higher Education: An Alternate Proposal.' *Social Scientist* 38, no. 9/12 (September–December): 143–177.

Acker, S. and K. Oatley. 1993. 'Gender Issues in Education for Science and Technology: Current Situation and Prospects for Change'. *Canadian Journal of Education* 18 (3).

Adams, Ian. 1989. *The Logic of Political Belief: A Philosophical Analysis of Ideology.* Baltimore, MD: Barnes and Noble.

Adorno, Theodor W., Else Frenkel-Brunswik, Daniel J. Levinson and Nevitt Sanford. 1950. *The Authoritarian Personality.* New York, NY: Harper.

Altbach, Philip G. 1970. 'Student Movements in Historical Perspective: The Asian Case.' *Journal of Southeast Asian Studies* 1, no. 1 (March): 74–84.

Altbach, Philip G. 1979. 'Introduction: Student Activism in the Seventies.' *Higher Education* 8, no. 6 (November): 603–607.

Altbach, Philip G. 1984. 'Student Politics in the Third World'. *Southeast Asian Journal of Social Science* 12 (2): 1–17.

Ambani, Mukesh, and Kumaramnagalam Birla. 2000. 'Report on a Policy Framework for Reforms in Education.' Prime Minister's Council on Trade and Industry, Special Subject Group on Policy Framework for Private Investment in Education, Health and Rural, Government of India.

Ayyar, R. V. 2017. *History of Education Policymaking in India, 1947–2016.* New Delhi: OUP.

Baldwin, James. 1963. *The Fire Next.* New York, NY: Random House. pp. 9–10.

Basu, Somdatta. 2017. 'Jadavpur University Floats New PhD Entry Rules: Teachers Baffled.' *Times of India*, 25 February. Available at https://timesofindia.indiatimes.com/city/kolkata/jadavpur-university-floats-new-phd-entry-rules-teachers-baffled/articleshow/57340600.cms

Batabyal, Rakesh. 2014. *The Making of a University: JNU.* Mumbai: Harper Collins.

Bhattacharya, Sanchaya. 2019. 'Increasing M.Tech Fees: Only Part of a Solution as Structural Issues Remain Unresolved.' Expert Speak, *Observer Research*

Foundation Online, 17 October. Available at https://www.orfonline.org/expert-speak/increasing-m-tech-fees-in-iits-56715/

Bhushan, Sudanshu. 2011, August. 'A Plea for Liberal Education' (Seminar, issue no. 624). Available at https://www.india-seminar.com/2011/624/624_sudhanshu_bhushan.htm (accessed on 20 July 2021).

Bhushan, S. 2013. 'Higher Education in 12th Plan'. Economic & Political Weekly 48 (4): 17–19.

Bhushan, Sudanshu. 2016. 'Public University in a Democracy'. *Economic & Political Weekly* 51 (17): 35–40.

Brooks, Rachel, Mark McCormack and Kalwant Bhopal. 2015. *Contemporary Debates in the Sociology of Education*. Basingstoke: Palgrave Macmillan.

Brooks, Rachel, ed. 2016. *Student Politics and Protest: International Perspectives*. Oxford: Taylor & Francis.

Bordieu, Pierre, and Jean-Claude Passeron. 1990. *Reproduction: In Education, Society, Culture*. Thousand Oaks, CA: SAGE Publications.

Buradikatti, Kumar. 2017. 'Reports Reveal Violations by Colleges under Gulbarga University.' *The Hindu*, 3 December. Available at https://www.thehindu.com/news/national/karnataka/report-reveals-violations-by-colleges-under-gulbarga-university/article21255169.ece

Burd, Stephen. 2005, April. *GAO Fails to Gauge Results of Pell Grants*. Washington, DC: The Chronicle of Higher Education.

Campbell, Angus. 1964. *American Voter: An Abridgement*. New York, NY: John Wiley and Sons.

Castoriadis, Cornelius. 1991. *Essays in Political Philosophy*. New York, NY: OUP.

Census of India. 'State of Literacy.' In *Provisional Results 2011*, edited by the Government of India. Available at http://censusindia.gov.in/2011-prov-results/data_files/india/Final_PPT_2011_chapter6.pdf

Chafetz, Janet Saltzman, ed. 1999. *Handbook of the Sociology of Gender*. New York: Plenum Publishers.

Chatterjee, Krishnendu. 2019. 'Protests over High Costs of Learning Spreads from JNU to IIMC.' *News Nation*, 3 December. Available at https://www.newsnation.in/education/more/iimc-fee-hike-students-call-for-protest-to-go-on-strike-today-246157.html

Chattopadhyay, Saumen. 2018. 'Neo-Liberalism and Academic Freedom—The Emerging Scenario.' In *The Idea of A University*, edited by Apoorvanand. Mumbai: Westland Books.

Chomsky, N. (2012). 'The purpose of education'. *Learning without frontiers*, 28 June. Available at http://blip.tv/learning-without-frontiers/noam-chomsky-the-purpose-of-education-5925460

Cooley, H. Charles. 1902. *Human Nature and Social Order*. New York, NY: Charles Scribner's Sons.

Crossley, Nick and Joseph Ibrahim. 2016. 'Network Formation in Student Political Worlds'. In *Student Politics and Protest: International Perspectives*, edited by R. Brooks. Abingdon; Oxford: Routledge.

Das, Suranjan. 2007. 'The Higher Education in India and Challenges of Globalisation'. *Social Scientists* 35 (3/4): 46–67.

Davies, Brian. 2012. *Social Control and Education*, Vol. 169. New York, NY: Routledge.

Deshpande, Vivek. 2019. 'Citing Poll Code Wardha University Expels 6 Students Who Wrote Letter to PM Modi over Lynching.' *The Indian Express*, 12 October. Available at https://indianexpress.com/article/india/maharashtra-varsity-expels-six-scholars-who-wrote-letter-to-pm-modi-over-lynching-6064880/?utm_source=Taboola_Recirculation&utm_medium=RC&utm_campaign=IE

Deshpande, Vivek. 2019. 'Varsity Revokes Expulsion of Students Who Wrote Protest Letter to PM.' *The Indian Express*, 14 October. Available at https://indianexpress.com/article/india/wardha-varsity-revokes-expulsion-of-students-who-wrote-protest-letter-to-pm-6067796/

Eagleton, Terry. 2015. 'Slow Death of the University.' *Chronicle of Higher Education*, 6 April. Available at https://www.chronicle.com/article/the-slow-death-of-the-university/

Ekehammar, Bo, Ingrid Nilsson, and Jim Sidanius. 1987. 'Education and Ideology: Basic Aspects of Education Related to Adolescents' Sociopolitical Attitudes.' *Political Psychology* 8, no. 3 (September): 395–410.

Erikson, E. H. 1980. *Identity and the Life Cycle*. New York, NY: W.W. Norton & Company.

Feldman, K. A. and T. M. Newcomb. 1970. *The Impact of College on Students: An Analysis of Four Decades of Research*. San Francisco, CA: Jossey-Bass.

Filipini, Michele. 2017. *Ideology: A New Approach*. London: Pluto Press.

Foucault, M. 1980. *Power/Knowledge: Selected Interviews and Other Writings*. London: Penguin Random House.

Freire, Paulo. 2017. *The Pedagogy of the Oppressed*. London: Penguin Books.

Fuller, Steve. 2000. *Governance of Science: Ideology and the Future of the Open Society*. Berkshire: Open University Press.

Fuller, Steve. 2004. *Thomas Kuhn: A Philosophical History for Our Times*. Chicago: University of Chicago Press.

Geoghegan, Vincent, and Rick Wilford. 2014. *Political Ideologies*. Fourth edition. New York: Routledge.

Ghosh, Shatarup. 2017. 'Education Getting Worse under Didi's Tenure.' *India Today*. 5 April. Available at https://www.indiatoday.in/education-today/featurephilia/story/bengal-education-system-316390-2016-04-05

Giddens, Anthony. 1983. 'Four theses in Ideology.' *Canadian Journal of Political and Social Theory* 7, no. 1/2: 19.

Giroux, Henry. 1983. *Theory and Resistance in Education: A Pedagogy for the Opposition*, p. 145. South Hadley: Bergin & Garvey.

Giroux, Henry A. 1985. 'Toward a Critical Theory of Education: Beyond a Marxism with Guarantees.' *Educational Theory* 35, no. 3, 313–319.

Giroux, Henry A. 1986. 'Solidarity, Struggle and Public Sphere: Beyond the Politics of Anti-utopianism in Radical Education, Part 1.' *The Review of Education* 12, no. 3, 167.

Giroux, Henry A. 1998. *Teachers as Intellectuals: Toward a Critical Pedagogy of Learning*. USA: Bergin & Garvey.

Giroux, Henry A. 2009. 'Democracy's Nemesis: The Rise of the Corporate University.' *Cultural Studies, Critical Methodologies* 9, no. 5: 669–695.

Giroux. Henry A. 2016, 2007. *University in Chains: Confronting the Military-Industrial-Academic Complex*. Boulder: Paradigm Publishers; New York: Routledge.

Goradia, Abha. 2019. 'IIT Students Plan to Protest against M.Tech Fee Hike.' *The Indian Express*, 9 November. Available at https://indianexpress.com/article/education/iit-students-plan-to-protest-against-mtech-fee-hike-6110770/

Gottlieb, D. 1964. 'Sociology of Education.' *Review of Educational Research* 34, no. 1: 62–70. Available at www.jstor.org/stable/1169567 (accessed on 7 February 2020).

Gudavarthy, Ajay. 2018. *India After Modi: Populism and the Right*. London: Bloomsbury Publishing.

Gudavarthy, Ajay. 2019. *India after Modi*. New York: Bloomberg Press.

Habermas, Jurgen. 1987. *Towards a Rational Society: Student Protest, Science and Politics*, translated by Shapiro. Cambridge: Polity Press.

Habermas, J. and J. Blazek. 1987. 'The Idea of the University: Learning Processes'. *New German Critique* 41: 3–22.

Habib, Irfan. 2017. *Indian Nationalism: The Essential Writings*. New Delhi: Aleph Book Company.

Hall, Stuart, and James Donald, eds. 1986. *Introduction in Politics and Ideology*. Oxford: OUP.

Hall, Stuart. 1983. 'The Problem of Ideology, Marxism without Guarantees.' In *Marx: A Hundred Years on,* edited by Betty Matthews, 82–83. Atlantic Highlands: Humanities Press.

Hans News Service. 2019. 'All India Students Federation Opposes Fee Hike in Engineering Colleges.' *The Hans India*, 24 June. Available at https://www.thehansindia.com/news/cities/hyderabad/all-india-student-federation-opposes-fee-hike-in-engineering-colleges-540507

Hans News Service. 2019. 'Fee Hike for Law Courses Flayed.' *The Hans India*, 16 October. Available at https://www.thehansindia.com/news/cities/hyderabad/fee-hike-for-law-courses-flayed-573222

Hans News Service. 2019. 'Telangana Government Constitutes 11 Member TFRC.' *The Hans India*, 28 June. Available at https://www.thehansindia.com/telangana/telangana-government-constitutes-11-member-tfrc-541860

Hensby, Alexander. 2014. 'Networks, Counter-networks and Political Socialisation: Paths and Barriers to High-cost/Risk Activism in the 2010/11 Student Protests against Fees and Cuts'. *Contemporary Social Science Journal of the Academy of Social Sciences* 9 (1): 92–105.

Heredia, R. 1996. 'Tribal Education for Development: The Need for a Liberal Education'. *Journal of Education and Social Change* 10 (1–2).

Hoare, Quintin, and Smith Nowell Geoffrey, eds. 1971. *Selections from the Prison Notebooks of Antonio Gramsci*. London: Lawrence and Wishart.

HT Correspondent. 2017. 'Jamia Rolls Back Fee Hike After Students Protests.' *Hindustan Times,* 7 February. Available at https://www.hindustantimes.com/cities/jamia-rolls-back-fee-hike-after-students-protest/story-IrOD6kRNCfEG-bNwHRAfE0I.html

Humboldt, W. von. 1970. 'On the Spirit and Organisational Institutions in Berlin'. *Minerva* 8: 242–250.

Iftikaar, Fariha. 2019. 'Most DU Colleges Hike UG Course Fee.' *Hindustan Times,* 19 June. Available at https://www.hindustantimes.com/education/most-du-colleges-hike-ug-course-fee-check-details-here/story-E35YwpN5mXqyJrS-Syw6TjI.html

India Today Web Desk. 2016. 'FTII to Propose Fee Hike, Age Limit: Students Oppose.' *India Today News*, 30 September. Available at https://www.indiatoday.in/education-today/news/story/ftii-pune-344068-2016-09-30

Indiresan, J. 1999. 'Campus -Community Linkages: A Dialogue on Diversity'. In *Diversity and Unity: The Role of Higher Education in Building Democracy*, edited by M. Cross, N. Cloete, E. Beckham, J. Indiresan and C. Musil. Cape Town: Maskew Miller Longman.

IQAC, Jadavpur University. 2017. 'Annual Quality Assurance Report 2016–2017.' Available at http://www.jaduniv.edu.in/upload_files/iqac_file/1538375070-1.pdf

Jain, Rupam, Lasseter Tom. 2018. By Rewriting History Hindu Nationalists Aim to Assert their Dominance over India, 6 March, Reuters. Available at https://www.reuters.com/investigates/special-report/india-modi-culture/

Jessop, B. 2002. *The Future of the Capitalist State*. Oxford: Blackwell.

John, Maya. 2013. 'Critiquing Reforms in Higher Education: Understanding the "Education Question" in India.' *Social Scientist* 41, no. 7/8 (July–August, Special issue: The Four-Year Undergraduate Programme in Delhi University): 49–67.

Jose, Jinny P. 2019. 'Fee Hike: IITians Are Feeling the Pinch.' *The Hindu BusinessLine*, 3 December. Available at https://www.thehindubusinessline.com/specials/india-file/fee-hike-iitians-are-feeling-the-pinch/article30148946.ece

Jost, John. 2006. 'The End of the End of Ideology'. *American Psychologist* 61 (7): 651–670.

Kaiser, Fred M. and Robert Lilly. 1975. 'Political Attitudes among Students: A Small College Experience'. *Adolescence* 10 (38, Summer): 287–295.

Kapur, Devesh and P. B. Mehta. 2019. *Navigating the Labyrinth: Perspectives on India's Higher Education*. Hyderabad: Orient Blackswan.

Kaushal, Ravi. 2018. 'What's Ailing Delhi University?' *News Click*, 23 May. Available at https://www.newsclick.in/whats-ailing-delhi-university

Kavish, Priyanka. 2019. 'Why Fee Hikes Are Death for Education in India.' *Sabrang India*, 25 November. Available at https://sabrangindia.in/article/why-fee-hikes-are-death-education-india

Kerlinger, Fred N. 1984. Liberalism and Conservatism. *The Nature and Structure of Social Attitudes*. Hillsdale, NJ: Erlbaum.

Kimberlee, Richard H. 2002. 'Why Don't British Young People Vote at General Elections?' *Journal of Youth Studies* 5 (1): 85–98.

Kimiko de Freytas-Tamura. 2017. 'George Orwell's '1984" Is Suddenly a Best-Seller.' *New York Times*, 25 January.

Klemenčič, Manja. 2014. 'Student Power in a Global Perspective and Contemporary Trends in Student Organising'. *Studies in Higher Education* 39 (3): 396–411.

Klinenberg, Eric, (Excerpt and Interview). 2019. 'Populism Can Be Beaten by Libraries, Really.' *The Economist*, 31 May. Available at https://www.economist.com/open-future/2019/05/31/populism-can-be-beaten-back-by-libraries-really

Koshy, Jacob. 2017. 'Fee Hike Massive Say IISER Students.' *The Hindu*, 10 June. Available at https://www.thehindu.com/news/national/fee-hike-massive-say-iiser-students/article18957199.ece

Kulkarni, Tanu. 2019. 'Bangalore University Increases Affiliation Fees to Overcome Revenue Crunch.' *The Hindu*, 29 July. Available at https://www.thehindu.com/news/cities/bangalore/bu-increases-affiliation-fees-to-overcome-revenue-crunch/article28740179.ece

Kumar, Rajesh. 2016. 'Colleges Affiliated to IP University Fee Hike.' *Daily Pioneer*, 12 August. Available at https://www.dailypioneer.com/2016/delhi/colleges-affiliated-to-ip-university-hike-fee.html

Kumar, Udaya. 2016. 'The University and Its Outside.' *EPW* 51, no. 11 (March 12): 29–31.

Kundu, Indrajit. 2019. 'Teachers See Red over Mamta's Proposed Gag Order for State Run Colleges and Universities.' *India Today*, 18 April. Available at https://www.indiatoday.in/india/west-bengal/story/teachers-see-red-over-mamta-s-proposed-gag-order-for-state-run-college-and-universities-1215646-2018-04-19

Lecompte, Margaret D. 2014. 'Collisions of Culture: Academic Culture in the Neoliberal University.' *Learning and Teaching: The International Journal of Higher Education in the Social Sciences* 7, no. 1 (Spring, Special Issue). 57–78.

Lipset, Seymour Martin. 1960. *Political Man: The Social Bases of Politics*. New Delhi: Doubleday.

Lipset, Seymour Martin. 1967. 'University Students and Politics in Underdeveloped Countries'. In *Student Politics*, edited by Seymour Martin Lipset, 3–53. New York, NY: Basic Books.

Lohumi, Bhanu, P. 2019. 'Shell Out 16k More for BEd.' *The Tribune*, 21 November. Available at https://www.tribuneindia.com/news/archive/shell-out-rs-16k-more-for-bed-863776

Lukács, Georg. 1971 [1923]. *History and Class Consciousness: Studies in Marxist Dialectic*, trans. Rodney Livingstone. Cambridge: MIT Press.

Lukács, Georg. 1968–1981. *Gesammelte Werke*, Darmstadt: Luchterhand.
Luckmann, Thomas, and Peter L. Berger. 1967. *The Social Construction of Reality: A Treatise in the Sociology of Knowledge*. New York: Anchor Books.
Lynch, William T. 1994. 'Ideology and the Sociology of Scientific Knowledge.' *Social Studies of Science* 24, no. 2 (May): 197–227. Available at https://doi.org/10.1177/030631279402400202.
Madhukar, Ritu. 2019, 1 July. 'Students and Faculty React to UGC's Move to Do Away with the Black Robes'. *The Wire*. Available at https://livewire.thewire.in/campus/students-and-faculty-react-to-ugcs-move-to-do-away-with-black-convocation-robes/ (accessed on 20 July 2021).
Mahajan, Shobhit. 2018. 'Of Pain Waves, Plastic Surgery & Panchgavya: The Quest for Hegemony in the Natural Sciences.' In *The Idea of A University*, edited by Apoorvanand, 23–33. Mumbai: Westland Books.
Mammo Muchie, Noklenyangla, Rajiv Mishra, and Fayaz Sheikh. 2016. 'A Utopian University: Ideas, Imaginations and JNU.' *The Thinker* 70: 72–75.
Mannheim, Karl. 1955. *Ideology and Utopia: An Introduction to the Sociology of Knowledge*. Boston, MA: Mariner Books.
Mansbridge, Jane J. and Aldon Morris, eds. 2001. *Oppositional Consciousness: The Subjective Roots of Protest*. Chicago, IL: University of Chicago Press.
Markam, Santoshi. 2020. 'The Alienation of Adivasis From Our Identity, or How I Unlearned My Hinduisation.' *The Wire*, 12 August. Available at https://thewire.in/culture/alienation-adivasis-identity-culture-hinduisation-education
Martin, J. L. 2015. 'What is Ideology?' *Sociologia, Problemas e Práticas*, no. 77: 9–31. https://doi.org/10.7458/SPP2015776220.
McClintock, C. G. and H. A. Turner. 1962. 'The Impact of College upon Political Knowledge, Participation, and Values'. *Human Relations* 15 (2): 163–176.
McCoy, Lilian. 1998. 'Education for Labour: Social Problems of Nationhood'. In *Forming Nation, Framing Welfare*, edited by Gail Lewis, Chapter 3. New York, NY; Oxford: Routledge.
McCrum, Robert. 2009. 'The Masterpiece that Killed George Orwell.' *The Guardian*, 10 May. Available at https://www.theguardian.com/books/2009/may/10/1984-george-orwell
McLaren, Peter. 1988. On Ideology and Education: Critical Pedagogy and Politics of Empowerment. *Social Text* no. 19/20 (Autumn): 153–185.
McLaren, P. 2005. *Red Seminars: Radical Excursions into Educational Theory, Cultural Politics, and Pedagogy*. Hampton Press.
Mead, H. George. 1934. *Mind, Self and Society*. Chicago, IL: University of Chicago Press.
MHRD. 2006. 'Lyngdoh Committee Report'. New Delhi: MHRD, Government of India.
Ministry of Human Resource Development. 2006. 'Report of the Committee Constituted by Ministry of Human Resource Development, Government of India, as per the Direction of the Hon'ble Supreme Court of India to Frame

Guidelines on Students' Election in Colleges/Universities.' Available at http://dbrau.org.in/attachment/LyngdohcommitteeReport.pdf

Ministry of Human Resource Development. 2019. *All India Survey on Higher Education* (2018–2019). Available at http://aishe.nic.in/aishe/viewDocument.action?documentId=262

Ministry of Statistics and Programme Implementation of India. 'Chapter 3.' In *Social Statistics*. Available at http://www.mospi.gov.in/sites/default/files/reports_and_publication/statistical_publication/social_statistics/Chapter_3.pdf

Minnis, J. 1990. 'Adult Education as Socialization: Implications for Personal and Social Change.' *The Journal of Educational Thought (JET)/Revue De La Pensée Éducative* 24, no. 2: 88–94. Available at www.jstor.org/stable/23767963 (accessed on 5 February 2020).

Mishra, Singh. 2015. 'Continuum of Ignorance in Indian Universities.' *EPW* 50, no. 48 (November).

Nair, Rukmini. 2015. 'Why IIT Founder Nehru Wanted Arts for Engineers'. *NDTV*. Available at https://www.ndtv.com/opinion/why-iit-founder-nehru-wanted-arts-for-engineers-1208945 (accessed on 20 July 2021).

Narayan, Badri. 2016, 20 February. 'What Ails Student Politics in India'. *Catch News*. Available at http://www.catchnews.com/india-news/what-ails-student-politics-in-india–1455984365.html (accessed on 20 July 2021).

Nayyar, Deepak. 2017. 'The Degradation of Indian Universities through Politics.' *Livemint,* 9 March [2016]. Available at https://www.livemint.com/Opinion/t7Wpt9fu57OIimiSwuwVRM/The-degradation-of-Indian-universities-through-politics.html

Nehru, Jawaharlal. 2008. *The Discovery of India*. Noida: Penguin.

NEHU. 2014. 'North-Eastern Hill University Fortieth Annual Report 2013–2014.' Available at https://nehu.ac.in/public/uploads/NEHU_Annual_Report_2013-14.pdf

NEHU. 2018. 'North-Eastern Hill University Forty-Fourth Annual Report 2017–2018.' Available at https://nehu.ac.in/public/uploads/Annual_Report_2017-18.pdf

New Education Policy. 2020. 'MHRD, Government of India.' Available at https://www.education.gov.in/sites/upload_files/mhrd/files/NEP_Final_English_0.pdf

Newman, Henry. 2016. *The Idea of a University*. Scotts Valley, CA: Createspace Independent Pub.

Niazi, Shuriah. 'Ministry Back Pedals on "gagging" Rules for Academics.' *University World News*, 26 March. Available at https://www.universityworldnews.com/post.php?story=20181026124012244

North-Eastern Hill University. 2016. 'Notification: Revision of Fees for Courses.' 7 August. Available at https://nehu.ac.in/announcement/display/188/Notification-Revision-of-fee-for-all-coursesprogrammes-in-the-University

O'Sullivan, Dennis. 1991. 'Socialisation, Social Change and Ideology in Adult Education.' *The Journal of Educational Thought* 25, no. 3 (December): 227.

Orwell, George. 'Notes on Nationalism.' The Orwell Foundation. Available at https://www.orwellfoundation.com/the-orwell-foundation/orwell/essays-and-other-works/notes-on-nationalism/

Orwell, George. 1984. *Notes on Nationalism*. Penguin Books and Orwell Estate.

Pant, H. 2008. 'In Defence of Liberal Education'. In *Beyond Degree*, edited by I. Pande, 168–177. New Delhi: India International Centre.

Park, Charles. 1980. 'Preachers, Politics and Public Education: A Review of Right Wing Pressures against Public Education in America.' *The Phi Delta Kappan* 61, no. 9 (May): 608–612.

Parsons, Talcott. 1959. 'The School Class as a Social System'. *Harvard Educational Review* (Fall). Reprinted in *Social Structure and Personality* (1964) and in *Education, Economy and Society* (1961), edited by A. H. Halsey, Jean Floud and Arnold C.

Patel, Sujata. 2004. 'Higher Education at the Crossroads.' *Economic & Political Weekly* 39, no. 21 (22–28 May): 2151–2154.

Pathak, Avijit. 2019, 31 August. 'Politics on the Campus'. *Tribune*. Available at https://www.tribuneindia.com/news/ archive/politics-on-the-campus -825477 (accessed on 20 July 2021).

Pathak, Avijit. 2020. 'Rethinking Education in the Age of Totalitarian Politics.' *The Wire*, 21 January.

Pathania, Gaurav. 2018. *University as a Site of Resistance*. Oxford: OUP.

Payne, E. 1927. 'Education and Social Control.' *The Journal of Educational Sociology* 1, no. 3: 137–145. https://doi.org/10.2307/2961744.

Pender, Stephen. 2007. 'An Interview with David Harvey.' *Studies in Social Justice* 1, no. 1 (Winter).

Pilkington, Hillary and Gary Pollock. 2015. '"Politics Are Bollocks": Youth, Politics and Activism in Contemporary Europe'. *The Sociological Review* 63 (S2): 1–35.

Pinner, Frank A. 1972. 'Students—A Marginal Elite in Politics'. In *The New Pilgrims: Youth Protest in Transition*, edited by Philip G. Altbach and Robert S. Laufer, 281–296. New York, NY: David McKay.

Plato. 2018. *Laws*. Translated by Benjamin Jowett. Rockville: Wildside Press.

Popper, Karl. 2002. *Conjectures and Refutations*. New Delhi: Routledge South Asia Edition.

Powell-Price, J. C. 1945. 'The Present State of Indian Education.' *Journal of the Royal Society of Arts* 93, no. 4,700 (14 September): 534–546.

Prakash, Ved. 2007. 'Trends in Growth and Financing of Higher Education in India.' Economic & Political Weekly 42, no. 31 (4–10 August): 3249–3258.

Purkayastha, P. 1989. 'Science, Falsification and Ideology.' *Social Scientist* 17, no. 3/4: 22–30.

Ramani, Meeta. 2017. 'Karve Institutes Fee Hike is Illegal: SPPU.' *Pune Mirror*, 14 July. Available at https://punemirror.indiatimes.com/pune/civic/karve-institutes-fee-hike-is-illegal-sppu/articleshow/59584041.cms

Redmann, Jennifer. 1988. 'Children's Literature, Education and Ideology in the Weimar Republic and Nazi Germany.' *Teaching German* 31, no. 2 (Autumn): 131–137.

Reisch, George. 2019. *Politics of Paradigms The: Thomas S. Kuhn, James B. Conant, and the Cold War 'Struggle for Men's Minds*. Albany: SUNY Press.
Ryle, Robin. 2012. *Questioning Gender*. Thousand Oaks: SAGE Publications.
Sahni, Rohini, and V. Kalyan Shankar. 2015.'What Does an MA Know: Postgraduate Learning Deficit and Diploma Disease in Social Sciences.' *EPW* 50, no. 31 (August).
Salmi, Jamie. 1992. 'The Higher Education Crisis in Developing Countries: Issues, Problems, Constraints and Reforms.' *International Review of Education/ Internationale Zeitschrift für Erziehungswissenschaft/Revue Internationale de l'Education* 38, no. 1 (January): 19–33.
Sanyal, Sanjeev. 2016. 'The Left Paralysis.' *The Week*, 21 February. Available at https://www.theweek.in/columns/guest-columns/the-left-paralysis.html (accessed in September 2019).
Sarfaraz, Kainat. 2019. 'Ambedkar University Students Want Fee Hike Review.' *Hindustan Times*, 29 November. Available at https://www.hindustantimes.com/education/ambedkar-university-students-want-fee-hike-review/story-E8PwwW18PkGBhtGC9TUwjO.html
Sargent, John. 1944, January. 'Post-War Educational Development in India' (Report by the Central Advisory Board of Education; also Sargent Committee Report). New Delhi: Ministry of Education, Government of India.
Satia, Priya. 2019. 'In Trying to Defy Colonialism, Draft NEP Walks the Path of Colonizers.' *The Wire*, 20 July.
Seaton, Jean. 2018. 'Why Orwell's *1984* Could Be About Now.' *BBC*, 25 May. Available at http://www.bbc.com/culture/story/20180507-why-orwells-1984-could-be-about-now
Sengupta, Amit, Jesani, Lara and Matthew Jacob. 2019. 'Indian Campuses Under Siege: A Report.' People's tribunal on Attack on Educational Institutions in India. Published by People's Commission on Shrinking Democratic Space.
Sharma, Unnati. 2019. 'Not Just JNU, Several Institutes Across India Are Witnessing Student Protests.' *The Print*, 20 November. Available at https://theprint.in/india/its-not-just-jnu-several-institutes-across-india-are-witnessing-student-protests/323297/
Sharp, Rachael, and Jacqueline Lewis, and Anthony Green. 2017. *Education and Social Control: A Study in Progressive Primary Education*. Oxfordshire: Routledge.
Shimbori, M. 1979. 'Sociology of Education'. *International Review of Education/ Internationale Zeitschrift Für Erziehungswissenschaft/Revue Internationale De L'Education* 25 (2/3): 393–413.
Singh, Mohinder, and Rajarshi Dasgupta. 2019. 'Exceptionalising Democratic Dissent: A Study of the JNU Event and Its Representations.' *Postcolonial Studies* 22, no. 1: 59–78. Available at https://doi.org/10.1080/13688790.2019.1568169.
Snow, David A. 2001. 'Collective Identity and Expressive Forms'. In *International Encyclopedia of the Social and Behavioral Sciences*, edited by Neil J. Smelser and Paul B. Baltes, 2212–2219. London: Elsevier.

Staff Correspondent. 2016. 'After IITs NIT Fee Hiked to Rs 1.25 Lakh from Rs 70,000 per Annum.' *The Economic Times*, 24 June. Available at https://economictimes.indiatimes.com/industry/services/education/after-iits-nit-fee-hiked-to-rs-1-25-lakh-from-rs-70-000-per-annum/articleshow/52907233.cms?from=mdr

Staff Reporter. 2016. 'Calicut Varisty Decides to Rollback Fee Increase.' *Times of India*, 13 June. Available at https://timesofindia.indiatimes.com/city/kozhikode/calicut-varsity-decides-to-rollback-fee-increase/articleshow/52736532.cms?frmapp=yes&from=mdr

Staff Reporter. 2016. 'Jamia Milia Islamia Faces Students Ire over Fee Hike.' *Times of India*, 6 April. Available at https://timesofindia.indiatimes.com/home/education/news/Jamia-Millia-Islamia-faces-students-ire-over-fee-hike/articleshow/51711950.cms

Staff Reporter. 2017. 'JNUSU Protests against UGC Norms Outside HRD Ministry.' *The Hindu*, 6 April. Available at https://www.thehindu.com/news/cities/Delhi/jnusu-protests-against-ugc-norms-outside-hrd-ministry/article17835218.ece

Staff Reporter. 2017. 'IGNOU Courses Fee Hike Opposed.' *The Hindu*, 12 December. Available at https://www.thehindu.com/news/cities/Delhi/ignou-courses-fee-hike-opposed/article21444596.ece

Staff Reporter. 2017. 'Jamia Milia Islamia Students Call off Strike on Hostel Fees.' *Times of India*, 17 September. Available at https://timesofindia.indiatimes.com/city/delhi/jamia-students-call-off-strike-on-hostel-fees/articleshow/60861851.cms

Staff Reporter. 2018. 'After Jadavpur Sit in Students of Presidency University in Kolkata Protest over Hike in Counselling Fee.' *The Indian Express*, Edex Live, 13 July. Available at https://www.edexlive.com/news/2018/jul/13/after-jadavpur-sit-in-students-of-presidency-university-in-kolkata-protest-over-hike-in-counselling-3417.html

Staff Reporter. 2019. 'IIT Council Meeting 2019: Thrust to Improve Rankings and Fee Hike.' *Timesnownews.com*. 28 September Available at https://www.timesnownews.com/education/article/iit-council-meeting-2019-thrust-to-improving-rankings-fee-hike-for-m-tech-courses-and-other-key-points/496496

Staff Reporter. 2019. 'Kolkata Visva Bharati Students Withdraw Protest over Admission Fee Hike.' *The Indian Express*, 23 May. Available at https://indianexpress.com/article/education/kolkata-visva-bharati-students-withdraw-protest-over-admission-fee-hike-5743212/

Staff Reporter. 2019. 'MBA Students in Lucknow University Protest Sudden Hike in Semester Fee.' *Times of India*, 3 September. Available at https://timesofindia.indiatimes.com/city/lucknow/mba-students-at-lu-protest-sudden-hike-in-semester-fee/articleshow/70952718.cms?from=mdr

Staff Reporter. 2019. 'Why Are Students Protesting over Fee Hike in JNU.' *BBC News Hindi*, 19th November. Available at https://www.bbc.com/hindi/india-50469921

Stouffer, S. A. 1955. *Communism, Conformity, and Civil Liberties: A Cross-section of the Nation Speaks Its Mind*. Lincolnshire: Doubleday.

Sundar, Nandini. 2018. 'Academic Freedom and Indian Universities.' In *The Idea of A University*, edited by Apoorvanand. Mumbai: Westland Books.

Sundar, Nandini. 2018. 'Academic Freedom and Indian Universities.' *Economic & Political Weekly* 53, no. 24: 48–47.

Suri, R.K., and Harpreet Kaur. 2009. *Reservation in India: Recent Perspectives in Higher Education*. New Delhi: Pentagon Publishers.

Tedin, Kent L. 1987. 'Political Ideology and the Vote'. *Research in Micropolitics* 2 (1): 63–94.

The Indian Express. 2018, 13 July. 'After Jadavpur Sit-in, Students of Presidency University in Kolkata Protest over Hike in Counselling Fee'. *Edex Live*. Available at https://www.edexlive.com/news/2018/jul/13/after-jadavpur-sit-in-students-of-presidency-university-in-kolkata-protest-over-hike-in-counselling-3417.html#:~:text=The%20institution%20of%20national%20eminence,%2C%20which%20was%20%22unjustified%22%20 (accessed on 21 July 2021).

The Indian Express. 2019, 23 May. 'Kolkata: Visva Bharati Students Withdraw Protest over Admission Fee Hike'. Available at https://indianexpress.com/article/education/kolkata-visva-bharati- students-withdraw-protest-over-admission-fee-hike-5743212/ (accessed on 20 July 2021).

Thompson, John. 1987. Language and Ideology: A Framework for Analysis. *The Sociological Review* 35, no. 3: 517–536.

Tilak, B. G. Jandhyala. 1997. 'Five Decades of Underinvestment in Education.' *Economic & Political Weekly* 32, no. 36 (September 6–12): 2239–2241.

Touraine, A. 1971. *The Post-Industrial Society. Tomorrow's Social History: Classes, Conflicts and Culture in the Programmed Society*. New York, NY: Random House.

Tripathi, Akhilesh. 2019. 'Students Protest against Fee Hike in Allahabad University.' *Patrika* (e-paper). Available at https://www.patrika.com/allahabad-news/students-protest-in-allahabad-university-against-fee-hike-1552484/

Upadhyaya, Sugeeta. 2007, 13 January. 'Wastage in Education'. *Economic & Political Weekly* 42 (2).

Vidyarthi, Aparajita. 2018. 'Students of FTII Protest Fee Hike.' *Pune Mirror*, 13 January. Available at https://punemirror.indiatimes.com/pune/civic/students-of-ftii-protest-fee-hike/articleshow/62479311.cms

Visvanathan, S. 1998. 'Democracy, Plurality and the Indian University', in M. Cross. N. Cloete, *et. al.* (ed.), *Diversity and Unity: The Role of Higher Education in Building Democracy*, Maskew Miller Longman.

Visvanathan, S. 2000. 'Democracy, Plurality and Indian University.' *Economic and Political Weekly,* 35(40), 3597–3606.

Wang, Vivian, 2021. 'Hongkong's Lesson to School Children, No Questions Asked.' *New York Times*, 24 February. Available at https://www.nytimes.com/2021/02/24/world/asia/hong-kong-national-security-law-education.html

Weiss, Meredith, and Edward Aspinall. 2012. *Student Activism in Asia: Protest and Powerlessness*. Minneapolis: University of Minnesota Press.

Welton, J. (1982). "Schools in the welfare network," *Child Care Health and Development* 8: 271–282.

Wexler, Philip. 1982. 'Structure, Text and Subject: A Critical Sociology of School Knowledge.' In *Cultural and Economic Reproduction in Education: Essays on Class, Ideology and the State*, edited by Micheal Apple, 285, 17. London: Routledge and Kegan Paul.

Woolcock, Joseph A. 1985. 'Politics, Ideology and Hegemony in Gramsci's Theory.' *Social and Economic Studies* 34, no. 3 (September): 199–210.

Zemsky, Robert. 2003, 30 May. 'Have We Lost the Public in Higher Education'. Washington, DC: The Chronicle of Higher Education. Available at https://www.chronicle.com/article/have-we-lost-the-public-in-higher-education/ (accessed on 20 July 2021).

ABOUT THE AUTHOR

Sushree Panigrahi has a PhD in Sociology from JNU. Her areas of interest are forced migration, culture, gender, media, education and critical thought. In a career spanning over 16 years, she has worked in reputed research institutes, international non-governmental organizations and think tanks. Early in her career, she worked in International Centre for Peace Studies and National Council of Educational Research and Training. She then moved on to join Action Aid International, working on developing an Asian programme for women, children and sex workers living with HIV/AIDS. At BBC Media Action, she led a multi-state research for a women-empowerment-based radio programme. She has been associated with RGICS as Fellow and Senior Fellow since 2011. She has published articles in national and international journals on gender and media, forced migration and ideology and women. She has also published papers on healthcare, fee hikes in universities, spending on higher education and fake news. She has written numerous policy and issue briefs on matters of contemporary relevance. She has presented papers in national and international seminars and participated in workshops, delivered guest lectures and led research projects.

INDEX

academic freedom
   administrative work and rules, 226–231
   designing and assigning courses, 224–226
   recruitment, 220–224
   research, 226–231
academic merit, 20
Academic Performance Indicator (API), 207
Akhil Bharatiya Vidyarthi Parishad (ABVP), 5
Allahabad University (AU), 56
All India Youth Federation (AIYF), 109
Altbach's argument, 155
Ambani–Birla report on education, 188–190
Ambedkar Periyar Study Circle (APSC), 4
and quality control in higher education, 203–206
anti-English movement, 203
Anti-Terrorism Day, 78
attendance and biometric, rules, 229

Banaras Hindu University (BHU), 6, 56
Birla–Ambani Report, 202

campus politics
   point of discussion, 66–70

celebration in universities, 249–251
Central Civil Services (CCS) rules, 230
Citizenship Amendment Act (CAA), 5, 102
compulsory attendance rule, 144
compulsory education, 229
Constitution Day/Samvidhan Divas, 75
course designs, 209

democracy and dissent, 117
democracy in university, 18

Economic Survey of India, 2018–2019, 199
education
   Altbach's view on student community, 66
   Berger and Luckmann's view, 12
   composition of the student community, 114
   functionality and purpose, 16
   Giroux points out about state funding, 20
   Gramscian idea, 71
   latent functions, 143
   life on campus, 59–66
   Lilian McCoy's write-up, 14
   Newman's views, 17
   Plato defined, 11

restricted to classroom, 98
rewriting history and scientific temper, 89–99
socialization, 13
Social mobility through, 14
Udaya Kumar points out, 21
education in India, 199
education system, 1, 42
   ABVP, 5
   campuses conflict, 4
   conflicts within, 29
   Jamia Millia Islamia, 6
   paradoxes, 9
   violence in JNU, 6
   Vishwa-Bharati University, 5
Ek Bharat Shreshtha Bharat, 76
elementary education, 202
Encyclopaedia of the Social Sciences (1937), 144
Essential Services Maintenance Act (ESMA), 231
expenditure on education in India, 186

faculty power, 222
Federation of Central Universities Teachers Associations (FEDCUTA), 231
fee hike, response and impact, 190–198
female students, protest, 150
Freire, P. book *The Pedagogy of the Oppressed*, 217
Freire, P. teacher and student relations, 218–220
French Revolution saw study of ideology, 47

gender, 141
   conservative ideas, 145
   discriminatory rules, 148
Giroux, H.A. corporatization (funding of universities and courses), 223
global disenchantment with education, 199

gross enrolment in higher education, 186
gross enrolment ratio (GER), 156

habitualization, 217
higher educational institutions, conflicts, 8
Higher Education Commission of India (HECI)
   UGC debate, 210–214
higher education system, 200
hostel rules, 139

idea of university, Newman's view, 17
ideology
   Adams' point of view, 44
   Adams writes, 50
   Altbach's view on student community, 66
   concept, 46
   cultural construct, 51
   defined by Giddens, 45
   Destutt de Tracys perspective, 47
   Filipinis viewpoint, 47
   function defined by Seligar, 49
   Giroux writes, 53
   Gramscis view, 47
   human affairs by Mannheim, 46
   John Thompsons view, 49
   life on campus, 59–66
   Mannheims point of view, 45
   Marxs concept, 44
   Pondicherry University, 56
   relation with life experiences, 46
   Stuart Hall and James Donalds framework, 48
   Williams, Giroux and Wexlers definition, 45
Indian system of education, 186
Indonesian student movement, 110

Jawaharlal Nehru University (JNU), 6
   discussion on student politics in campus, 60

protest, 115
violence, 6

Karnataka Universities Act, 2000, 220
knowledge, 20
knowledge economy, 19
Kothari Commission (1966), 188

labour class
  Lilian McCoy's write-up, 14
life on campus
  political affiliations and political activity, 59–66
literacy rates
  SC and ST, 157
  ST, 159
Lyngdoh Committee, 120–124

Maharashtra Universities Act 1994, 122
Mandal Commission agitation, 112
Manusmriti (Ancient Hindu Code of Law), 7
massification of higher education, 201
Moot Court Committee, 149
Moot courts, 149
moral standards, conflicts, 142
Muslim students
  Jamia Millia Islamia, 173

NASSCOM–McKinsey Report of 2009, 200
National Employability Report for Engineers, 2019, 200
nationalism
  contemporary, 80
  discussion, 71
  George Orwell's note, 71
  India's freedom struggle, 73
  Orwells viewpoint, 72
national politics, 204

National Register of Citizens (NRC), 102
Nav Nirman Andolan (Reconstruction Movement), 112
New Economic Policy, 202

Punjab University
  indirect election, 120
paradox of homogeneity, 10, 98
paradox of student activism, 9
Pinjara Tod (break the cage) movement, 39, 150
political control, 208
post economic liberalization, 201
Poush Mela, 5
Prison Notebooks, 47
  Gramsci wrote about teacherstudent ratio, 51
private universities, 207
Progressive Students Organisation (PSO), 109
protest
  Ambedkar University, 150
  AU, 152
  DU, 150
  female students, 150
  Guwahati University, 152
  Jamia Millia Islamia, 151
  JNU, 150
  Kashmir University, 152
  Kottayam Medical College, 153
  Rajasthan University, 153
  SPPU, 152

quoist system, 155

Radhakrishnan Commission, 187
reservations
  AU, 167–168
  Banaras Hindu University (BHU), 166–167
  Bangalore University, 176
  Calicut University, 175

DU, 169–170
education and jobs, 156
enrolment in P.G and Ph.D, 164–166
Gulbarga University, 173, 175
IIT Delhi, 179
JNU, 176–177
JU, 170
NIT Warangal, SPBU, IIT Chennai, NIT Kashmir, Guwahati University, 179–181
North East Hill University (NEHU), 170–173
OU, 168–169
Punjab University, 177–179
Periyar University, 163
Pondicherry University, 163
recruitment, issues and controversies, 181–184

Sargent Report of 1944, 198
status on education, 187
Savitribai Phule Pune University (SPPU), 65, 74
Scheduled Caste student enrolment, 156
skill gap, 189
Slow death of the University, 19
socialization, 13, 141
  Berger and Luckmann's view, 13
  conflict theories, 143
  discipline and social control, 142
  education, role, 142
  families and school, 148
  feminist movement, 141
  view, 143
State
  functions defined by Gramsci, 52
  nationalism and ideology, 70–73
status quoist education, 1
Structural Adjustment Programme, 201
Student Federation of India (SFI), 109

students
  Bangalore University, 68
  Calicut University, 81
  disillusionment with politics, 137
  Gulbarga University, 80
  Jadavpur University (JU), 67
  science on national anthem and patriotism, 84–89
  SPPU, 74
Students Federation for Freedom of Tamil Eelam, 114
students movements in Asia
  All India College Students Conference, 108
  Burma and Vietnam, 111
  Emergency in 1974, 111
  history, 107–118
  Indonesian student movement, 110
  Lyngdoh Committee, 120–124
  Nav Nirman Andolan (Reconstruction Movement), 112
  relationship between state and students union in India, 118–120
  students view on political activism and activities on campus, 124–138
students' movements in Asia
  AIYF, 109
  PSO, 109
  RPI, 112
  SFI, 109
  VRSF, 112
students union
  Chinese government in 1998, 101
  linkages, 103
  need and acceptance, 100–107
  post Independence, 100
  protest at Tiananmen Square, 101
  Reformasi Movement of 1998 in Indonesia, 101
  resurgence of student activism, 101

Such a Long Journey, 8
Swachhata Hi Seva, 75
system of social control, 145

teachers
 conversation with, 216
 executive councils, 231–236
 ideology and science, 252–258
 ideology and taught, 236–243
 students union, role, 243–249
 valuable insights, 216
The German Ideology, 44
trilemma of Indian Higher Education, 201
typfication, 217

unemployability, 200
university
 Batabyal and Nayyars views on politics, 136
 composition of academic councils, 40
 composition of the student community, 114
 conversation on caste in Gulbarga University, 63
 democracy, 18
 democratic space, 18
 Giroux, H. A.
  viewpoint, 71
 Haragopal, G. view on human-rights activist, 117
 life on campus, 59
 meaning defined by Habermas, 22
 point of discussion in campus, politics, 66–70
 politics, 136
 student organizations, 116
 vision basis, 17
 write-up by Bhushan, 18
University Grants Commission (UGC), 75, 187
 letter to vice chancellors of all universities, 77
utopia, 45

Vande Mataram
 controversy, 79
vernacular languages, 203
Vidharaba Republican Students Federation (VRSF), 112

World Bank Report (1994), 201